ENDORSEMENTS AND COMMENTS ABOUT *BrainStyles*®

Marlane Miller's *BrainStyles* does a wonderful job of helping each of us understand who we are and become the best "us" we can possibly be . . . without having to become someone else!

~ Leonard A. Schlesinger, PhD
George F. Baker, Jr. professor of business administration
Harvard Business School

Relationships are *the* reason we agree to live and love. Miller has eased the struggle by defining understandable and usable tools that can create transformation. She walks us through the creation of healthy partnerships, while leaving our unique personalities intact. Of particular interest is her ability to blend the spiritual components of the task with the intellectual, the emotional and the clinical realities of everyday circumstances. Her book outlines a specific system for coping with our differences and highlighting our strengths. What a gift! It should be in every employer's and family's library.

~ Judith K. Kyle, PhD, licensed professional counselor
diplomat, **American Academy of Forensic Examiners**

Anything that we do is best done when we live within our gifts. Marlane Miller made this exact point in terms of *BrainStyles* long before it was popular in the development literature. Her current book gives testimony that her message applies to the most important aspects of our lives, loving relationships that give us meaning. *BrainStyles for Lovers* is a most welcome gift to all of us who long for warm, intimate, and loving relationships and who need to hear the message that we can have all of that without having to give up who we really are!

~ Larry Peters, PhD, Professor, Neeley School of Business
Texas Christian University, Fort Worth, TX

This book combines three great ingredients—concepts that are grounded in theory, a framework that is useful for helping readers make sense out of their own relationships, and real-life stories that make the application of *BrainStyles* easy to visualize. I've already started applying some of the things I learned—not just to my marriage, but to some of my co-workers and friends. Thanks, Marlane!

~ Linda L. Hoopes, PhD, psychologist and consultant
former director of research, **ODR Consultants**, Atlanta, GA

I've personally found the *BrainStyles* concept to open a rich, untapped resource of diversity within our work group. The rewards were definitely worth the time and energy investment.

~ Tom A. Muccio, vice president, customer business development
Procter & Gamble Worldwide

You know P&G is so big on training, and in my five years there, I went to dozens of training sessions each year. But your *BrainStyles* program has had the biggest impact on my life, and it is the one I fall back on continually. Please do not take this as flattery, but as honesty. In fact, when I first started in my position at the university, I had difficulty working with our president, so I asked him to do your *BrainStyles Inventory©* to help me understand where he was coming from on his reactions and his decision making process. He did and it was very beneficial. I've been here seven years now.

~ Carol Woodward, director of marketing & public relations
former **Procter & Gamble** employee, **University of Mary Hardin-Baylor**
Belton, TX

BrainStyles is a common denominator across all humankind regardless of gender, race, ethnic origin, etc. It is something that brings diverse people together on common ground.

~ Henry Ho, customer business development manager for Asia
The Procter & Gamble Company, Hong Kong

Your book has helped me tremendously and made me understand exactly why I am feeling so totally frustrated when people can't see it when I "get it" so quickly and easily. Your points on communication are so perfect and right!

~ Janet Hoy, senior project manager
architectural firm, Sydney, Australia

This is an important book whose ideas will help managers and employees better understand each other. It's a "must" H.R. book.

~ Stanton H. Goldberg, vice president, human resources
Ciba-Geigy Corporation

There has been, it seems, a library of books published in the past several years aimed entirely at encouraging us to improve ourselves and to change. The message has been that if we do not change we will not be able to meet the demands of an ever-changing world. How refreshing now to read *BrainStyles* by Marlane Miller, who, instead of encouraging us to change, gives us the tools and guidance to discover and affirm who we really are—how we think and how we respond. From there, Ms. Miller teaches us how to recognize and affirm the people we love and work with, leading them to a better, more sensitive, and more effective way of being. I recommend this book as a tool for both life and work.

~ James A. Autry, author, *Love and Profit* and *Confessions of an Accidental Businessman,* retired president of the magazine group of the **Meredith Corporation**

From phrenology to Myers-Briggs tests, systems for explaining personality share a weakness: messy divisions between categories. There's an endless number of personality attributes, and nearly as many possibilities for grouping them. Dallasite Miller fights this tendency by focusing her system on the way people make decisions. . . .

~ "Help Yourself," a column by Mike Maza
The Dallas Morning News, 2/2/1997

. . .[W]hen I was reading the description of my *BrainStyle* I had to do all I could not to burst into tears!!! Because, like the person described in your book[1], I felt that FINALLY someone knew what was going on in my "weird" mind . . . . I wasn't weird; I was OK; I AM OK!!! You have no idea what a relief it was to find at 35 that this is the case. At 35 I feel like my life is just beginning!!! . . . I now feel like I don't constantly have to apologise [*sic*] for who I am, to others and myself. . . . I feel vindicated, liberated. . . .

~ Andrea Bulacios, personal assistant for the city of Casey
Melbourne, Australia

I have read Polish version of book and I have to say . . . it is great! This book changed my life. I was always thinking that I was not right. Now I can see that there are other people like me and that they are even successful. My plan is work on my strengths. I am hoping that since not to cry on my non-strengths any more [*sic*]. I have understood that I cannot be Conceptor or Knower. And it is OK. I am Conciliator, and I have something to offer that other people do not have. Thank you for giving me hope.

~ Aga (Agnieszka Sypniewska), **MBA student, Poland**

Your book has had the deepest impact on my coaching and on my own personal life. When people hire a coach, it is often because they feel an urgency to change

---

1.*BrainStyles®: Change Your Life Without Changing Who You Are*[SM], Simon & Schuster ©1997.

themselves rather than the situation they are in. They are intrigued when I suggest to them the most efficient way to change could be to not change! It is amazing how *BrainStyles* can help all of us to reconnect and empower our true selves.

~ Catherine Beau-Wedemeyer, *BrainStyles* coach, formerly an executive with Bosch Industries and Andersen Consulting, **Frankfurt, Germany**

This is a whole system for living. I use it with my family, friends, and people at work. Knowing *BrainStyles* has made me more secure with people, especially new customers, who [*sic*] I have to get to know in a pressure situation.

~ Dan J. Carrithers, product manager
The Dexter Corporation, Detroit, MI

BrainStyles . . . is an exciting book that provides new insights into the way people's brains are structured to make decisions.

~ Bill Gardiner, book review, "Holistic Management in Practice"

This material changed my life! *BrainStyles* filled in the gaps that were missing for me in all the other systems I've studied—including the Meyers-Briggs test and numerous other personality systems—with real validity. This is really break-through stuff because it explains how someone thinks *now* in such a simple way, you can use it immediately to improve and work much more effectively as teams.

~ John P. Fullingim, director
The Addison Marketing Group, Dallas, TX

Over the last six years, *BrainStyles* and the principles associated with it have helped me develop higher performing teams: teams that possess a full range of skills to manage and lead all aspects of business . . . I think *BrainStyles* helps us understand and value diversities like never before. The differences in race and gender have become second to how people think as I deal with them. That's what my organization really needs.

~ Gary Weihs, division distribution manager
Pepsi-Cola Company, NY

Becoming aware of my strengths empowers me to do what I do well, and not to spend time trying to become something I'm not. This has been very powerful for me and my relationships with and expectations for other people.

~ Steve Trozinski, North American logistics manager
Monsanto Corporation, St. Louis, MO

Marlane Miller's insightfulness and interpretation of four basic right-left brain personality types is outstanding. If previously you have been confused or unsatisfied with all the other 5 . . . 6 . . . 7 . . . 8 . . . or 16-fold typologies, *BrainStyles* is the book for you! It is mind-enlightening, and quite personally engaging. . . . This book is NOT a neurological guidebook nor a postgraduate thesis like other personality assessments can be. . . . I look forward to more books from this author.

~ Michael Adam, psychology research director, **Los Angeles, CA**

BrainStyles has changed my life as a trainer. In the past, I felt that some of the students were resisting my training. After I have identified the *brainstyle* of the student I can adapt my training to their style and the way they process information. Some of my students have said after training, "Now I know why I am the way I am. There isn't anything wrong with me after all." *BrainStyles* has been tremendous for my work team. The bickering has been replaced with, "This is their *brainstyle,* we need to communicate in the way that they understand best."

~ Linda Monk, Express Personnel Services regional operations trainer
Rochester, MN

First of all, I think that the *BrainStyles* test and literature is not only applicable in business situations, but I also find it very useful in my personal life as well. After reading this book, I bought another and gave it to my fiancée to improve the odds of our marriage being successful.

I would strongly recommend this book to anyone who has a genuine interest in improving the performance of those around them and their teams.

In my work setting, I will endeavor to apply these principles. I will first have to focus on myself, but I think that finding others' strengths and bartering with them to cover my "non-strengths" will be beneficial to our whole team.

~ Comments from three Southern Methodist University MBA students
Dallas, TX

"Leading From Strengths with *The BrainStyles System*®" has been presented several times each semester this year to graduate MBA students through the Business Leadership Center, Southern Methodist University. The participants' ratings for the course are among the highest received for our courses. . . .

All students discussed the usefulness of the seminar to enhance their personal lives and relationships. I heartily endorse *BrainStyles* as part of an educational curriculum. It provides a very useful tool for developing personal leadership as well as a foundation for collaborating with others in teams.

~ Paula Hill, director, Business Leadership Center
Edwin L. Cox School of Business, **Southern Methodist University**

BrainStyles™

for Lovers

For Wendy and Robert,

May you re-discover what
true lovers you are —
All the best,

Marlane Miller

BRAINSTYLES™
for Lovers

CREATE PARTNERSHIPS THAT CHANGE YOUR LIFE
WITHOUT
CHANGING WHO YOU ARE℠

MARLANE MILLER

BROWN BOOKS PUBLISHING GROUP
DALLAS, TEXAS

BrainStyles for Lovers
© 2004 by *BrainStyles*, Inc.

Manufactured in the United States of America.

For information, please contact:
Brown Books Publishing Group
16200 North Dallas Parkway, Suite 170
Dallas, Texas 75248
www.BrownBooks.com
972-381-0009

ISBN 0-9634406-2-4
LCCN 2003096948
2 3 4 5 6 7 8 9 10

DEDICATION

This book is for Linda Bush,
a woman who makes dreams come true,
first in her own life,
next, in the lives of all those she meets, teaches, and knows.
She, more than anyone, has taken this work and made it live
in her own family
and then in the minds and hearts of others.

READER'S BONUS

DON'T LOAN YOUR BOOK!

YOUR PURCHASE OF THIS BOOK ENTITLES YOU TO MORE PERSONAL INFORMATION AND INSIGHT AT NO ADDITIONAL COST.

Before you read any further, you may wish to learn something more about your own natural gifts as defined in *The BrainStyles System*®.

In order to do so, go online to www.BrainStylesforLoversQuiz.com and enter your code: A194BrS5 and TAKE THE FREE *BRAINSTYLES*® QUIZ (adapted from the original BrainStyles Inventory© 2.0).

Your answer will direct you to a specific chapter to find out more in depth about that brainstyle to determine if it describes you at your best.

Additionally, you may want to gain some insights about how you approach relationships that may have been hidden from your own view until now. COMPLETE THE FREE QUIZ TO DEFINE YOUR IDEAL PARTNER (adapted from the original *BrainStyles Inventory*© 3.5). Your answer will direct you to specific chapters included here to deepen your ability to create and build a spiritual partnership.

BOTH QUIZZES ARE FREE. EACH IS AVAILABLE AT
www.BrainStylesforLoversQuiz.com
Don't forget to enter your code!

CONTENTS

ACKNOWLEDGMENTS

T hank you to all the magnificent people who have opened their lives to my prying questions with such generosity of spirit and time. Thank you also to those who were such terrific listeners, readers, and editors over the six-plus years of birthing this book. Some of these include:

LINDA BUSH, partner, friend, storyteller, facilitator: You are one who lives what she teaches. I don't know if I could have done this without you. Your contributions are living testimony to how grand you are.

FRAN DI GIACOMO: Thank you for being such a living example of the power of spirit to create and sustain life and art. I could not understand the world or the purpose of things if you were not in my life. Thank you for being a living Master, a friend, and an inspiration.

CHRISTOPHER RUSSELL, businessman, visionary, wise beyond your years: You are another Conceptor who has made my life and work grander than I could have imagined. You are a gift.

VICKI RUSSELL: who carefully and wittily not only shared your insights and support for *BrainStyles*, but inspired me to move on to a "book you could share with your friends." I hope this one works.

VIC AND MARY ANN SASSONE, an extraordinary couple who let Love win and let me tell about it: How glad I am to know and work with you.

PAUL SOBCZAK, now married, with more wonderful stories to tell as only he can tell them to show how being yourself can truly bring happiness: Thank you for letting me tell all the men what a real guy looks like on the inside.

BOB COSNER AND CHERYL WILLIAMS-COSNER: Thank you for your trust, your openness, and your simple honesty about the things in life that count the most. I am honored to have gotten to know you and share a peek into your amazing lives.

ROGER PARKER: Thank you for stepping forward from the audience so long ago and far away and introducing your brilliance, your heart, and your vision to me. You are an inspiring gentle man whose impact on others I have witnessed firsthand.

BRUCE WERTZ: You not only walked me to my car on the very first night of my book tour, you opened your life to me and others so candidly that no one can fail to look more deeply than the surface when reading about you. You break all the stereotypes for tough business guys by showing who you really are.

ELLIE LUCE, you of the refined and laser intellect, the jaw-dropping insights: Thank you for showing what nurturing means from a whole different perspective, so crucial for working women today. You are an executive of living, not merely a professional executive. I am the richer for knowing you and wearing a boa.

FRANCENA T. HANCOCK, PHD, coach, wise woman, supporter, writer, and one who always, always has time for me (and others) to focus the illumination of your immense intellect and experience: Thank you for your cheers when I needed them.

PAMELA MURPH, a wise mother, wife, and businesswoman: Thank you for showing the way that faith and graciousness work to realize the real value of marriage. Your unfailing optimism and kindness shine on every single person you know. I am so grateful to be one of them.

MANCY AND KEVIN KIRKLAND, who prove that love conquers all: It was such a pleasure and honor to join with you at the beginning of what is sure to be a wonderfully fulfilling lifetime commitment. Thank you for such openness and sparkle.

CHAD KRISHER, you of the Fit and the Brave, with heart of the lion and the gentleness of Real Men: I salute you and the family you have loved into being. Thank you for sharing your personal look at life; I know it was not easy doing so—but since you "don't read" it won't be so bad to have it all in print.

DEBRA WILLIAMS, healer and teacher: Thank you for such a living, breathing picture of romance and spirituality.

BEVERLY FORTÉ: You give us all the gift of your vision and strength. Bless you for being so generous with your loving wisdom, fired by physical limits.

DONNA WIEDINMYER: Thank you for your bodacious and enthusiastic response to my work, your insights, not to mention your introductions and endorsements. Coming from a woman of your credentials, it meant a great deal.

NADINE BELL: *All* editors should have your heart and your tenderness. You helped me fall in love with writing all over again.

LYNNE HAYNES, you gentle, caring lady: Thank you for listening for so many hours to the roughest of drafts and being so supportive. We talkers would implode were it not for gracious and kind listeners like thee.

YVONNE CLEARNESKY: Your spirit and support light up the darkness of the Internet. Thank you for your continual illumination.

JUDY FORST: You're so much more than a friend, you're a true sister of my soul. You live your love. Thank you for always, always being there.

MY BROTHER GREG: Thank you for your steadfast and loyal support, your willingness to go forward no matter what, and your continued openness.

FRANK CAMPBELL: I learned so much from you. I wouldn't have been able to write were it not for your wise and endless patience, clarity, and care.

And lastly and mostly, to all the other committed folks who have spent their time, their money, and their heartfelt energy in teaching *BrainStyles* back to me as well as to others: Thank you, Dieter Albrecht, Cholifah and Taufik Bahaudin, Catherine Beau-Wedemeyer, Alisha Chappell, Constance Clancy, Pam Cosby, Charlene Graeber, Dessie Leff, Linda Monk, Antonio Rios, Joy Simmons, Stephanie Stanfield and the ever-wonderful Rita Marsh, Jerald Wilks, and Richard York. Not to mention "Marcy" and "Melinda."

AUTHOR'S NOTE

~~~~~~~~~~~~~~

There will always be a before *and* after. *I am writing the
day of 9/11/2001. 9-11. Our call for help. Oh God.*

~~~~~~~~~~~~~~

We are in crisis in America. In the midst of this day, things changed for all Americans. I feel such horror, such grief. Traditionally stoic, detached New Yorkers have come together in open caring and comfort. Concerned colleagues in Britain, Europe, and China have contacted me by e-mail with expressions of terrible sadness. Much of the world has come together, as British Prime Minister Tony Blair put it, to "stand shoulder to shoulder" with us in the face of this terrorist attack. I weep all day. Call family. Going into town, I hug people I barely know in quiet streets.

Just one week ago, the headline article in a national Sunday magazine read "Why Are We So Angry?" "Road rage, sky rage, sideline rage" are shown with vivid examples of brawls and even one death where "a Massachusetts father—angered over rough play during his son's hockey practice—*beat another father to death as their children watched.*" [Emphasis added.] "A sense of helplessness can trigger rage," according to the expert cited. "That's why we kick ATM machines."[1]

That expert is wrong. We don't resort to rage in our daily lives because we feel helpless but because we have forgotten the purpose for our lives. Acting like

---

1. *Parade* Magazine, 9/2/2001.

spoiled infants wanting what we want NOW, America has been told to grow up in the harshest possible way by terrorists who speak for those who not only hate us but also want us to feel what they feel and suffer as they are suffering, by living in fear and worrying about survival. Our response to the attacks and losses has been almost universal in our turning to one another. In our insular world, we had forgotten our Selves. We had lost perspective, focusing on what does not matter. Now we return to what does: family, neighbors, colleagues, people everywhere. The last words of those heroic, dying passengers on the hijacked planes were for their families: *I love you.*

We had forgotten these were the most important words in our lives. Today the whole country is saying *I love you* to one another; rescue workers are working endlessly; people are standing in line for three hours to give blood even when it isn't needed; stricken strangers are instant friends. We are united in our pain. Things are different. We have been killed on our own streets.

Today we are returning to what counts, to what unites us, to why we are here. Our warriors take up their protection of us with nobility, faith, and a focus that reminds me of my dad and my husband, braving their own fears to make sure we're safe. They love us by protecting us. Military wives and kids face the camera and say, "It's their job" and send their husbands and daddies out to die.

We are returning to the best of ourselves. Our heroes are finally the real ones, not those in Hollywood: regular folks doing remarkable, courageous things smack in the face of death.

REMEMBERING WHAT COUNTS. Ten days after the tragedy I read of some four hundred couples canceling their filings for divorce in Houston, Texas. Marriages all over the country that had been postponed are now on the docket. "No more time to wait," said some newly-called National Guardsmen. Twenty-somethings who were hotshot equity and bond traders officing on Wall Street and in the World Trade Center were interviewed on television and talked about the shift—well, complete revision—of their priorities.* One young man said he was always rather arrogant about the fact that he had been at the top of his class, was a bond trader with a six-figure salary, and earned a large annual bonus. His peers agreed that they had cared only about the stock market and their own careers. The speaker continued by saying he had met a New York City fireman after the tragedy that killed his colleagues

---

* In a *USA Today* feature one month later, a survey measured the shift in priorities from Before, when Career was top of the list, to After, when Career was 10th and Family ranked 1st.

and friends. With tears in his eyes, the bond trader said, "I was embarrassed to tell him what I did for a living." All the group nodded. Eyes were full.

Living in this world is a game of survival. We now see that living safely to pursue our dreams sometimes costs us the greatest price of all. I believe it is also our blessing to get beyond survival and show those who envy us how to live a loving life that is free and then invite them to join us in the fullest expression of their lives. As one woman sighed to me in the midst of this day, "If they only knew we want them to have the same lives and happiness *we* have."

To move forward into true happiness, we all need to act from the best within us—all the love and purpose the horror of 9/11 brought forth. We need to do more than "get back to normal."[2] The state of fear-filled normalcy for Americans and most of the globe is far from acceptable. We must continue to let go of our precious grudges, treasured life stories of wounds and hurts, and the complex history for why we must suffer in our closest partnerships. We must rethink our own life stories and create them anew with love and forgiveness.

There is nothing new to learn. There is a lot to let go of.

It's time to make a difference where it really counts with those we would call when our planes are going down, the people we worry over and try to fix, the very ones we get mad at instead of remembering just how much they mean to us.

Let's get on with it.

---

2. Seven months after 9/11/01, a headline in *USA Today* trumpeted, "How rude and aggravating: Nasty drivers, irate parents, recorded greetings are a 'national problem.'" A survey by a nonprofit group reported ". . . 79 percent of Americans agree that the lack of courtesy careening along the country's highways and ringing in its collective ear is a 'serious national problem.'" This time the story "gained no further interest." The father who beat his son's soccer coach to death went sorrowfully to jail. Airline passengers helped a flight attendant subdue a would-be bomber who had explosives in his shoes. We wait patiently in lines at airports.

A BrainStyles™
Affirmation

I have all the strengths within me right now
to solve any problem I face.

My natural abilities are my focus, which
I apply lovingly and responsibly.

I learn from mistakes and criticisms to grow
with others and master my own wisdom.

I know that by trusting my natural abilities
I can contribute powerfully, caringly, and
responsibly to others, regardless of whether
they recognize this at the time or not.

I release the need to please others or adapt
to their wants, and commit to serve them
with the best of me by looking for
and bringing out the best in them.

I release the past and liberate myself
to be who I really am.

INTRODUCTION
WHAT THIS BOOK HAS TO OFFER YOU

You may be one of those people who has an inkling that the purpose of life is to join in some way with others, even those others who are cantankerous, obnoxious, bewildering, and often deeply offensive. You may be one of those who knows, without knowing how you know, that there is a better way. Conflict, blame, fear, breaking up and making up, and loving so hard it hurts are just not where you want to stay.

WHAT YOU'LL GET HERE. The material in this book is based on more than fifteen years of study of neuroscience (the brain and its functions), genetics, 30-plus years of study of group and individual behavior, adult learning, organizational behavior, and—significantly—a 20-plus year study of spiritual and religious principles and their applications with others of all faiths. The result is a meld of science and ancient wisdom, which asks you to look at the human experience anew. Those who have engaged with *The BrainStyles System®* have experienced transformations in their lives by becoming aware of the most intimate thing they do as humans: *think*. By engaging with *BrainStyles*, you will become aware of, and be able to define, how both you and your lover think about things—especially stressful, critical turning points in your relationship— based on the latest research in brain processing, genetic studies, and their psychological applications. You will be shown how to apply hard-edged knowledge with respect and love within the most challenging learning laboratory you face every day: your personal relationships. You will be shown how honoring your gifts above all will allow you to transcend the limitations of your hardware by embracing them. You will, as so many others have done, be able to transform irritations, stress, and anxiety into renewing and nurturing events and respectful, expansive partnerships with less work. More ease. More confidence. More impact. Less time. Less effort. More peace and fulfillment.

WHERE THIS BOOK IS GOING. SOME DEFINITIONS.
With what gifts I have, I offer this book to whoever wishes to continue remembering what counts, to whoever wishes to seek a longer-range perspective in the holy arena of partnerships.[1] I am using the word partnership intentionally to mean a connection that occurs when two complete human beings join together to create a purpose larger than themselves. In this kind of partnership, a spiritual bond is joined. The health and lives of both partners expand exponentially: in the ideas each considers, the risks taken, the confidence demonstrated, the reach each attains, the goals set and successes achieved, and most importantly, the lives each touches with love.

This is what true love is. This is what one's True Love can bring. It can begin for singles at any age, continue for newlyweds, or for those who have been married for 20-plus years as my husband and I have been.

Make no mistake: I am not claiming the Perfect Marriage for myself. I am claiming a partnership that has fewer shallower valleys and many more peaks, deeper joys, and much, much less conflict than in our first eight years together or ever before in my life. We take turns being the steadier, more spiritual partner, as one of us faces life's challenges. We have learned to see love that exists beyond form.

In a spiritual partnership, each looks for and lovingly speaks to the mastery within the other, rather than his or her problems, mistakes, or non-strengths. Each partner knows the best of the other and holds that idea steadfast on his or her behalf in their daily lives. Children who are born into these kinds of partnerships act differently. They know and can live from their wisdom, the gifts that allow them to perform where they have the most to offer, especially at home with their parents. Children learn naturally how to be considerate and respectful, for this is how they are treated and honored. When schools do the same, discipline problems disappear as the true strengths of the students are acknowledged, developed, and given expression.

---

1. I owe these distinctions to an extraordinary personal coach and teacher, Susan Hayword of Carbondale, Colorado.

We have relationships with business associates, plumbers, acquaintances, and others in our lives where we have measures and goals and make deals. Relationships are defined as those interactions where I ask for what I want from you (if I have you over to dinner, you reciprocate); enter the relationship for what I can get; and when I don't get it, it is upsetting, a breach of our (stated or unstated) contract. In families with relationships, others are there to complete us, to fill our needs, to make us whole. Our children are dependent upon us for things, for love and approval of their performance. When they don't behave as we wish, we withdraw our approval and teach them to "improve," which amounts to changing who they are to fit our model.

To benefit from this book, it is not necessary to have a faith in any religion or higher being. I can assure you that if your partnerships become more friendly and respectful, your family becomes more pleasurable, and one or two others become your greatest pleasure, you will have lived a wonderful, successful life that will touch many. If your marriage can be a place where two minds join for a larger purpose, the world will be more loving, one life at a time. If we use the examples of Gandhi, Jesus, Buddha, and Mohammed, that strategy seems to be quite effective.

If we want things to change globally, we must start locally, intimately, with the biggest challenge of all: creating peace and love in our own homes.

SECTION I:

DEFINE YOUR GIFTS
IN A NEW WAY

CHAPTER **1**

BECOME A LOVER

~~~~~~~~~~~~~~
There is no order of difficulty in miracles. One is not "harder" or "bigger"
than another. They are all the same. All expressions of love are maximal.
—*A Course In Miracles*, Text, 3
~~~~~~~~~~~~~~

THE ORIGINAL *BRAINSTYLES* INSIGHT

We had agreed to write a book together, my husband and I. Well, we would hire a writer, he would outline his concepts, and I would "coordinate the project" by adding examples and editing. I knew there was going to be a lot more to my part than that, I could feel it in the pit of my stomach; but I deeply wanted to have a project that we could do together. I had been commuting to New York from Dallas for the first five years of our marriage. It was now three years later, and we still had separate workday lives.

It was the initial 1988 meeting with our wonderful Deliberator writer/editor, Jane Albritton, who was to write the opening three chapters and a book proposal for our first book on *BrainStyles*. She sat with head down at the table's end while David and I went at it. He was quite irritated and saying something like, "You are interrupting me AGAIN; you are the most difficult person to deal with I have ever met; NO ONE talks to me like you do"—or something like it—as I was thinking, "Who IS this obnoxious horrible male chauvinist domineering pigheaded jerk? Why have I married him? Omigod, is it going to be like this forever?"

My CEO husband was dominating the meeting. We were talking about the very field I had studied my whole career—human development—and I had things to say, important comments to add to this topic that we'd discussed for the past six years, and he wasn't the least bit interested. I was appalled. Furious. He was not even considering my words—or my feelings, for that matter.

Then a thought somehow occurred to me (probably out of desperation): What if I applied what we were writing about? What if I tried practicing what we were about to preach; namely, what if I stopped focusing on what he was saying and how he was saying it, and instead looked for his gifts? I was aware of my vision shifting. Without trying, I just listened. I was suddenly conscious of the stunning concepts this man was presenting. They sounded new, fresh, exciting. I have no recollection of what I said in the next set of interactions; I was just there, doing what I did naturally, without posturing or "trying to communicate effectively." The next thing I knew, he was listening to me intently; I was incredibly impressed with him in an entirely new way. The only comparison I could make was the feeling I'd had when I first fell in love with him. I knew in an instant why he was admired by so many employees and friends. I realized I admired him too. I had lost that in the distance, in the day-to-day of problem solving and arguing and "communicating" for hours (we are both pretty passionate debaters).

Later I realized more of what had happened in that moment when I had chosen to look beyond irritating behavior: I had stopped competing to have the brilliant ideas, to be the expert, and listened instead to the brilliance he brought. My fear of being stupid or not having enough to contribute to our project was revealed (to me), released, and completely overwhelmed by an opportunity to use my true strengths, as I was to learn later. I had stopped focusing on me and my unmet needs to see "weakness" in another. Instead I focused on him, totally, as I recognized his strengths. And I found them. I found the very heart of our relationship at the same time. I had used no techniques or skills, no hours of discussion, no therapy, no self-help tactics; I was honestly there, present, listening with an open mind, and *miraculously!* he responded in kind! Everything appeared to have changed between us and yet nothing had changed in either of us. This was nothing less than a miracle: a shift in our relationship from one of criticism and fear to one of love and acceptance.

From that day forward we have never had the fights or heated "discussions" of the first eight years of our marriage. Things changed. I respected him for his gifts, deeply and truly. He amazed me with his regard for my contributions in a way I had tried to achieve by "being smart" and never really accomplished. Our marriage deepened. Shortly thereafter we launched a project to redecorate part of our home. Previously this would have led us straight to divorce court. However, using the emerging concepts of *BrainStyles,* we collaborated and completed the entire yearlong trial of remodeling with NO fights. I rest my case for *The BrainStyles System* on this one example.

~~~~~~~~~~~~~~~~~

The greatest way to live with honor in this world
is to be what we pretend to be.
—Socrates

~~~~~~~~~~~~~~~~~

NO MORE PRETENSE. BECOME A LOVER. I don't intend to tell you how to love or respect another—you already know how. My intention is to use research and experience to guide you to let go of what you've put in the way of the loving outcomes you deeply desire. You simply need to recall your own magnificence, as well as the magnificence of those around you. Use that perspective to define yourself and your family and create your legacy. Whatever your profession, at home you are a lover, not a fighter. You already have what it takes to be and bring out the best within each of you.

As a sixteen-year-old gay, black adolescent said to me, "It takes courage to be yourself." I trust you to have that courage. The courage you need is fueled by love, not righteous indignation or brilliant answers. It requires courage to live the paradox of being one of a kind, yet being one of the human family. *Each of us is one of a kind connected with the whole.* Celebrate the fact; don't make it better or worse. We *must* connect with and celebrate others to be fully alive. By doing so, we join together in a way that is loving and therefore holy. Creating a partnership is a sacred act. We do so when we apply our best, the natural gifts we already have within, to be truly ourselves, serve our partners, and contribute to the world.

The foundation for what you are reading and are encouraged to practice comes from the following list of principles. Living them, I can attest, will change your life without changing who you are. You will give yourself permission to have sustaining, loving relationships that have no limitations. By honoring those you love, you will expand your very soul.

THE BrainStyles PARTNERSHIP PRINCIPLES

- You can't change anyone, including yourself. Honor gifts above all; respect limitations.
- Successful relationships are ones entered into to see what can be given rather than gotten, from two who are complete rather than two who seek completion.
- Any relationship can be a spiritual partnership when two minds join to seek a common, loving goal.
- No relationship is accidental; its purpose is to practice forgiveness. This is why all relationships are precious.

    As we forgive another, we forgive ourselves and vice versa. Doing so, we heal the past and prepare for grander experiences in the future. Forgiveness takes place in the present moment and is complete when you realize there was nothing there to forgive in the first place.

- It only takes one to heal a relationship and transform it into a partnership.
- A partnership begins as each seeks the best within the other, rather than problems, mistakes, or defeats, and then honors that best over time.
- Everyone, with no exceptions, is capable of creating loving partnerships.
- In all situations, Love is the answer.

Your spirit seeks to join with others, to become part of a greater whole in order to realize fully who you truly are.

Your hardware must be honored so it can happen.

~~~~~~~~~~~~~~~~

I couldn't count it. I guess I just have a good ear.
—Ella Fitzgerald, one of the most celebrated jazz vocalists of the twentieth century,
who had no musical training, grew up in hardship, and just "started singing,"
commenting on her musical and rhythmic mastery.

~~~~~~~~~~~~~~~~

BrainStyles is a systematic approach to identifying your natural, hardwired, brain-based gifts that need attention rather than work and stress to nurture and grow. Defining your special gifts, your value and worth, is the platform upon which you stand when entering any relationship, whole and complete. Knowing who you are and who you are not allows you to be a lover in the fullest sense of that word.

BrainStyles teaches you how to reframe your "curses" into the blessings that they are. This approach that I live and teach—a philosophy and the tools to apply it—builds self-acceptance that can set you free to create a universe of people whom you respect for who they are and, just as importantly, for who they are not. As you do so, you live at ease with your own gifts and limitations. You expand out into life, fearlessly, by using your new wisdom to transform critical or fear-based reactions into more authentic, accepting responses. You give up expectations that just won't happen. You stop trying to change anyone—especially yourself.

~~~~~~~~~~~~~~~~

There is more in a human life than our theories of it allow.
Sooner or later something seems to call us onto a particular path. . . .
This is what I must do; this is what I've got to have. This is who I am.
—James Hillman, philosopher, author

~~~~~~~~~~~~~~~~

Marlee Alex, an Oregon writer, begins an article entitled "Listening"[1] by describing how her self-inflicted criticism turned her natural gift into an adolescent curse.

"I am a listener. Natural born. But I didn't always value this gift. In my teens I desperately wished to be like everyone else: bubbly, chatty, effusive. I even questioned if something was wrong with me because I was curious and quiet." What a discovery when she began to see what she could do with the very ability she used to disparage. "I am beginning to see how my ease in listening is

---

1. From *Aspire* Magazine, April 1997.

an art. . . . It's active, involving, participative. . . ." She lists what marvelous things being a listener provides. Without effort, she elicits stories, revealing the inner worlds of others just by being herself and doing what she does most naturally. The difference between Marlee and most of the rest of us? She is being herself with purpose; she does what she does on purpose.

Marlee volunteers at a women's prison. What does she do? She is "present"; literally she just sits around, being available, as she nonverbally communicates her acceptance of the women and where they are in life. Mastering her gift of being a quiet introvert,[2] she has developed her own art. Applying a gift in this way, she is a Master in the fullest sense of the word.

And there's more. Previously dreading social events, Marlee says, "Now before going to a party, I just tell myself to listen with affection. My attitude is 'Tell me more.' The result is [that] a person shows me his soul." Social life now holds no fear. Marlee has discovered a career, a way to serve in the community, a whole lifestyle of being confident in what she has to offer. With a simple shift, what was invisible is now a celebrated asset. Her true self, the best of her, is in the spotlight making her own and others' lives richer and more satisfying.

It would seem most of us just stumble upon our gifts—without training, extra stimulation in preschool, or even a very supportive environment.

A *brainstyle* describes the way you think and use your brain most naturally and effortlessly to do what you do best. In our western culture, a *brainstyle* is what is invisible to us. We focus on what we need to improve, fix, change. "Self Help" is an industry. Isn't this ridiculous? The self needs no "help." Our "self" only needs permission—permission that comes from within—to be and do our best. Knowing this prevents dependencies where the ego seeks to become whole by choosing just the right person to round you out and give you what you're missing. You can enter a relationship for what you have to offer, not for what you can get. By doing so, you are in a creative partnership that has no limits to how fully you can grow together.

> BRAINSTYLE CLUE: You are not your hardware. You are in charge of how your hardware serves you. Clarity about your *brainstyle* allows you the perspective to run your internal programs.

---

2. About 25 percent of the population are introverts, or those who have a more active internal life than their counterparts, the extroverts, who are stimulated by the external world and interactions with others.

SURRENDERING TO YOUR STRENGTHS IS A SPIRITUAL ACT.
You free your intuition, creativity, focus, and become generous with your abilities as you free yourself to be who you are capable of being. Strengths expand naturally; you expand naturally by honoring your strengths—in your capacity to love, learn, and lead from a loving center. You become powerful in the choices you make. You stop feeling victimized. Doing what you love to do, you go to work with passion, eagerness, curiosity, and a willingness to see what you can make of the puzzles you confront. You learn from others instead of defending yourself from their "abuses"; you contribute to your family by using your natural abilities lovingly to realize the life rewards you really seek with those you care about the most. This is not sacrificing, helping out, or being sympathetic. It is honoring yourself for who you are and making your gifts available to others. It is honoring others whom you live with by loving them equally for who they are and who they cannot be.

Living in this way is peaceful. Giving yourself permission to be lovingly authentic permits calmness, and eliminates conflicts and stress. An Indian guru, Swami Chidvilasananda, in her book *Inner Treasures*[3] says ". . . contentment does not lead to inactivity. On the contrary, it is the state that allows every activity to come to fruition. When you perform action from the source of contentment, it has beauty and sanctity. When you perform action out of anxiety, nervousness, and twenty cups of coffee, then that's what you give to the world."

Sounds simplistic. It *is* simple to say—it's not always easy to live.

---

3. 33–34 (©1995, SYDA Foundation).

Become a Lover

Brave enough to be
authentic, vulnerable, and trusting;

Loving and wise enough to look past
what is said and done
to the very best of the other,
regardless of the past;

Strong enough to create a partnership
grander than goals and more than an alliance,
especially in the face of setbacks and loss;

Capable enough to require the best
outcome for each of you;

Committed enough to make
your dreams come true;

Open enough to expand them together.

Celebrate the best of what is.

Be willing to fall in love every day.

~~~~~~~~~~~~~~

THE REAL WORLD

In the real world that lasts beyond us,
     of beauty,
     of wisdom,
     of love, not fear,
       there is no *good, better, best,*
There is simply correcting mistakes.

Time is made to know you.

The Way You Oughta Be
Is The Way You Are.

Your mysteries,
Your stories, your missteps, your laughter
Are the songs that teach me
     I can sing too.
My heart and mind look beyond
     what my eyes can see.

We are One in spirit.

In the real world,
You are your brilliance,
     not your flaws.

August, 1998

~~~~~~~~~~~~~~

CHANGE YOUR LIFE, DON'T CHANGE WHO YOU ARE

~~~~~~~~~~~~~~~

No two people in the world are exactly alike. [However] genetically, we are all very much alike. Your genetic endowment is 99.9 percent identical to that of the stranger you passed in the street earlier today. Indeed, it's only that remaining 0.1 percent—one part in a thousand— that distinguishes you from any person who has ever lived.
—*Mysteries of the Mind,* Richard Restak, MD, National Geographic Press, 2000

~~~~~~~~~~~~~~~

DEFINING YOUR GIFTS WITH *BRAINSTYLES*

Looking behind behavior to what drives it, you come instantly to the brain and its genetic hardware. Recent worldwide genetic studies verify all humans alive today have a single, common African ancestor. Yet your brain is unique, like a fingerprint, made up by DNA common to every other human who has ever been born. The brain also defines your abilities and limitations. A description follows to help you identify those abilities and limits in a new way.

> *BRAINSTYLE CLUE:* A *brainstyle* describes the way your brain processes **new** information in order to **make a decision** and allow you to take action.

Taking action is a natural process, and—until you learn to watch out for it—it seems a lot like remembering what to do. But it is very different when you use your natural gifts. You are more like you and less like anyone else. You probably don't get along with anyone else as well at the time you are using your *brainstyle* to think, unless you appreciate each other's gifts and rhythms. It is when you are using your natural way of thinking that you want time for yourself to think and say and feel in your own way. When you don't get to do any of these things, you can get testy. Or you may have learned to hide behind glazed eyes.

DECISION-MAKING. Scott Turow, in his novel *The Sins of the Fathers,* describes what decision-making requires for a judge. For those in new decision situations whose *brainstyle* does not naturally sort and evaluate new material quickly, this character may be speaking for you and describing how you handle decisions in a stressful situation:

> Decide, I tell myself, as I so often do. In this job, deliberation is respected. Indecision is not. My work, in the end, is simply that, deciding, saying yes or no. But it's hard labor for the natively ambivalent. There's no other job I know of that more reliably reveals the shortcomings of a personality than being a judge. The years roll on and life seems like this more and more, that choices don't really exist in the way I thought they would when I was a child and expected the regal power of adulthood to provide clarity and insight.   (pp. 79-80)

Have you also felt overwhelmed, angry, frustrated with yourself or the stupidity and stubbornness of others when it's time to DO SOMETHING?

It can be easier than this.

A BRAINSTYLES OVERVIEW. A *brainstyle* defines how your brain uses information when you are most naturally yourself, using your neural hardware in the quickest, easiest way you have available to think through information, process feelings, retrieve experience, and access your problem-solving abilities when deciding to take action. When you think about it, your relationships are put to the test when you must decide on something together. Stress is most likely to occur in those times when the wedding must be planned, money is involved, a deal must be closed, or any commitment must be made. Knowing your *brainstyle* means knowing a central fact about yourself that illuminates your decision-making, whether you are a judge in court or you do your judging on everyday matters. Knowing how you make a decision provides a core of information about all the stressful times in your life. Using the *BrainStyles* roadmap to your gifts allows continual forgiveness for what you don't do well.

But wait, there's more: Knowing how others make decisions gives you the basis for understanding, forgiving, and then relating to others in a respectful way that isn't phony or contrived. When you give up trying to be and do it all equally well, and berating yourself for not living up to your ideals, life can be easier, richer, and more satisfying. No, you won't just lie around making excuses. Living from within your hardwired gifts is not only a relief but also the basis for your personal motivation, integrity, clarity, and success. Your leadership. Defining your gifts and their boundaries automatically creates a need for partnership that is vital to your life. Applying these principles can recreate a marriage, as I should know. I learned firsthand how to apply what I was trying to teach and write about at home.

> *BRAINSTYLE CLUE:* We access different areas and functions of our brains with greater or lesser speed.

TIMING AND CREATING OUR REALITY. According to measurements made in the 1980s, our brains register approximately *one in every hundred incoming stimuli.* The implications of this finding are profound. Whatever is out there talking at us, appearing before us, or trying to influence us in some way, we sort and select in order to understand it. Thus we create our own reality in our heads. It isn't Mom's reality, a teacher's reality, or a friend's reality; it is our own interpretation of events, created by our own synthesis of right and left brain information-processing, that sets our thoughts and feelings in motion.

> *BRAINSTYLE CLUE:* A *brainstyle* defines the most efficient (fastest) way your brain uses information by drawing upon specific regions that specialize in certain processing functions. The areas you access fastest and easiest define your natural gifts.
> Decisions, values, and perceptions are all biased by how you sort the information. For example: If you take in information and break it down into literal, provable pieces, you see the world as a series of literal, provable events.
> *In short:* The way you take in and file information defines the way you view reality, express it, and prefer it to be expressed to you.

WE CREATE REALITY . . . IN TIME. To prove this further, in recent experiments at the Salk Institute, neurologist Dr. Eagleman reported, "Snap your fingers in front of your eyes, and that to you is the moment now, but in fact, that event happened well in the past." The light had to reach your eyes, and the sound had to reach your ears. And then both signals get processed by the brain and put back together so that they look simultaneous. "But it's nothing but trickery on the brain's part. And it has to go through a lot of effort to make it come out right." When asked how this all happens, one scientist says that it's all "just an illusion, and things are not actually all that coherent." Metaphysical teachings put it like this: "Projection creates perception." In other words, *I wouldn't have seen my reality if I hadn't believed it was going to happen in the first place and then sorted out the facts to prove it.*

> *BRAINSTYLE CLUE:* A fact is a perception waiting to be disproven.

Add to this information what a Harvard microneurobiologist reported in a lecture at the Aspen Institute in 1997: "A piece of the brain the size of a grain of rice contains axons twenty miles long." Axons transport the messages that get sent from one part of the brain to another as we think through information. That information moves at about sixty miles an hour (on average). Of course, after the first cup of coffee you might reach the speed limit, but metabolism has some of us in second gear most of the time or in hyperdrive and hyperactivity, given our biological energy level. The reality we see has to come in through our senses to be processed across miles of brain "wiring" (neural synapses) to reach and connect specialty areas that deal with images, sounds, and specific memories in order to think about and respond to every single event every single minute. And we take all this for granted.

> *BRAINSTYLE CLUE:* Your genetically-based hardwired gifts work according to your own special timing. Becoming aware of your *brainspeed* timing is the basis for taking charge of your hardware.

To get a better understanding of what we use to see the world, let's take a quick peek into what's in our heads, at least in terms of brain hardware and what it does. Then we'll appreciate just how magnificent this two-and-a-half- to three-pound part of our body is, how it serves us, and why we see reality as we do.

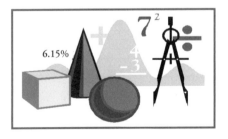

BRAINS 101: THE LEFT HEMISPHERE OF THE BRAIN. *I think, therefore I am*[1] could be the motto of this side of our brains.

The left hemisphere *interprets* the world for us. Its job is to create a position out of that interpretation that makes us right rather than loving. As Dr. Michael Gazzaniga[2] says, "The left brain weaves its story in order to convince itself and you that it is in full control."[3] Another prominent neuroscientist, Dr. Antonio Damasio, says that the "left cerebral hemisphere" makes up verbal narratives that "do not necessarily accord with the truth."[4] We lie to save our ego-identity— don't tell me you haven't done it—and look good according to some standard we made up. It is the side that, metaphorically, watches out for our survival, and literally *keeps us alive* by registering fear and articulating what can go wrong and how to prevent it. The left brain is the little voice that nags, critiques, worries, is skeptical, doubts your worth, and criticizes and compares your thighs, hairline, and stomach to hers or his. It is the side that expresses emotions as judgments, often through projecting the unexpressed feelings onto our partners: "He doesn't love me." "He's always critical." "She always whines." "Why am I still with him/her?"

> *BRAINSTYLE CLUE:* The left side of the brain performs what we are aware of as conscious thinking with words. It is the hemisphere that allows us to measure and speak, judge and organize, and be logical by seeing the cause-effect relationship between events and actions.

This is the side of the brain that many philosophies try to leave behind so that we can live permanently from the other side of the brain, which is the side that allows us to just BE. Ask yourself how long you would stay alive on this planet if you were without your left brain. How well would you get along in the human community, let alone in a relationship, if you had no ability to perform with language, space, or time?

> *BRAINSTYLE CLUE:* The left hemisphere gives us the ability to perform in this world, in time, to be aware of dangers, to be able to speak, problem-solve, measure, investigate and organize rational solutions. We learn with the left side of the brain by taking in information and sorting and analyzing it.

---

1. Philosopher Rene Descartes used this statement to "prove" our existence. Sadly, most of us don't know what to replace it with; for Americans it might be *I perform; therefore I am.*
2. Codiscoverer of the functions of the left and right hemispheres of the brain, along with Roger Sperry.
3. *Scientific American,* July 1998, 51.
4. Alexander Star, *New York Times Magazine,* May 7, 2000, 31.

The left hemisphere is the logical side of the brain, which looks for cause-effect relationships and therefore controls our lives. People who have the easiest and quickest access[5] to this side express their caring and nurture very literally. They protect *(Watch out!)* and fix things by analyzing, sorting, naming what's wrong or missing, and generating the consequences *(if you keep doing A you'll always get B, so do this to get C)*. This cause-effect thinking communicates largely by using *blaming* as a frequent communication. Yes, blaming is the language of this side. Think about it: how do you get to the cause of a problem? (Who did this? Why did you do it?) The answer can then be found so the cause can be prevented next time. Thus this brain hemisphere is the one that gives us apparent control (through thinking in words and symbols that are literal and have boundaries), so this is the side that tries to control others. *(Put this there. Clean up your room. Why did you forget my birthday?)* With our left brains we make demands. We achieve and compete, measuring our progress and worth.

> *BRAINSTYLE CLUE:* The left side of the brain laughs. Left-brained humor observes the obvious in new and surprising ways, uses puns and wordplays. Surprises cause startled laughter. The right brain helps by knowing the correct association; the left side sees the error. Right-brained humor builds associations, exaggerations, and creates outlandish mental pictures that make us laugh.

The left brain makes jokes by observing illogical and obvious things and making surprising connections about them[6]. Think of a comedian like TV star Jay Leno, who presents headlines in the paper that have double meanings that are puns. The left brain reads, compares, then analyzes the unintended and laughs. Think of right-brained comedian Robin Williams and humor writer Dave Barry[7]. Each creates guffaws from making outrageous associations, painting outlandish pictures with metaphors, and exaggerating to an extreme, providing a right-brained picture that overrides analysis and blows apart our normal associations.

A detective's job is to apply the left brain to observe literal facts, describe, analyze, sort, put events in a sequence, and solve a crime, all without getting personally involved. The firemen, emergency workers, and police who went into the burning World Trade Center towers were "just doing their job"—with left-brained skill, goals, and detachment.

---

5. That is, the largest amount of neural connections to a certain area of the brain.
6. "He was so dumb, he took a ruler to bed to see how long he slept." "Take my wife. Please."
7. ". . . the mental capacity of an eggplant . . ." ". . . a brain that rattled around in its head like a BB . . ."

> BRAINSTYLE CLUE: The left side of the brain learns and stores your personal measures for quality, your standards for personal worth and performance.

When I first began to write for publication, my left brain got enormously busy shouting out all my worries and fears of being "naked on the page" with internal critiques: "No one will believe you! How can you prove that? Who are YOU to say any of this?" It harped and whined and shrieked on my mental radio. If I tried to tune to another station, the voice was only more insistent and demeaning. A huge victory for my life as a whole was to learn how to use it for the overall goal. Using my left brain's "voice" (thoughts with words that compare and measure) to serve rather than bully me has become one of the biggest gifts of writing. I finally figured out my inner critic was there to keep me alive; it was bringing up what was threatening. How could I use its concerns? It was asking me questions that I didn't have the answers to. I then decided to tune it in on purpose. The challenges were loud and clear; I only needed to find out the answers and put them down on the page and *voila!* a more credible, provable result. My left brain was satisfied. My fantasies of brutal critics lost their power. I then knew I'd done a job according to my standards, which is the job of the left brain to impose. The result? I was never asked a question about what I had written that I hadn't already put to myself. The difference? Others were always nicer to me than I was.

Now that I have made friends with this gift, it is one of the biggest sources of peace for me. My challenges are mentally posed in a much kinder, gentler tone, and others' challenges are much easier to entertain. *Really.*

> BRAINSTYLE CLUE: The left hemisphere of the brain has the ability to say no, set limits, observe specifics, measure performance, and worry about the future. The left hemisphere of the brain measures, operates within, and creates structure.

The left brain wants to create and observe *impact.* This boundary-setting side of the brain *(Don't. Stop. Keep away.)* thus continually evaluates and compares what is observed, heard, or felt *(He is too close, I was faster than he was),* and so acts as our judgment machine to monitor and regulate our existence and interactions. To create change, the left side of the brain demands movement, effort, uses the "will," and articulates our internal intention to push on a thing or person to realize a tangible goal, or get what we want in measurable terms. As I have said, the left brain's job is survival and protection. Left-brainers we live with and love dedicate themselves to these things on our behalf.

THE LEFT-BRAINED STEREOTYPE REVISITED. When you think of someone who is "left-brained," who comes to mind? The math whiz? The technocrat? The nerd? The hard-nosed, no-nonsense attorney, corporate whiz, or engineer? Well, you're right. AND you should also consider the writer, the photographer, the artist who paints or re-creates people or things in *realistic* portraits, landscapes, and vivid still-lifes. And before you continue to use the most common stereotypes of what left-brained folks do, here is an example of how a very left-brained man applied caring and "heart" with a right-brained woman dealing with personally loaded issues in her divorce.

THE LOVING LEFT-BRAINER. "I want to call up his attorney and tell that S.O.B. *my* side of the story." Melinda (a pseudonym) was mad, righteously indignant over "years of being left out, looked over, and given the short end of the stick." She had had it "up to here." She had decided it was time to tell her soon-to-be ex-husband just how unfair and selfish, and, and . . . well, you get the idea. Her right-brained emotions were overwhelming, imperative, and demanding left-brained action to make that phone call—in short, to *DO something!* She wanted her husband's attorney to *understand* (translation: to actually *feel* the full magnitude of her emotions). She was furious that her lifetime was being boiled down to some (left-brained) financial statements and legal papers. "YOU CAN'T FIT WHAT I FEEL ON PAPER!" she stormed into the phone.

Listening to the recap of how this very left-brained gentleman handled her call, you may also be struck with how the structured, factual, literal ones care for, nurture, or protect with as much kindness and love as those who touch and hug and speak more directly of their feelings.

"You have every right to call and tell him your side of the story," her attorney responded in what can only be described as a neutral tone. She said the very tone he used gave her pause. In *BrainStyles* terms, we would say that pause allowed her to access her left-brain logic, or to consider the cause-effect consequences of what she was about to do. She had enough foresight to suspect there might be consequences that she wasn't presently considering.

"You've spent so long on the phone with him, what do you think will happen if I call him now?" she asked more hesitantly.

"I personally don't think it'll do much good. All he'll do is tell you your husband's side of the story. He'll tell you why he deserves the money more than you do. You'll just get upset at this, and so will he." Melinda thought her attorney probably said more than this, but she couldn't really remember. What she did hear was a very rational, nonjudgmental position (quite different from her own, she noticed) that allowed her to see herself rather starkly from the other side. Hers wasn't a pretty nor a powerful position. In fact, she assessed (getting quite logical indeed), she would likely create a fight and end up losing. Even if he did give in, she thought, how would that be, being placated? She realized, she said, just how kind the logic was that was coming over the phone; just how many times over the last six months she had longed to strike out, to "let 'em have it"; and with persistent rational counsel she had held her peace and instead worked toward a balanced solution. She was embarrassed. She then fully acknowledged that this legal and financial arena required her *non-strengths*. She did not make the call. Listening to someone who was far stronger in drawing from the left brain allowed her to balance her emotions with logic and analysis.

THE FEARFUL LEFT-BRAINER. Those who draw predominantly from their left brains do have their downsides. For instance, they sometimes get their opinions and the facts confused. Their opinions are right; ergo, they are just being factual. They structure everything, state it in a way that is either "dry"—lengthily sequential and full of history and specifics—or black and white. No runs, no hits from your side; no errors from theirs. On the defensive, reality is what they say it is, and it always somehow describes a reality that makes them a hero or a winner and you a loser. However, loving the Logical Ones by honoring their gifts allows these remarkable folks to apply them for your benefit—to love and respect you—just as in the example above.

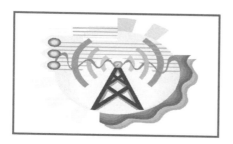

BRAINS 102: THE RIGHT HEMISPHERE OF THE BRAIN. The right brain allows us to integrate ideas, feel attraction, make connections, and bond. The right brain learns directly from experience, processing exactly what is available to the senses. So our right brains store experiences, whole and complete, and relate one thing to another to give us holistic *wisdom* as opposed to linear *intelligence*.

> *BRAINSTYLE CLUE:* The right brain processes information all at once, through all the senses available (holistically) as a whole total impression or *experience.*
>
> The right brain perceives emotions, or the behaviors on face, posture, and skin that show reactions to outside events. It then associates external events with internal memories, presents emotions to interpret personal meaning (seeing how it applies to me), and learns to guide thought and behavior in this way.

The right brain experiences its beliefs as self-evidently valid (experience is truth); thus beliefs based on experience are *very* difficult to change. We draw from this side of the brain when we are unrelievingly stubborn, unconvinced by logic and facts; we just know what's right for us. So we live with the gal or have unprotected sex and forget what our folks said, to learn from our mistakes when things don't work out, as they told us they wouldn't. The right brain changes slowly with repetitive or intense experience. Trying to convince with words doesn't work on the nonverbal, imaging side of the brain. (Remember the exhausting, fruitless religious/political monologue volleys with the hard-headed folks in your own family?)

The opposite is true with our logical hemisphere, which, once it is shown a rational or contrary answer, can change in an instant and start in a new direction. Am I crazy, or isn't it the ones who promote love, world peace, and harmony who are often preoccupied with Change! Progress! Growth! and find it horrifically challenging to accept *what is* as perfection? The core ability of the right brain is to perceive things exactly as they are. It is the left-brained interpretation of reality fueled by fear that is the ego's tool to make us adapt, try to change what is, and perfect others and ourselves with harangues and nagging.

This does not mean the left brain is the same as the ego, nor that people who draw more from the left brain are more egotistical. Neither does it rule out that the left hemisphere of the brain is the outward servant of the ego, whose job is to learn things to make us smarter, earn money to make us safer, direct activities to make us more popular, and survive happily. However, we have a higher authority within us to direct the left brain in how we complete our mission. We can choose to shift our perception from one of measurement and critique to merely demean to one of measurement and critique to clarify and build.

> *BRAINSTYLE CLUE:* The right side of our brains allow both intuitive wisdom and thick-headed, stereotyping stubbornness.

Often the right-brained can approach an intuitive, experience-based subject such as trust as an all-or-nothing decision: We either trust her immediately, impulsively, full out, or not. Family matters become self-fulfilling prophecies and biases towards others as fact, as in, "I knew she'd say that, she's always said that."

> BRAINSTYLE CLUE: The right brain thinks quickly, priming for immediate action. It also makes leaps that associate one idea with another in random ways. The right side of the brain experiences unreasonable anxiety and unexplainable love.

When using the right brain, you envision the end, leap to conclusions, and care about how things will come out. This is the source of our vision, in the highest, deepest sense (as in Martin Luther King Jr.'s "dream"). The right brain creates a mental image, locks on to it, and is bitterly disappointed if you don't attain it. This does NOT mean that if you have quick and dominant access to the right brain, you can change your mind quickly. It does mean you can get excited about a new idea and its possibilities (brainstorming) and look like as if you're changing your mind or going along with the program early on. Later comes a different story.

The right brain operates differently according to the emotional state produced in reaction to others or the situation, by sensing and rapidly interpreting events, interactions, and nonverbal cues based on experience, unencumbered by logic or analysis. Thus people can decide they like or dislike someone in four seconds, experience prejudice against a group, or create a stereotype as a natural survival mechanism (a quick fight-or-flight response based on what we remember as a threatening situation).

This side of the brain controls movement and so takes over after we learn to execute a skill by giving a feeling of being on automatic pilot, in "the zone," outside of time, and at one with the universe as parts of the left brain literally shut down. The imaging ability of this hemisphere creates leaps in thinking, while giving us the perception of access to the Unknowable and Infinite through prayer and meditation. Images "pop up out of nowhere" to be intuitive flashes, assumptions, and expectations for others. Those with a great deal of access to these gifts can lock on to their inner pictures and idealize, hope for the best, be unrelenting, enthusiastic optimists and be vulnerable to disappointment with the less-sexy, measurable results. These same gifts inspire with visions of what might be, use passion to preach and convert, create melodies, or write songs and paint abstract creations that have never been seen before. When the right brain is primarily involved, we call it Art in some form. The Art of War, for instance, is the strategy of leaping ahead of your opponent. The Art of Politics is intuiting what another is after and either helping or thwarting his or her goal.

> BRAINSTYLE CLUE: The right brain experiences life passively or automatically (as if we are seized by our emotions).

Feelings of losing control and being overwhelmed or terrified are taken in and processed by the right brain. These feelings can be bounded by and limited with left-brain words—an explanation, a diagnosis, the rules to limit an event—as the words make an experience measurable and therefore endurable.

Empathy and visual imagery, the tools of the counselor and inventor, are the strengths of this hemisphere. The right side of our brain loves. It is our connection to the whole, to ideas that go beyond proof, to the unfathomed and unfathomable with leaps of insight and intuition. It operates with and creates images, leaping about the boundless mindscape of dreams. Its language is the unstated, the associative and random.

> BRAINSTYLE CLUE: The right brain thinks in terms of associations, patterns, connections, and so speaks in associations (i.e., "this reminds me of"), and uses similes and metaphors (this is like that, a "blue sound," etc.). People who tell stories with lots of interruptions and lack of sequence, or who lose the point, are trying to convey what is stored in their right brains without words.

This side of the brain seeks connection and may just be applying the simpler principles of attraction and repulsion in dealing with people and ideas, based on emotional and sensory input as well as experience.

The right brain thinks in terms of broad categories and patterns (overlooking the distinctions to focus on similarities), thus allowing tolerance of differences, instant intimacy with others, and falling in love with people, objects, professions, and new ideas. This is why those who are predominantly right-brained seek and are attracted to harmony and comfort, turn to meditation and prayer, reading, or a soothing touch to feel well. They avoid conflict and "harsh, toxic people," who confront or label or demand.

> *BRAINSTYLE CLUE:* The right hemisphere of the brain KNOWS but cannot speak.

Yet all these gifts are dependent upon the structure and language of the left brain—the measuring, analytical, critical side—for expression. And so the dilemma of the right-brained in Western culture: the right-brained are the airheads, the left-brained are the big winners and moneymakers. In cultures where the unseen and unknown are prized, the right-brained take their place much higher in society as heads of the organization, family, or faith; the ones who have the indefinable spirit, contacts, the juice, the charisma.

LEFT- AND RIGHT-BRAINED FASCISTS. The right-brained think they must teach their opposites how to be more feeling, or express their feminine side, and all those things that intuitives can do naturally. This is a wholly worthless exercise.

The left-brained think they must shock the flaky ones into seeing reality, the facts of the situation, and the measurable, concrete consequences of their actions. This is also, for the most part, a wholly worthless, endless exercise. Yes, rocks are hard and water is wet, and you cannot yet drive off a cliff and survive, it's true. However, in relationships, the only thing that matters is getting the things out of the way that prevent the expression of love between you.

Accept the fact that the expression of love is channeled by *brainstyle* hardware. Give up demanding your way as the right way and making others wrong in the way they express themselves.

Look for love. It's always there. Always.

HONORING THE RIGHT BRAIN. In general terms, the right brain is often called "the heart" and the left brain "the head." And as we all know, the heart ultimately rules the head, overcoming a lack of IQ with the love of a thing that conquers disciplines in all fields, making the ultimate decision because, well, we just felt it was right. Don't we all know of a brilliant person who never got off the ground with his (left-brained) genius for lack of the ability to sell his ideas or include others?

If, as physicists tell us, the known universe (including our own bodies and possessions) is 90 percent space, how will the left-brain principles of friction, combustion, logic, and force act upon it to take us beyond our present boundaries out into that space and the infinity that awaits? The task must surely demand the gifts of the inarticulate right brain whose very milieu is space, without time or limits, and which operates beyond quantum wave or particle, beyond the known.

THE FEARFUL RIGHT-BRAINER. Fear drives emotional demands. Loud and long-winded, sullen, resistant, scheming or demanding, the frightened right brain can override logic to propel deception for personal and short-term gain, attention, and ego-centered goals. You've winced at the right-brained gossips, whiners, or anxious drama queens who are masters of tragedy, as they have boasted about their own conquests and verbally maimed their selected competition to stir up other egos, making revenge and retaliation their "only choice." Their lives really are soap operas, their problems insolubly locked onto selected painful emotional memories which they carry without benefit of healing, from any loving sources of wisdom, external or internal.

But enough about the worst. The right brain can replace images when directed to. Healing begins with loving acceptance of one's gifts. Meet Judith, a woman who has suffered a lifetime of anxieties over her worth and impact, overlooking and undervaluing her true right-brained gifts to arrive *here*.

THE RIGHT-BRAINED MASTER. There was to be a wedding, a marriage of two families—one from the left coast, one from the right—who had never met until the day before the Big Day. Tension was everywhere with The Questions. Would anyone like anyone else? Would they survive this event and make the kids happy? How could they come out looking good, or at least avoid making complete idiots of themselves?

In stepped the right-brained mother of the groom, Judith, a woman who had raised a family to adulthood, and now, in her mid-fifties, describes herself as a jack-of-all-trades, master of none. "I've done many things over my life (cooking, entertaining, art, playing the piano, running an art gallery, sales and marketing, raising a family) but none of them have ever been with mastery," she says. "I have always wondered just what I could really do well." This is a typical remark by those with the most access to the nonverbal side of the brain: Their work in life is, for the most part, the art that is immeasurable.

For most of us, it would be difficult to describe the impact of Judith's gifts as we observe the wedding and its attendant social events. Her natural strengths and their impact were assumed, part of the white noise of social life.

At this wedding, from the very first meeting, the other family was included in every activity seamlessly, effortlessly, by this jack-of-all-trades' gift. ("She's such a nice person. My, isn't she friendly.") The first meeting was dominated by her warmth and laughter, eye contact, handshakes, offers of help. The strangers were actively shown positive regard in the face of their somewhat stuffy behavior that honored formalities and procedures. She was "only being considerate." She accommodated their needs and manners. She offered. "What do you need? How can I help?"

Her laughter melted the iciness of the group as she enjoyed the dumb jokes and attempts at socializing by those not so adept in the liquid movements among guests as she. For everyone at this wedding, she smiled; she *listened*. Everyone there, especially the oldest and the youngest at the party who might feel awkward or left out, was attended to, seated, asked after.

It was apparent that her natural abilities to make relationships, to connect with others and their needs and feelings, had created a loving center—first for her own family, and now a second one. At this particular event, others often were in charge. Would they have done as well if she weren't there to give the encouragement and gratitude that she did? Would the dinner have been served as well? Of course. Would the guests have all smiled and behaved themselves nicely? Of course. Would there have been the same ineffable feeling to the affair? Undoubtedly not.

The one with the ability to know her feelings and put them at the service of the total group won the day. She *is* a Master of her gifts, having used all the many "trades" she has practiced over the years as vehicles to deliver her social skills lovingly, to make life a joy for those who are better at other things.

DON'T FORGET YOUR

FREE READER'S BONUS

Define your *BrainStyle* and your Ideal Lover

See page xiii for more information

CHAPTER 3

THE PROBLEM IS TIMING. THE SOLUTION IS TIMING

~~~~~~~~~~~~~~~

Relationships are dances in time, with leaders and
followers continually seeking a rhythm together.
—*BrainStyles®: Change Your Life Without Changing Who You Are^SM, 45*

~~~~~~~~~~~~~~~

BRAINSTYLES AND TIMING

Besides *brainstyle*, personal pace and energy level are the most powerful bonding agents or sources of friction between people. Timing in the brain is just one expression of our energy level to use the hardware we have, zipping back and forth between the left side and right side of our brains.

High-speed people drive projects and make things *move*. They try things. They never seem to relax; they just go to sleep. It's 120 mph or Stop. They also frustrate easily and can trip over themselves with their energy, spilling things, ideas, and people in their exuberance to move quickly. They never get enough done in a day, have too many ideas, are too urgent too much of the time, wish fiercely, and dream big. Slower pace brings a more thoughtful demeanor, time to listen, to pick up on the end of sentences, to wonder and worry about things, to chew the entire meal, to make meals an event, to plan more carefully. A more deliberate pace allows one to take more time for whatever his gifts are: introspective ones spend more time looking inside, decisive folks spend more time fixing things, heady ones dream up ideas and solutions to things, to explain major problems to those who take the time to move thoroughly and methodically through the day to prove that it was the tortoise, not the hare, who triumphed.

Learning about timing and brainspeed will give you a powerfully constructive way to re-evaluate people and inherent gifts. Integrating that knowledge into the larger context of healing relationships will give you peace.

In Western culture especially, fast is smart and cool; slow is dumb and dumber.[1] Having the answer on the tip of your tongue is therefore prized over the thoughtful, slower response. There are exceptions, of course. I am famous in my family for the quick, decisive direction: "No, don't turn here." "Are you sure?" "Yes." Lately many of my quick, decisive directions have been completely and thoroughly wrong. I'm not proud of this. However, my timing is as much a part of me as my eye color. My timing promotes blurting, "*Yes*, this is it." Then, of course, you know someone who ponders things forever, so that when he says something everyone stops and listens, giving him more than his due just because he considered so long before offering his pearl.

Timing is central to how we express ourselves and live in the world.

TIME AND PERCEPTION. Imagine we can draw time on a line. Labeling the line with familiar terms for our perceptions of events, it would look like the figure below. (Note: *brainstyle* terms are added where they occur in time.)

~~~~~~~~~~~~~~~

TIME

Time O____ 1st time___ 2nd ___ 3rd___ 4th ___ 5th ___ *** ___ 15th *** ___ 20th ___ 50th___

NEW	*FAMILIAR*	*ROUTINE*	*EXPERTISE*
BrainStyle exhibited		Learned, rehearsed, cultural behavior	Mastery of strengths, growth in spirit

~~~~~~~~~~~~~~~

Brain research and daily observation confirm that we handle new incoming information in an entirely different way than we handle familiar information.

---

1. Fast is considered so much better, in fact, that being busy and racing around is exalted, with wireless, hot-synced digitized beeping toys that interrupt meals or anything else that requires focus to enjoy. We don't have time for picking a mate; we artificially inseminate or adopt children so we can keep working, hiring our childcare. Leisure time is scary, because doing and busyness come before being and relating.

Initially, we use our brain hardware actively to engage with or to process information received. We do so with our natural timing to access the areas of our brains that we can reach easily and quickly. Later we draw from memory to recall what we have already processed, learned, and stored when we want to do the same thing again. This learned, or stored, information allows us to be social and polite, work in a job that builds to a career, make fewer "mistakes" with the second child, and eventually accumulate enough stored information to allow the title "expert" or at least "experienced."

~~~~~~~~~~~~~~

BEHAVIOR

Time O___ 1st time___ 2nd ___ 3rd___ 4th ___ 5th ___ *** ___ 15th *** ___ 20th ___ 50th___

NEW	*FAMILIAR*	*ROUTINE*	*EXPERTISE*
authentic, original, vulnerable	polite, rehearsed, defensive	unconscious, righteous	skilled, expert, or master

natural strengths	**learning in non-strengths**	**mastery**
so quick, they are invisible	*what we learn*	*what we contribute from life experience*

~~~~~~~~~~~~~~

In fact, what is easiest for us is invisible to us. We, therefore, focus on what we must struggle with. So we often create a reality that is defined this way: What *I* can do without even trying = right; what you say and think = stupid or hurtful. But the truth is, we just process information differently and can never create a universe the same as anyone else does. This is the biological reason why others with different hardware—especially in stressful situations—ask, "If I can do it, why can't you?" Because our gifts are invisible to us, we expect others to know what we mean or treat us as we would treat them. We focus on problems and prescribe effort to solve them; when we work hard at something it has more value to us in this ego-driven system of struggle and drama.

To live a life of effort, we must forget the "fact" that every genius or zillionaire slides into her discipline using gifts with ease, transported by the love of the work to carry the day, inspired to overlook effort and transcend the difficult. Those who focus on and nurture their natural abilities may live quiet lives, lives not of desperation or perspiration but fulfillment and satisfaction, well grounded in who they are, forgiving of who they never could be.

> *BRAINSTYLE CLUE:* We are in such a hurry to become experts, we continually commit two fundamental errors to create lives of struggle and frustration: 1) We overlook our strengths. 2) We focus on our non-strengths. By doing so we lose the essence of ourselves.

When we get bogged down with career and relationships, it is because we make these two mistakes:

1. We overlook our natural gifts.
2. We focus on non-strengths, or what we can't do well.

This is the time when competition—trying to be better in non-strength areas than someone else— appears to be the only solution; and fighting, struggling, and effort the means to get what we think we want. (A fairly limited goal, when you think about it.) It's stressful, uphill, and makes relationships into superficial alliances and tradeoffs, *politics* in the mean sense of the word.

In this paradigm, we expect others to make us feel better (with the same approach as we would use). When they don't, we blame them for making us feel unworthy, inept. We tell them they are "acting just like a woman" or "thinking just like a man." We compare ourselves and come up short. Or we judge them and feel vastly superior. In all cases, we are isolated and cut off, first from our own gifts, and then from everyone else's.

> *BRAINSTYLE CLUE:* Relationships are dances in time.

Each of us has our own gifts and our special timing in which we operate. You lead, you follow, you make music together, in rhythm, over time. And as you practice, you perform more easily and efficiently for longer periods of time with a wider diversity of people. Even relatives.

THE RHYTHM TOGETHER. In one marriage, Dave is a rocket-paced left-brainer, and his wife JoAnn is a slow-paced right-brainer. She drives 25 mph in a 35-mph zone; he never gets below the speed limit. Dave takes paperback novels along for evenings out at restaurants so he'll have something to read when JoAnn goes to the ladies' room. Their occasional arguments are based on pace: she cannot, will not, match his speed. He wants faster (logical) decisions from her, which she cannot give him. Yet when she gets clear on an issue, her husband marvels, "She just goes out and does it. She just went out, and the second house she saw, she bought. It was incredible." How did that happen? "I finally got clear on what the emotional issue was that was holding me back," said JoAnn . . . after years of agonizing over where to live. Their love has had to work around their extremely different paces. It took years to learn to dance to one another's rhythm. Why? Dave admits that JoAnn gives him an anchor, a steadiness and comfort to his life that he might have overlooked had he not slowed down. JoAnn laughs as she says that Dave is sure entertaining ("never a dull moment") and brings movement and excitement to their lives. They have put timing differences aside in activities where their daughter sets the pace. They have negotiated to have a part of the week where each gets to live at his/her own pace: Dave eats and runs; JoAnn lingers over coffee at home. Dave sleeps less and goes for an early run, JoAnn reads her books late in an adjoining room so he can go to sleep early. They make family time special and romantic.

> *BRAINSTYLE CLUE:* Timing is the problem. Timing is the solution.

Since conventional wisdom has it that fast is smart and slow is stupid, and traditional wisdom tells us that patience is a virtue and haste makes waste, which is it? Your own *brainstyle* timing propels personal perceptions of smart and stupid, wise and wasteful. If you are naturally fast-paced, know that your rapid finger-drumming and quick interruptions don't just intimidate others who have a slower pace, they prevent them from thinking and giving you their best. If you are naturally slower paced, know that your pace not only wears out others who need to move more quickly, it also prevents them from sorting and processing as ably as they can.

SOME TIPS ON TIMING:

- When a big issue comes up, do not insist that you sit down and discuss it to the end. Allow for timing.
- Prepare for the topic by warning the more thoughtful one of a need for a discussion.
- Allow the right-brained person to review the topic several times.
- Get clear on common goals first with the fast, left-brained person.

In the chart below, there is a guide to help you open to some new possibilities for managing timing, a key factor in relationships.

The graphics illustrate quantity and speed of access at *Time Zero* for each *brainstyle.*

Observe and Define a *BrainStyle* When There Is a New Event (at *Time Zero*):

A Knower *brainstyle*	A Conciliator *brainstyle*	A Conceptor *brainstyle*	A Deliberator *brainstyle*
Draws from the left brain first to quickly answer with logic or analysis.	Draws first from the right brain to respond/react with emotion.	Draws randomly from both sides of the brain to simplify or reconstruct new information.	Draws from memory to first assess (compare to a standard) before reacting or analyzing.
Sorts information into A or B, black or white.	Imagines possibilities or rejects the whole idea.	Reframes things into a concept.	Sorts information into elements for understanding.
Simplifies. Diagnoses. Prioritizes. Sets boundaries. Fixes it.	Keenly aware of other's reactions and interactions. Seeks to bring harmony.	Simplifies, tests, and generalizes.	Establishes a plan to organize what needs to be done.
Decides facts now. Feels later.	Feels now. Reacts now. Decides (commits) later.	Invents solutions in a random way using trial and error. May feel and/or judge now, act later.	Prepares to do the right thing.
Does not revisit the decision; takes action. Does not spend time reviewing, agonizing, or rethinking nearly as much as any other *brainstyle*.	Acts now. May redecide soon afterward, however.	Decides on a hypothesis to define the future and direct further decisions.	Doesn't react or decide until has "enough" info. Implements decision and reviews steps.

*All Charts© 1997, 2003 *BrainStyles*, Inc. No reproduction without permission. *www.brainstyles.com*

~~~~~~~~~~~~~~~~

Micro Predicts Macro: *BrainStyle (Time Zero)* Response Predicts Lifestyle.

A man I'll call Lloyd, a "left-sided" Deliberator,* is a fast-paced, left-brained man in his forties. In all he does he moves quickly, talks fast, reacts with rapid answers, EXCEPT in new situations. Then he must "go back to the beginning and review the data" so that he can create a straight, logical, mental line from the start to the current point in order to decide what to do next. Lloyd has to have things in order, his own sequential mental order,

*See chapter 7.

in order to think them through. In his work life, he says that he thinks outside the box and moves the ball forward as he competes to get to the goal first. In his personal life he loves lots of activities and going lots of places that are fun and stimulating to visit. If you look more closely, however, he goes outside the box by building on what he has learned, tried, and tested to get to the next rational step. Because he has a lot of energy, he can do this more quickly than others with similar gifts and so can call himself creative as a thinker—if you stretch things a bit. However, his ideas come from what he knows and has tested; new ideas are rigorously challenged until he reviews and understands each component, often needing the endorsement of an expert whom he trusts. His wife brings in new friends and destinations for travel to his life; he plans trips with similar itineraries in different destinations, but his most comfortable destinations are with longtime friends and familiar places.

What might we predict about Lloyd from his *Time Zero* reaction? That his basic lifestyle will have predictability and a structure to it that he loves to repeat and perfect. That he is reliable and will not go too far astray in his lifestyle, values, or choices. When asked to teach something he knows about, he is in heaven and you are in for a lesson that you'd better want, because you're going to get all the background and instruction so that you can do it, and do it well. Once when a man with Lloyd's *brainstyle* who particularly loved to ballroom dance was asked to teach a nervous friend who had never learned to dance, the process and the results were extraordinary. Because this *brainstyle* likes reason but hates confrontation, especially in new things, he was exquisitely sensitive, gentle, non-threatening, and went step by step to introduce the woman, who was all left feet, to move little by little from the box step to a foxtrot in about two hours. She found it painless. He was terribly gratified. He was at his best.

Dori is predictably unpredictable. With a very right-brained Conciliator *brainstyle* (see chapter 5), she is naturally spontaneous, often playful, and unfocused at first. Sometimes in new situations (*Time Zeroes*) she will react emotionally and spontaneously, sometimes calmly and coolly, by responding with something she has learned on the topic. Most often, however, her infectious laugh bubbles out or a red-faced indignant reaction comes. She says what she feels. She is scattered and tries to fight many fires at once. Thus her life reflects her many interests and ability to respond to many stimuli without getting too attached to any one of them. She reads any number of books in the broad field of personal growth she is best at and most interested in. She attends many workshops that she "always get[s] something valuable" from attending. She loves to travel, mostly to meet people and expand a large network of contacts and friends. She has been married three times, lived in a number of places, and now in her sixties, still loves to explore life, locations, and opportunities. Dori has convinced her husband to be more adventurous, "explore his inner Warrior," and sell their home, move, and travel for a few years. Her *brainstyle* reaction at *Time Zero* predicts a lifestyle.

As you observe *without judgment* what happens for you when confronted by new information, you can begin to manage your unmanageable future. By accepting and building on what you will do most naturally and most easily from your hardwired gifts, you can move into a lifetime that suits you and allows you to contribute in the most natural way for you. You can give up interpreting your life as one defined by external events. You take charge. You appreciate yourself. You stop trying to change others or the world around you.

~~~~~~~~~~~~~~~~

APPLYING BRAINSTYLES AT TIME ZERO TO LIFE SITUATIONS. This story was shared by Linda Bush, MA, master facilitator of *The BrainStyles System*.®

While my husband, Gary, and son, Karl, waited for me in our boat, I gathered up towels, sunblock, and a hat, and tiptoed through the wet grass to the dock. Stepping around a mound of mud where the shore met the dock, my foot slipped out from under me and I went down, slamming my other leg into the edge of a dock plank. I crept back up on the dock and tried to lift the bruised and bloody shin to lessen the pain and swelling. Muffled curses crossed my lips. I heard my husband call, "What happened?" while my son stood with open mouth, motionless. "I slipped," I squeaked.

Now they slowly came toward me. Gary, the Knower, the logical problem-solver, looked at the shin, the wet heel marks on the dock plank, and stated simply, "See, that's why you never walk in the direction of the planks, only across the planks, especially when it's wet."

His next few comments described how he'd have built the dock to prevent such accidents. Still wincing and crying, I watched him in amazement. Luckily, I knew that a Knower at *Time Zero* first sorts the information into logical and meaningful patterns to create a solution. Did I expect sympathy and a hug? Were I not in pain, I would have laughed.

Meanwhile, nine-year-old Deliberator Karl came closer, frowned at my wound, and gave me a reassuring hug and kisses around my shoulder, then helped me hold the leg up for relief. He suggested ice and a clean towel to stop the bleeding. He said repeatedly, "You'll be OK, Mommy," and asked, "Does it hurt bad?" He brushed my bangs back and said, "Let's go get ice from Grandma. Come on, you can do it." Then he turned to his dad and surveyed the dock planks and nodded with understanding as his Knower father continued problem-solving.

I limped away alone to get ice and smiled through the tears at the responses, knowing my husband's way of caring was to do what he did, not what I would have done.

> *BrainStyle Clue:* Different gifts and different timing. Each brings different lessons. Each gift is its own blessing, its own curse. It's up to you how to perceive it.

What do we do when our timing is quite different from another's? What is the bridge between you and another?

Relationships exist and unfold in the moment. When you stop rehearsing, contradicting, or being busy, just stop, then you can focus on gifts rather than appearance to discover who is really there. Or perhaps you become self-aware. You stop thinking about how you look or sound. In that space, you listen for *how* they are thinking, as Linda did in the middle of her bloody shin episode. Only then can you acknowledge the other's gift, or add to it, or underscore it. Then you can contribute authentically from your gifts. This takes time and timing.

Ram Dass said, "There is a place within us that is timeless. We have the opportunity to connect with that place when we go beyond our personality, beyond our body and its sensations, its aging, to our natural selves." In *BrainStyles*, we call it focusing on strengths, with a heightened awareness in the moment on what we do naturally, effortlessly. Moments expand, become joyful. Miracles occur naturally.

We contribute from who we are instead of who we are supposed to be.

~~~~~~~~~~~~~~~

Stress stops when you've arrived there. Being present means giving up the low buzz of anxiety about the future we keep anticipating all the time. Being present means taking time to feel feelings like pain, sorrow, and joy, which take longer to experience than does the whiz of our thoughts. When these feelings crop up (and anger and anxiety have a faster rhythm than pain or sadness), we think we need to hurry faster, to catch up, to solve

*problems more quickly. Actually, the solution is counterintuitive. You need
to slow down so you can feel what is going on. This allows you to expand the
moment. Even with a deadline, it will feel like you have more time.*
—*Timeshifting: Creating More Time to Enjoy Your Life,*
Stephan Rechtschaffen, MD (Doubleday, 1996)

~~~~~~~~~~~~~~~

TIME

Time O___ 1st time___ 2ⁿᵈ ___ 3ʳᵈ___ 4ᵗʰ ___ 5ᵗʰ ___ *** ___ 15th *** ___ 20ᵗʰ ___ 50ᵗʰ___

NEW	*FAMILIAR*	*ROUTINE*	*EXPERTISE*
BrainStyle exhibited	Learned, rehearsed, cultural behavior		Mastery of strengths, growth in spirit

~~~~~~~~~~~~~~~

MANAGING YOUR TIMING. DÉJÀ VU ALL OVER AGAIN. Earlier
we learned about the expression of *brainstyle* gifts in time. A *brainstyle* occurs at
Time Zero (an event seen as new or unfamiliar), then Learned Behavior, then
Expertise or Mastery occurs as you take in new information, store more and
more, and apply it over time. Being the wizened expert is the prize for most of
us. You are the one with the answers at last, the guru, the teacher. When you are
an expert, however, you also have two choices to make regarding your wisdom.
Either you can use your natural strengths to serve others by expanding the topic
and/or the relationship, or use your gifts to be right and make others stupid or
wrong. Mastery, especially as it relates to time and timing, is when you are *purposefully* aware of being at *Time Zero*—an unfamiliar situation where you do not
know what to do. Using a conscious sensitivity and inner alertness to your own
natural responses, you will be able to draw from your initial emotion, insight,
solution, concept, or diagnosis of the moment, pause, and THEN combine it
with the "learned behavior" or expertise you have gained over your life to reach a
much wiser, more potent response. You manage your timing AND expertise by
honoring and therefore managing the hardware that created it, rather than being
managed by it.

➤ You don't just react defensively when your husband/friend/sister has just
said something "outrageously offensive" to you. You allow yourself a
forgiving moment when you allow your reaction; feel it, appreciate it, and
then respond.

➤ When you don't have an answer, you pause, and affirm that it will come.[2]

You strive to offer the best of all that you remember with the full power of your gift behind it. Here are some examples.

Francena, a Deliberator of heightened sensitivity, says at times that she must withdraw from a client or topic or conversation in order to process the information. Thinking and then writing allow her to respond with the full force of her powerful intellect to offer an analysis of the person's life or situation along with questions that she has culled from the many she generates initially. Her clients gain structure and clarity from her carefully crafted direction in a series of steps (a methodical sequence) that her *brainstyle* offers best.

Linda, the Conciliator who described her vacation *Time Zero* above, pauses in the moment of a painful fall while Knower hubby problem-solves the planking on the deck rather than comforts her, and in full awareness of their differences (her stored information) accepts her initial emotion, laughs forgivingly rather than shrieks accusingly, limps for help, and releases her past knee-jerk reaction of getting mad at him for doing things his way in new situations. Later she offers the full force of her strengths (i.e., empathy, bonding with others, synthesizing information) to keep the relationship with her husband loving. She also learns from the situation and uses the example of family reactions in a new situation to teach her clients and friends to realize more forgiveness and understanding in their lives. Linda is living masterfully, rather than emotionally, demonstrating her larger Purpose for living as she does so.

Charlene, a Deliberator married to a high-energy Conciliator, has learned to offer him her planning to anchor his go-for-broke, spontaneous adventures on their boat to realize more satisfying, well-stocked trips. She takes the time she needs, in the moment, to offer her plan without stopping his enthusiasm. Their boating adventures are safer, allowing her to act as more of a partner and for both of them to have more fun.

~~~~~~~~~~~~~~~~

2. Research on memory supports this confidence as one of four factors which aid memory. Telling oneself, "I can remember," and "I know I can recall" gave tested subjects greater recall. For more information on memory, read Daniel Schacter's book, *The Seven Sins of Memory* (Mariner Books, 2002) or go to www.brainstyles.com for an article drawn from several sources on how to manage your memory.

AT TIME ZERO, ALLOW TIME FOR BRAINSTYLE STRENGTHS. WITH A . . .

KNOWER . . .	CONCILIATOR . . .	CONCEPTOR . . .	DELIBERATOR . . .
Realize the first decision will come fast and won't change very much.	**Refuse** a quick decision.	**Allow** time for specifics. Get interim decisions.	**Don't ask** for a quick decision in a new area.
Offer your goals early.	Allow the left brain time to add logic and consider facts.		
Don't argue methods or history.	Expect changes.	Ask questions that elicit his thinking rather than facts or history.	Offer goals, alternatives early.
	Be supportive.	Fill in details.	Provide interim deadlines to manage progress.
Look for her gift of clarity and focus to define what is unclear. See how she defines, structures, and sets limits to problems.	Look for his integration of differences, his personal touch, the brilliance and warmth.	Notice how he has taken something overlooked or simple, given it depth, and taken you somewhere new.	Notice how she organizes the idea or breaks it down into doable pieces. Listen to her questions that often identify what's missing or is inaccurate.
Acknowledge this.	Appreciate this and he will offer more.	Get excited with him.	Watch how she anticipates risks to keep you safe.

All Charts© 1997, 2003 *BrainStyles*, Inc. No reproduction without permission. *www.brainstyles.com*

CHAPTER 4

THE KNOWER[1]

BRAINSTYLE

~~~~~~~~~~~~~~~~~

Winning isn't everything. It's the only *thing.*
—Coach Vince Lombardi, Knower

When I'm quiet, I'm just quiet. When he's quiet, it means something.
—A Knower wife's comment about her Deliberator husband

~~~~~~~~~~~~~~~~~

The brain diagram above is an attempt to portray what is going on for this *brainstyle* in a new situation. The smaller arrow denotes a delay in timing and lesser access to the emotional, imaginative right brain. The larger arrow depicts the faster access to and greater output from the gifts of the left hemisphere of the brain, to give more logic, analysis, black-and-white conclusions at first pass with new information.

> BRAINSTYLE CLUE: The *BrainStyles* database shows that Knowers are nearly 13% of the population, with approximately 65% male, 35% female.

For example: a Knower artist paints literal, real things. Fran, a Knower artist, took four days to use her left-brained abilities to re-create on canvas the face and hand of a man with a gaze so lifelike your eyes are riveted to his and

---

1. The name of this *brainstyle* came from the dictionary definition, *to perceive with certainty.* It is only a coincidence that the word "know" is associated with "know-it-all" and "to know" the answers.

you look for smoke from his cigarette. It took Fran *four months* to create the abstract, ill-defined background (requiring right-brain access).

Another illustration of this brainspeed timing and access: tough on the outside (first); a cream puff on the inside (later, more privately and selectively).

Because of this brain access, Knowers are best at bringing practical, fact-based, crisis decision making quickly in new situations compared to the other *brainstyles*. If you are a Knower, those who are quick with their feelings (where you are slow) therefore slow you down, get in the way of your natural timing and process, and drive you nuts if you don't know how to use what they offer. Because the left hemisphere of the brain is the side with speech, the Knower's answers can come faster and more articulately than others'. If you are not a Knower reading this chapter, how do you feel about the following people?

➤ Dr. Laura, who "tells it like it is" (Dr. Laura Schlessinger, American radio talk show advisor who crisply clarifies the rules of morality and religion for her listening audience; the one who Deliberator *brainstyle* and TV personality Barbara Walters tallies as "hurting" people);

➤ Judge Judy (an officer of the court who has become a famous TV personality for her no-nonsense approach in sorting out small claims issues between litigants with her hard-edged rulings on the law); or

➤ H. Ross Perot, billionaire entrepreneur who founded the computer consulting company EDS, known for its military structure and discipline.

Each is an example of the Knower *brainstyle*. And because they are Knowers, they are also controversial.

NOTE TO OTHER *brainstyles:* If you get nothing else here,

1) Realize that **all *brainstyles* can look, act, and talk like Knowers** when they are in a field in which they are expert.

2) If you study this chapter, your conclusions about people with these gifts may change from being slurs and labels to a more respectful view of their remarkable gifts.

3) You can stop calling everyone who gets on your nerves a Knower.

KNOWERS IN A WORLD OF NON-KNOWERS. Three different editors said I should remove the reference to Laura Schlessinger ("Dr. Laura") in this chapter. Why? Too annoying, too opinionated about religion, the family, and morality. She is way too offensive, they said. "If you're gay, you're *wrong*. If you're living together, you're *wrong*," said a young co-habiting hairstylist quite heatedly when Dr. Laura's name came up. "I just cannot stand anyone that narrow-minded."

Disagree with her values, which Dr. Laura rigorously applies to problem situations, but get past her presentation: She is a perfect example of the gifts most hate—and the gifts most need. What other *brainstyle* could take on the questions she gets and give an answer so clearly in one minute or less? Not any. The problem? People of different *brainstyles* overlook the value a Knower can bring: Her answer is a clear *starting point.* You can take it or leave it. What is invaluable is the simplicity and focus she has brought to the tangled issues of, say, parenting, wedding mania, step-parenting, adultery, drug abuse in the family, and on and on, with a simple clear response.

Listening more closely, what I hear from Dr. Laura are rules being applied in a black-and-white fashion to family and marital problems. Listeners consult her for "moral advice." Here are some examples of her clear and direct advice[2]:

~~~~~~~~~~~~~~~~

Dr. Laura: I ask all women with your dilemma: Do you want to stay married? Woman caller: Yes.

Dr. Laura: Then you must make him feel welcome when he comes home, not like an intruder in your life. Hugs and kisses. Brownies. Get the idea?

Caller: Yes. You're right. I haven't been doing that.

~~~~~~~~~~~~~~~~

Male caller: I've been married 29 years, and I can't stand it anymore. I want a divorce. My life with her is hell, and I just called to see what you'd say.

Dr. Laura: You need to seek counseling to find a way to work things out for the sake of your family.

Caller: But I hate her.

Dr. Laura: We live in a culture that would support you in ending this marriage because you feel like it. But I don't support that point of view. You vowed before God to stay married, and to honor your pledge, you need to seek an alternative and work it out. You called me, I'm giving you my opinion.

(Click. She ends the call and takes the next caller.)

~~~~~~~~~~~~~~~~

---

2. Advice, NOT consultation or suggestions. Either take it or don't. She believes in the tenets of her religion (Judaism) and asks others to live up to their own faiths. If you don't have one, she suggests you choose one, or at least live according to moral guidelines of honesty, consideration for others, and personal responsibility.

Most people in this *brainstyle* are compared with the verbal and emotional sensitivities that are the strengths of other *brainstyles*. H. Ross Perot, labeled explosive, paranoid and grating, is well-known as a billionaire entrepreneur who founded and ran his company EDS[3], it was said, like a boot camp. However, he's the same man whose caring paid for the helicopter rescue of his employees stranded in Iran. His founding of a third party to seek the U.S. Presidency not only gained a huge following of loyal supporters but made the financial health of the nation a priority for the first time. Later, he also became infamous for his fears of conspiracies based on an old grudge held against the Bush family, which made him the butt of many jokes. The paranoia that other *brainstyles* see in Knowers is a result of their gifts in logic (looking at the world for cause-effect relationships) applied on a large scale. Logic looks for what can go wrong in the world in order to ensure our survival with logical solutions. The grudges are decisions made and held with the same hardware that creates unswerving loyalties.

Often labeled *abrasive, inconsiderate,* and *scary,* as a Knower you're a black-and-white thinker, and you seem not to care how others feel about what you offer. Take it or leave it. Other *brainstyles* need to consider what they would do without the champions of ideas and answers that do NOT pander to the consensus or the politically correct. As a Knower, you're well aware that you are a small minority of upstream-swimmers who are continually maligned and isolated. You demand. You challenge. You have a way of confronting that could be styled Take No Prisoners. When immature, you only use the cause-effect logic of the left brain to blame. When mature, you modify your logic with caring values to create broader solutions.

"I've noticed in many Knowers that when things don't go their way, they assign blame to others, often with amazing, conspiracy-type explanations. . . . [My son], who is now 11, is also a Knower, and we have seen from an early age when things have not gone well for him, he has come up with elaborate stories of other kids persecuting him. I have been fascinated by how much he can sound like adults that I work with!"[4]

This is what I know about you: You talk tough; yet, surprise! your deepest concerns, your most proud accomplishments, focus on the inner person.

---

3. Electronic Data Systems has 140,000 employees and is second to IBM in the computer field with $21.5 billion in revenue. EDS was the first computing company to sell expertise instead of a product.
4. Mike P., a Deliberator dad and executive who is well-versed in *BrainStyles*®.

~~~~~~~~~~~~~~~

I'll tell you the secret to what made that company [EDS] successful.
I've said it before, and nobody's paid any attention to it, so they won't
start now. It all comes down to the spirit of the people within the
company. We built a company with huge spirit.
It had nothing to do with technology.
—H. Ross Perot, in an interview about the success of the company
he founded forty years before, that literally created the computer services
industry. *Dallas Morning News*, May, 2002

~~~~~~~~~~~~~~~

TO THE NON-KNOWER: If you have another set of gifts, you can still relate: You feel like a Knower every time you are clear, decisive, focused, and right about the answer. Everyone feels this way when they get to know their field. This chapter reveals the real deal, the folks who offer these gifts quickly, naturally, and over their entire lifetimes.

My wish is for you to get past your demands for comfort in the way Knowers present their gifts, to uncover and value the extraordinary richness inside. I also challenge you to spend more time looking for the real *brainstyle* of those you dislike instead of immediately labeling them a Knower.

KNOWERS: WHAT YOU NEED TO KNOW. If you are a Knower, your speed may lead your ego to judge others as incompetent. You would be wrong about that. You would be right about the fact that you are often quicker to the punchline. That's what gets you into trouble.

Another thing that sorts you out in a crowd is the way you handle information. Perhaps you can relate to a newspaper column entitled "Share Torture: Let's keep intimacies to ourselves," written by *Dallas Morning News* columnist Maryln Schwartz, an often humorous and clearly left-brained observer of pop culture. She writes, "Lately I feel as if I'm in intensive therapy. It's not that I'm seeing a doctor. I'm just reading magazines and watching TV." Uncomfortable with hearing about people's feelings—the language of the right-brained—she says, ". . . here's a media alert. You are telling us more than we want to know. I'm sure these celebrities are going through some real pain. But I don't want to feel as if I'm part of their group therapy. Enough is enough." If you are a Knower, you might relate to her sentiments. It's not that you don't relate to others' pain, it's more that you consider that personal information should only be available on a Need to Know basis. And those who need to know are a select few who can do something about whatever the problem is. This is why it takes so long for all the talkers and sharers to get used to your private lifestyle: To them you are *cold, buttoned-up, secretive, controlling;* you know the words that have been laid on with a trowel to get you to change and share your secrets as they do.

It seems that from your point of view, the information that you prize most is information necessary to solve a problem or get from point A to point B. The ramblers and "sharers" distract, obstruct, and generally make a nuisance of themselves while they obscure the target. Easier to just do it yourself, isn't it, and leave all that blathering about personal lives and intimate details behind?

Cold. Aggressive. Mean. Can't work with anyone. Snob. No people skills. Insensitive. Tough. And especially, *Arrogant.* Familiar with labels like these? If you have these gifts, you're probably weary of people who have attempted to soften you up, open you up, teach you to communicate, or in some way try to get you to change who you are naturally. Why? Because they don't understand what your strengths are and how to take advantage of them. Instead, they just react to them.

Most Knowers are great advisors and counselors, but lousy at recognizing and expanding the gifts of other *brainstyles* who live and dream in other galaxies. Your best input is the direction and clarity you provide, along with your belief in another to find her own way. Doing so, you are a patient, caring, and practical supporter whose words carry great impact because you can lay out the future as a simple, doable adventure. How empowering!

Most Knowers are dismissed as being dismal with people, and so the real value they bring is lost. As a Knower, learning about your strengths allows you to make a choice about how you want to live your life as a whole. Do you want to use the magnificent hardware you were born with to limit your achievements to merely winning and self-promotion? Or will you, as Vince Lombardi did, not only inspire and motivate others, but also teach them how to realize their value through personal achievement? This is a moment-by-moment choice in every conversation, negotiation, interaction, and relationship. Your awareness of your *brainspeed timing* will make all the difference in how you manage relationships to allow you, with some very simple statements, to make stronger alliances and deal with people in a way that most in your *brainstyle* don't know how to do.

You know you're competent. You also know what an ally you can be in any relationship; how friends are friends, enemies, enemies, with no questions asked once you decide this is the way it's going to be. As one woman who is married to a Knower said, "Once he decided we were married, that was it for him. He never reconsidered. He even told me, once you're married, you're married. But when things aren't going well, I wonder a LOT of times if it was the right decision." The wife is obviously not a Knower and often second-guesses decisions. She has come to appreciate his clarity, steadiness, and incredible problem-solving ability and stopped looking at what he doesn't do to find a great deal more satisfaction in her marriage.

The following information will tell you why you do what you do well. In defining your abilities you'll quickly see the things you do that cause others so much trouble. You're *not* going to be asked to change. You *will* be offered a way to apply the strengths you have more effectively.

THE KNOWER: A SUMMARY OF STRENGTHS[5]

TIME ZERO →	SOON AFTER →	WITH PRACTICE →	EXPERT →
• Diagnoses the cause. • Sorts the facts into a few categories. • Analyzes for a few criteria. • Sets priorities. • *Simplifies it.*	• Decides. • Concludes: A or B. • *Simplifies.* • Confronts the problem. • *Solves it.*	• Sets up structured answers. • Runs the plan. • Controls the information. • Draws on others' strengths to complete the plan. • *Builds it.*	• Simplifies and solves chaos. • Starts or redirects a business. • Is a persuasive communicator. • *Directs it.*

➤ Knowers are the least apt to change their minds after *Time Zero* as they reach a rapid, factual, unemotional decision. Later, the right brain provides awareness of feelings, intuition, and the impact their decision may have on others.

➤ Since the left brain can change with lightning speed, the Knower needs a rational, usually logical reason to change course. This process can take time and requires establishing common interests and goals with the Knower.

➤ At her best in the beginning of something, a Knower's gifts can simplify and clarify how to reach a goal in the shortest amount of time.

➤ The Knower decides or concludes rapidly, based on facts, taking a topic or event to make it practical, more streamlined, and more efficient.

➤ The Knower's primary strength is seeing cause-effect relationships between unrelated things, allowing him to figure out logical solutions to complex and difficult problems.

➤ Knowers are excellent at directly addressing issues in order to reach a desired end with the least amount of emotion, worry, or regret. They spend the most time in the present or the future.

➤ Knowers are clear and logical communicators. They do best with facts and real things, and not as well with socializing and relationships with people where there is no clear leader, preferring a few close and trusted friends where they can be caring, fun, and not have to worry about being taken advantage of.

➤ Knowers prefer autonomy, working with their own direction, thank you, on their own self-directed projects, or clearing up the chaos others have created.

➤ A Knower's partner or parent must take charge, know what they're up to, or get out of the way.[6]

➤ Knowers have the classic entrepreneurial profile: self-starters, focused on the goal, with an ability to envision a practical and needed future for a worthwhile or money-making idea in the most efficient, direct, and measurable way they can think of.

➤ Knowers are either staunch allies or horrific enemies, one or the other. When the decision is made, it's made. Changing sides is NOT an easy process, and if it happens at all, it takes awhile. To reestablish trust, they must get new credible information and see how their goals are aligned with yours.

➤ Knowers love their mates and families by doing things for them. They demonstrate affection rather than talk about it. More than any other *brainstyle*, observations are keen about what is important to another and what needs to be given: a new appliance, time spent shopping with the wife (a dreadful activity for that particular Knower husband), time spent in sports with the children, paying bills and handling finances for aging parents. A Knower's care, private and unexpressed with words, is applied through action, romantic action at times, but rarely sweet nothings and poems.

---

6. Independent field sales, especially in technical fields, consulting, travel, contracting, building, the military, especially intelligence fields, police and investigative work, and medical diagnostics are all jobs that lend themselves to these strengths. Oh, and artists, film producers, technicians, photographers, journalists, and musicians have Knowers aplenty (music is appreciated by the right brain, learned and executed precisely by the left brain).

KNOWERS LOOK FOR OPPORTUNITIES TO:

- Control the information, and therefore the situation, in order to install a controlled, efficient, logical solution.
- Do it rather than talk about it.
- Achieve something tangible or measurable by solving practical problems, most often, that save or make money.
- Work independently.
- Make things simple and efficient.
- Create new solutions that make immediate sense.
- See it and tell it "like it is" without added emotions or lengthy explanation and history.
- Save time or set priorities by attending to events or things rather than lunching or socializing.

KNOWERS AS PARTNERS. Let me restate this. You're not a natural partner or team player who plays the same way other *brainstyles* do. To every relationship you bring a wealth of abilities, but you prefer to self-direct and be in charge, right? Since relationships as you conduct them are not typical of 87 percent of the population, how do you become more effective with people when there is no task to accomplish or project to finish? The problem is timing. The solution is timing. First allow for timing of the other *brainstyle, kindly.* You can then use your strengths wisely and responsibly by announcing what you can add and where you can add it. It is so easy for you to fall into *tell* and *sell* and *demand,* especially when things get out of your control or go wrong.

Your first inclination is to divide up the territory. When you see what needs doing in someone else's arena and know instantly what your partner is going to do to get off the track, stall, add problems, etc., this is a crucial time to offer your strengths. "Here's what might happen if we keep going; let's take a break and I'll make a quick outline," or "I want you to have a good experience here, and it might go easier if you consider this." You get the idea. You are fully capable of ramming the idea or solution to get it into their heads, showing them up with your speed, scheming, shortcutting, or cheating, and in general doing whatever it takes to be smart or to win. Don't do it.

Manage your hardware. Don't let it manage you.

MORE ON YOUR STRENGTHS: BULLETED, JUST FOR YOU, KNOWER DEAR.

➤ You're best at seeing how ideas will work, how to apply a principle to make ideas streamlined, or how to put a notion into practice.

This is what you can deliver consistently. When being harangued to change, you might remind the haranguer that this is what you have to offer, largely to the exclusion of other things. (Then create a *Strengths Contract,* as outlined in chapter 14.)

➤ You confront people and challenges directly and factually.

Others who draw more from the right side of the brain interpret your actions as brutal, abrupt, or aggressive. It's personal for them; it's a problem to solve for you.

> *BRAINSTYLE CLUE:* "Knowers and Conceptors will stab you in the front. Conciliators and Deliberators will stab you in the back."
> —Fran Di Giacomo, Knower, artist, wife and mother

➤ You're gifted in reaching an unemotional decision and sorting data unencumbered by feelings. You are more likely to be factually biased or opinionated rather than swayed by your feelings on a subject.

> *BRAINSTYLE WARNING FOR KNOWERS:* Do not confuse your opinions with the facts.

➤ You are an excellent priority setter. You quickly see what needs to be done to solve a problem from your perspective.

➤ You enjoy and are at your best working on one project at a time.[7]

➤ You set boundaries better than any of the other *brainstyles.* You can say no, quit smoking, diet, stop or start an activity or relationship whenever you decide to do so.

➤ You are least likely to be troubled by guilt and regret.

➤ You tend to be oriented to the present, call selectively on the past or precedent to support your case, and look forward to taking an idea or project in a straight line to win, nail it, get it done.

➤ You create adventures with a beginning, middle, and end. If you are a writer or speaker, musician or artist, you use your abilities to excite with

---

7. With some exceptions, Knowers appreciate the focus. Multi-tasking Knowers whom I've observed get things done efficiently if time is limited, yet attend to those several things one at a time.

realism, wit, and vivid images, which doesn't rule out science fiction or fantasy that is logically derived.

➤ You have the discipline to create your own image (weight, health, strength) as you think it should be, natural limit- and goal-setter that you are. If you still measure others against your gifts, you are showing your ignorance of genetics and brain-based abilities.

➤ You are often a ferocious competitor who loves to win and hates to lose. Your ability to measure progress as you drive to a goal puts you at an advantage in sports, for example. Only the left-sided Deliberator will match your focus, endurance, and will to win. This gift can be a curse in a family when your kids are expected to do the same.

➤ Your *brainstyle* strengths give you an edge in achieving "flow" in things you undertake. *Flow* is a condition of deep enjoyment where you can focus so completely on achieving a thing that you lose track of time or problems. But watch out for becoming a workaholic or isolated hobbyist, if you're more introverted.

➤ You are good at telling, directing, following, or making rules that aid efficiency and make a system work. *Bossy* might capture it.

➤ You want to preserve the values of those you care about, build on and maintain the fundamentals of your home now and in the future. Your gifts apply when working in and creating structure, so you create this at home and work[8] and can offer it as your gift.

➤ As a spouse or parent you often are the protector; you nurture by keeping others safe, anticipating what might go wrong and preventing or solving problems. As a homemaker you see and use efficiencies to create order, help others clear out the clutter, fix things before anyone knows about them, and do so without help.

➤ You're best at being literal and concrete in your communications. *No* means No.

➤ Rules mean what they say when YOU set them. Words are not personalized. That's why home can be your kingdom and work can be so frustrating. Many Knowers solve the latter problem by working alone, advising others as consultants, or joining an organization where the rules are followed.

---

8. As an entrepreneur, or in careers like law, the military, construction, engineering, graphics or art with tangible things, journalism, hardware, technical things and systems, among others.

> *BRAINSTYLE CLUE:* Remember, when the brain draws from one hemisphere, the other hemisphere just cannot perform as well. The gift of this *brainstyle* is to draw first and foremost from the side that uses the logic of the linear to get where it's going. Later comes the attention to emotions and other "peripheral stuff."

APPLYING KNOWER GIFTS TO MINEFIELDS: SUGGESTIONS FOR POLITICS IN THE FAMILY. DATING. HONOR.

➤ You "read" situations and people practically and selectively, watching for reactions to an agenda or statement. You know from experience how people's actions match their words. You have an ability I call "extrospection," or looking outside yourself to observe personal impact, say, of remarks of one person on another, or agendas that show up in a comment here, an opinion there, an alliance over there. You are a natural politician: You distill how people interact to move on issues from one side to another. *Extrospection* also allows you to learn from *others'* mistakes more easily than the right-brainers who need to have direct, personal experience to change their minds or direction. Use this ability to build your own code of honor rather than to point out others' flaws. You'll be sought out for your opinion and advice. Count on it.

➤ Focusing on a goal, you may act in a way to get what you want and quit once you get it. Since pretending is not your gift, and in fact you establish trust based on the congruence between what you say and what you do, why lie for a quick win and take a chance on losing the whole game? OK, victory is sweet. But remember, those other guys don't get mad, they get even.

➤ When in groups at home or work, you are undoubtedly proud of the fact that you can tease out others' hidden agendas or unstated personal issues quickly and form strategies to get to a goal based on that information. You do so with your keen observation of how words and behaviors match. This is the ethical quicksand you must make some hard choices about entering. If you work from fear, you will be climbing over the bodies of those you outmaneuver for your own gain at their expense. If you work from the love within you, you'll use your ability to pierce lies and maneuverings to bring clarity, boost others' awareness of their own capabilities, and go for a grander, longer-term win.

➤ Those you do really trust are few and far between, and once a person crosses the line and you consider them untrustworthy, you seldom look back. You might reconsider whom you are writing off. You never know when you might need to talk to her again. You might also learn something about yourself and your impact that would be life-changing by reevaluating what an "enemy" has to teach you.

PERSONALLY.

➤ Initially, you tend to approach relationships practically more than romantically, although once someone gets past your initial screening, you can be quite romantic and feel very deeply. (I'm not quite saying you're a sucker for a sob story. *Au contraire,* you tend to screen out so many, and take so few risks, that you probably miss many relationships that might have been terrific. When you think about it, speed dating is only another form of work; feelings take time.)

➤ Sexy? Well, certainly. Smoldering masculinity, short on the poetry, long on the values. Men Knowers I have talked to tend to buy things for their beloveds, romance without a lot of *schmaltz* and fluff, and are more straightforward and direct with advances. Women Knowers are often (not always) most openly sensual or sexy in speech and dress (a practical approach to mating), and short on the hard-to-get routine. And then, of course, there are Knowers who are not interested in the emotions and bonding required of an intimate relationship. They move on and don't have much more than a physical relationship with no strings.

➤ You're always looking for the best deal. Do you make offers that imply or state, "Take it or leave it"? You may get what you think is the best deal, when what you're getting is an answer to get rid of you. This may be the case if a number of people say yes and don't deliver. Watch a Deliberator make a deal. They are *amazing* at getting what they want and getting the salesman, son, or friend to still like them afterwards.

➤ Since you tend to be either friend or foe in a relationship, consider forgiveness as an opening in your life to let go of old baggage and clutter. Cconsider reopening some old doors you thought were shut permanently.

> *BRAINSTYLE CLUE:* Knowers, when you assess others' competence by asessing their speed and logic, you create interpersonal barriers, and set yourself up for loss, disappointment, and failed partnerships. The Big News for you is in the other *brainstyle* descriptions.

Many in your *brainstyle* are amazed to find out the gifts other *brainstyles* have behind their fuzzy, slow, incomprehensible, long-winded façades (isn't this what you call them?). The first step in leveraging your own abilities is to know more thoroughly what you have. The second step is to find out about those other guys, which also defines your own limitations.

MANAGING NON-STRENGTHS means allowing others to contribute to the plan or even to your solution. Really. Not just lip service. Your preference is to split up the turf to handle everything. "My husband (a Knower) calls it 'divide and conquer,'" says a wife. "We plan and then go different directions and check in on progress."

Here's what turf those other *brainstyles* can take to save or improve the day for you.

KNOWERS, YOU NEED THE DELIBERATOR in order to:

- assess the plan to see what's been overlooked.
- present ideas diplomatically, thoroughly, patiently, while seeing all sides.
- bring in the rules and precedents.
- build a consensus of ideas, gathering information and support.
- steady things, ensure continuity, bring in new information, and carry the idea through to the end.

KNOWERS, YOU NEED THE CONCEPTOR in order to:

- create a winning, more comprehensive future; they'll see people and concepts differently, give a new framework to systems and solutions that will include more input, potentially gain more commitment, and be broader-ranging.
- add passionate persuasion. Conceptors are excellent at introducing why change can benefit the whole person, system, family, etc.
- review communications (how to present your solution) for impact on people and plans (Conciliators will also be most helpful here).
- define a new direction, which may not be linear but can anticipate change.
- invent or start over, think the unthinkable in the realm of the possible. (Conciliators can think the unthinkable and not care as much whether it is possible or not; they relish an idea and love imagining possibilities.)

KNOWERS, YOU NEED THE CONCILIATOR in order to:

- get people involved and excited about your idea or plan, adding personal meaning to the factual necessities; they'll be great public relations support and personal cheerleaders. They will help you smooth things over or prevent personal flare-ups. They can articulate your unstated feelings.
- help see the personal, social, or political implications of the plan and explain them fully to others, adding excitement and personal relevance that

you leave out. They can also translate others' feelings to you.

- explain the *why* of the idea to others, especially in terms that are personally relevant or make the idea sizzle.
- brainstorm options for reaching your goal that include others, add fun, parties, neat and beautiful presentations, and the spin necessary to sell and get others behind it.
- add meaning, philosophy, symbolism, rhythm, color, and relationships to your logic and practicality.

A Summary of the Knower's Non-Strengths, Which Take Longer and Require More Effort. A *Short* List.

1. **SHOWING EMOTION.** You delay showing emotion, empathy, or enthusiasm compared to others, so others often label you as rigid or negative.

2. **WORKING WITH ABSTRACTIONS.** You don't work as well with nuance, the unspoken messages, symbolism, abstractions, or ambiguity as much as the right-brained do. Socializing, poetry, the abstract (as in "intellectually abstract") forms of art and literature, for instance, take more effort and great patience on your part.

3. **BEING FANCIFUL.** You don't create images, imagine as many possibilities, or make up stories readily. Your humor is often in the delivery. You get and offer punchlines as a matter of course and don't get fancy along the way.

4. **SHOWING PERSONAL SENSITIVITY.** You may notice quickly, but don't respond to as many cues and interpersonal dynamics as readily as others, so the raised eyebrow of your father-in-law during dinner isn't relevant until he actually says what his problem is. Many interpret this as insensitive. This doesn't mean that once you know of something important to another you won't embrace it or provide it. Ignoring a problem is often your way of showing consideration. Or boredom. This means your greatest gift is your time, which is Big News to other *brainstyles* with different timing.

5. **TAKING RISKS.** You are a cautious risk-taker, tending to reason out the future, and you can miss opportunities when focusing only on the downside or negative consequences.

6. **GENERATING ALTERNATIVES.** Since you don't create wild ideas or a lot of alternatives readily, preferring to stick with your own A or B answer, you may tune out the right-brained folks until they get to the part where they turn their support into enthusiasm for you or your project.

7. **ACTING AS A PARTNER OR TEAM MEMBER.** You don't tend to be a team player, collaborator, or partner, or support others' agendas. Let's face it, you like to be in charge.

8. **GENERATING AN INCLUSIVE VISION.** You won't believe this is the case until you work or meet up with a true Conceptor. However, your vision is the most practical and realistic one around. Conceptors add other dimensions and leap into new possibilities that are outside your scope.

9. **DETAILS.** Details and steps to get somewhere new can be mind-numbing for you until you see their use. Until then your speed can shut out new topics and facts to close opportunities for those who are potentially your best allies.

10. **MULTI-TASKING.** Exploring a range of new topics. Taking care of several things at once is distracting for you. You are best from start to finish. Others are better at "multi-tasking"; you focus, preferably on one thing at a time. Those who bring up new subjects, taste their way through topics without depth of analysis or are fascinated by the new, exhibit a non-strength of yours.

> *BRAINSTYLE CLUE:* To leverage your strengths, get beyond your ego's desire for being right, in control, and winning by defeating another.

GIVEN YOUR NON-STRENGTHS, HERE ARE SOME TIPS FOR MANAGING RELATIONSHIPS:

1. Tell people what to expect from you. Explain the benefits you can provide with focus, solutions, and direction, and tell them they will probably be better at making the relationship go than you will, which does NOT mean you don't care.

2. Take responsibility. Know that you look outside yourself for causes to problems. You are most likely to blame others or the situation and ignore your own contribution to the mess. *Hold yourself accountable first.*

3. People have trouble with you because of your speed in deciding about what the outcome should be. If you get others inputs to the goal, then guarantee to apply their strengths throughout a project, your partner/spouse will love this and you. She will value the clarity you bring even more when you point out how you need her strengths to get a better result. Oh, and the plan will have more commitment and you'll have a happier home.

4. You already know that people will do things the way *they* want to and their strengths allow. Stop judging their pace. Don't compare one to another. Coach.

Motivate by pointing out the goal and how their gifts can get them there.

5. When considering a new project or idea where a lot is at stake, let your partner pose the upside potential and think about it for a while. Reconsider. Don't decide a go/no go at the moment. Your *brainstyle* loathes taking risks, especially financial ones, because risks are illogical and the future unpredictable. Set a budget, a curfew, the limits on what you can tolerate, and let your partner or your child go for it. You *know* they have to learn their own lessons. Letting go is a challenge that matures you.

6. When your partner is terrific at brainstorming, wait to add practicality or application. Otherwise you may be seen as an idea-squelcher when offering the downside for their new ideas. The people who cannot focus are those whose right brains are flooded with ideas and stimuli, and as they deal with fanciful or far-out subjects, they just may come up with a breakthrough that can take you new places. Leave them alone until they get past initial creative ideas. Logic always follows insight. In fact, the real Knower leaders use their practicality to show the right-brained how to overcome self-doubt and analysis-paralysis to move ahead.

7. To get the right-brained to listen to your unassailable answers, you may need a personal story to illustrate what you mean. Describe the outcome in a way they can picture. Or if that is too much effort, ask them to do so: "Can you picture what I'm getting at?" Other *brainstyles* will not be sold on your pure, cool logic alone.

8. Present in small steps. Others take time to reach the conclusions you have reached because they see different elements of the plan (*not* because they're slow or stupid and you're intimidating). To fend you off, they'll say yes because they need time to decide. That's why they sometimes don't keep their word and end up blaming you for being too pushy. If you take time in the beginning, it will pay off later.

9. When around your family, let them know how their different *brainstyles* contribute to you especially. Acknowledging how each person's strength is needed and what each gives will make you an instant hero or heroine and show them where to grow. This is a way to prevent your lover from feeling left behind or unattended to.

10. When it's time for a family decision (time to move, buy a car, throw a party) give others as much time to prepare as you can. They need time to think and feel and imagine. Then they will help. Rather than decide up front how things will go, try acting as a guide. Set out the criteria for a success, bring focus, and

consider ideas kindly. Encourage your mate or your kids to discuss without you—not because you don't care (remind them) but because you're at your best at the very beginning of something, with problems as they arise, and at the very end—to simplify. Tell the talkers you want them to have time to feel comfortable discussing, creating alternatives, and working out the details. You can help get things done.

> BRAINSTYLE CLUE: *Timing* is the problem. *Timing* is the solution.

11. Use timing to keep the peace. Because you have quick answers, set goals first when required. Try to act as a facilitator for others so you can contribute focus while they shout out ideas and play with the fun stuff. If you help them get what they want because it's the right thing to do (not because you're sacrificing your time; you'll resent it and be a pain), you'll be revered.

12. Make a deal at the beginning with your beloved or your child when telling about their day or giving you the whole story so you'll have a win-win. You want the punchline. They want to talk and think things through with an audience. How can you create a time that allows the sensitive ones to feel "safe" with you? Their sense of being pressured by you has everything to do with your timing and impatience. Set the time aside and then hold them to it. *Timing:* It makes things bearable for you and doable for them.

13. Don't cheat. More than any other *brainstyle*, you have the strengths to maintain your discipline and follow your principles. Count all your strokes on the golf course and all the money in your account. Integrity goes beyond keeping your word; it also includes honest means to reach an honest end. Invest in your future by building your own character. Lead from your strengths. Apply your principles clearly and lovingly.

THE KNOWER
AS LOVER

KNOWER MEN: TOUGH CRUST. GOOEY CENTER. Word is now officially out that your tough exterior is not who you are inside.

> **NOTE TO NON-KNOWERS:** Don't let on you know this, they'll make it a point to make you sorry if you move on the information too soon or assume too much about how soft they may be.

You might mistake Jeff for a tough guy. He looks the part. Physically big and muscular, a former military man still with a crew cut, at 36 he initially seems gruff and a bit intimidating to talk to. He speaks in short sentences. Doesn't waste time. He is sitting outside when I see him, alone, bent over, having a cigarette. He dresses in a flak jacket and baggy chinos, to give the impression of someone you wouldn't want to meet in an alley.

His peers find him "difficult" to work with. He has no trouble getting an answer and making it stick. He doesn't socialize much or soften "the facts" to make them more acceptable. As he discusses his standoffishness he explains, "Why say anything? People just get mad at me or misunderstand what I'm trying to say." He adds, "Oh, yes, I get frustrated, so that's probably why I keep doing this," gesturing to his cigarette.

After talking with him on several occasions, with respect for what he brings and interest in what he thinks, it was easy for me to get past his gruffness. I was then able to ask him what success means to him. For him this was a deeper, much more personal question than I expected it to be. He mumbled his reply. He wasn't going to give up that privacy so easily. His answer was eye-opening, giving context for the rest of him.

He has, in the last two years, come to value a deep personal faith, and expresses it partly by action (of course), teaching Sunday school to eight-year-olds at his local church. His real criterion for meaningful personal accomplishment, he defines succinctly. "Success means being able to serve others—not make a million dollars." His tone of voice doesn't change from other parts of the conversation. I am clear that the lack of emotion has nothing to do with his intent. "But I couldn't do it longer than an hour or so a week"; he lightens the conversation to add, "I'm not that patient."

He is sharing his deepest values with me as much as anyone who ever wept over the revelation of a long-withheld secret. Most people miss the values underlying the actions because of the delivery. Most Knowers I have met are first in line to help with a cause, or are deeply concerned about others and how they (the Knowers) are seen in relationships.

Suddenly, I'd like Jeff on *my* team or teaching *my* kids. He'd rather touch someone's life than make money.

THE SOFT CENTER. Bruce is another tough guy. He has read my first book to get to know me, so the hard part for me—establishing credibility with his *brainstyle*—is over. He says, "I have never seen in writing so much information about who I am as a person. It was like you had a window into my mind and psyche and were able to watch and take notes." I told him that he seemed very open in our conversation. As he replied, he outlined his strict criteria for his trust and confidence. "What you don't know about me is I am a very private man. Few people other than family and very close friends know much about me or are ever invited into my home. Just to give you an idea, even though I've had the same housekeeper for years, she doesn't have her own key and only cleans while I'm there. From the emotional side, I am the 'cave dweller' as described in *Mars & Venus* and rarely, if ever, do I turn to someone for help in resolving personal issues or problems. So for me to share such details as I have with you, I have to be very comfortable with that person and I have to trust them—something I don't do very often. . . . [however,] I know that your questions are research-based and professional."

In the course of things, I find many other Knowers—the winners, the hard chargers, the tough guys and gals—have similar, secret, loving centers.

> *BrainStyle Clue:* Show Knowers respect by first and foremost respecting their need for privacy. Need To Know is their motto. To become a person who needs to know, you must take a chance. Offer your goals or purpose. Allow them time to establish that you mean what you say. Discuss some common interest. THEN ask more personal questions.

Once a Knower decides, he or she doesn't look back with the angst and guilt so common to most others. Bruce is such a husband, who married his teenage sweetheart when he was 19, she 17 and soon to have a child. Twenty-four years later he was still "head-over-heels in love with the woman I was married to and did everything in my power to keep the marriage together. I would have stayed with her the rest of my life. But she was unhappy, knew she was not in love with me, and wanted out of the marriage." Why? As Bruce heard it, "She felt like she had missed out on a major part of her life and she wanted to recapture it before she got too old." His non-strengths in the area of emotional relationships meant that he had missed her dissatisfactions. He "loved her enough to let her go" and then "finished raising" his youngest son of 14 by himself, a tough assignment.

> BRAINSTYLE CLUE: The focus in an argument or divorce is on the *non-strengths* of the other. *Comparisons* are the guns and bullets. The underlying motivation is the ego's feeling of lack and incompletion.

Comparisons launch and then create suffering; lovers become adversaries when gifts are overlooked and underfed.

Tired of the predictability, responsibilities of motherhood, and stability Bruce provided, his wife left to follow what she thought were her "heart's desires" into all the forbidden pleasures she hadn't enjoyed while married: sex with a lot of men, drinking, and country-western bars, with no kids to take care of. Her needs and appetites came first. She was 17 again. Years later she admitted to Bruce that she was intimidated by his "success, personal growth and knowledge, and felt we had grown apart." She acknowledged to him, however, "Not one time during our marriage was I ever condescending, called her (or made her feel) stupid or inadequate, and that I had always credited her with playing a role in the success we enjoyed." But Bruce didn't know how to assist her to express her feelings and learn from them, nor did she.

So, she hadn't grown with him. She had really seen their lifestyle as *his* success. To be fair, Knowers in general are not inclusive in the way that other *brainstyles* are; their natural gifts demonstrate independence, and so, it may be fair to say, may require a more self-sufficient partner who is committed to her own growth. The right-brained partners that Knowers often choose must be able to develop and manage most of the emotional side of the partnership. Bruce's wife wasn't able to do so.

In choosing your opposite, dear Knower, check your attraction against *brainstyle* strengths and values for the long term, as Bruce has learned to do.

> BRAINSTYLE CLUE: Want to stop any fight? Stop listening to the words, look for the love instead. Tell him of your belief in him. Help him grow by offering your gifts.
> Is she scared? Angry? Remind her of her strength in other, tougher situations, remind her you know her gifts, remind her of who she really is: her best self.

NOTE TO NON-KNOWERS: How much and how often a Knower openly demonstrates affection has little or nothing to do with how dearly the Knower loves his partner. The *brainstyle* is not a natural partner/pal/collaborator/sharer. The Knower's partner has a profound opportunity to see who she is and how she can be and feel complete as an individual without the overt support and constant inclusion of, say, the Conciliator or Deliberator spouse. Knowers show caring by deflecting attention and responding with what you think is important; their romance is bounded by what they can realistically deliver, and grounded in what they know is important to you.

When it came to the divorce, Bruce worried that his wife couldn't make it on her own[9]. In his view, she used the fact that he was still in love with her, "knew I would give her practically everything," and so she "ended up with 85 percent of our assets." His *brainstyle*-based conclusion: "That was my choice and I have no regrets." He'd put his worries to rest in the most measurable way he was able. It was over for him.

His values and abilities continued to take him to further business ventures, a comfortable lifestyle, and, as Knowers do, following the "rules" (of parenting in this case) by responsibly raising his son, leaving him with his only regret: that his son had no mom for his adolescence.

Over the last several years, Bruce's ex-wife has made five (naturally, he counted) overtures to reconcile. "Each time she asked, I would listen very carefully to what she said [Note the literal attention to detail], and . . . none included me in the equation. Statements like 'I want to come home,' and 'I want my old life back again' . . . [made it] obvious, even to a softhearted person like me, that she wanted [only] the stability and security back that I had provided for all those years and were now missing in her life."

No messy reconciliations, no break up-make up-break up scenarios for the Knower man whose gift is to set the boundaries, know his limits, have very clear

---

9. The left brain worries; the right brain is anxious. Remember? The left brain also measures, and so expressions of caring are often measurable: money, things given or built, and time.

values and deep feelings, and manage the deals and tangibles of life as best he can without being snookered. Soap operas are out for this *brainstyle*.

> *BRAINSTYLE CLUE:* Immature lovers often choose opposite *brainstyles* for personal completion. These partnerships require continual maintenance, and individual growth in natural gifts, to develop maturity. More mature lovers seek opposites more rarely, yet conciously with predetermined patience. Most choose commonalities, and especially similar values, in their partners. There is no way to lose, whichever way you choose.

CRITERIA FOR A PARTNER. Bruce dates now with much more insight than he had at nineteen. Whether he is the typical Knower man can be questioned, but his *brainstyle* can be predicted to have a list of criteria for a partner "as a package."[10]

- Lack of flashiness or flaunting of status. Showy exteriors put off many Knowers. Simplicity of presentation is valued; real value and worth need no explanation.

In Bruce's case, he dated a model whom he met first by e-mail, where he could learn of her intelligence, wit, and most importantly, about her values and thinking.

- Strong morals and principles. Knowers are best at streamlining things, taking efficient action, and following procedures so that clear principles and morals are the touchstones that separate right from wrong, good from evil, and make obvious what to do next. Those who don't have this kind of clarity are most often the ones who seek advice from the Knower, who can define boundaries and direction. When given a choice, Bruce now seeks similar values in a partner.

- Emotional security, independence, and self-worth. For the left-brained, emotional roller coasters can be worse than a turn-off, they can be deal killers.

His girlfriend of more than four years, the model who is now a close friend, loved the fact that Bruce didn't see her as particularly attractive, even though most men thought she was "drop-dead gorgeous." He was more interested in her values and character than her looks. OK, he says, it didn't hurt that she was attractive, but it was only a starting point. In his words, "After I'm attracted to a woman, there are qualities that must be in place to keep the relationship

---

10. He gets the whole picture when meeting someone and only breaks it down when pressed, the mark of a Knower.

going. . . . While a beautiful woman is a sight to behold, a woman who is beautiful and knows it and flaunts it is a turnoff for me. To me this would be the same feeling many women have about a man who has no looks or personality, but has money and power and flaunts it in order to get a woman." Bruce is a Knower who knows himself.

> *BrainStyle Clue:* It is easiest to stay focused on a Knower's behavior. Don't do it. The real treasure is the soft center. Be prepared to reveal yours first.

Knower Women: Anti-Heroines. The Knower women you will meet in this chapter make clear a profound lesson. If you are a woman Knower, don't pretend to be some feminine ideal from Venus. It's phony. No one will buy it. Be yourself. You are so impressive. So clear. So efficient. So great to talk to without all the fluff and clutter. Just be kind. Be honest. Allow influence. Use *timing*.

In the following example of a marriage, the Knower wife doesn't always sound kind, but many quotes are taken out of the context of the overall caring relationship. Like many professional Knower women, Ellen[11] is tough on the outside, a sucker for dogs and baby seals on the inside.

Partnership and Marriage as Seen by a Knower Wife: Mars and Venus In New Orbits. Ellen[11] is first of all an executive, let there be no mistake. When addressing the question, "What is marriage?" she immediately uses a business analogy to respond. "I saw that Carl had strengths I didn't have. I saw us as a team."

Ellen applied her view of their differences to the activities they enjoy: He loves planning vacations, searching out the luxury resort, the best restaurants; she only cares about adventure, uses a travel agent, sleeps wherever they have a bed for her, and swims with the dolphins. They take separate vacations annually; he for the quiet comradeship that suits his *brainstyle*, Ellen for the calm of nature that suits hers: he goes fishing and hunting in a lodge with friends, while she goes to the North Pole to watch polar bears with strangers.

As Ellen sees it, her Deliberator husband is a friend with everybody, writing frequent letters, talking and staying close to his family; she has little interest in spending her time this way (which is not a universal preference of Knowers). Ellen respects her husband for doing these tasks and doing them well. Knowers tend to be selective when making close relationships, as in all they do. Family is no excep-

---

11. Not her actual name, nor is "Carl" her husband's name.

tion for Ellen. Mutual respect for values is a must: she has parted ways with family members because of differing values.

There was romance, then marriage, then travel for each of their jobs, and then relocation for his job. Ellen gives a very detached description of events and interactions, focusing largely on her husband, as if by defining how he is different I will more clearly understand her in the black and white of the comparisons. This act defines her *brainstyle*: her hardware enables her to see clearly what is distinct and understand it by clarifying its boundaries, by defining what things are not.

Why did Ellen get married? He saw her as pretty and sexy; she saw herself as efficient, capable, and reliable. Being seen as pretty and sexy was new news that she does not comment upon, but it clearly got her attention.

Her husband is a very warm, right-sided Deliberator who has spent his career in the public relations business, a perfect fit for him as Ellen describes his diplomacy with people, making and maintaining contacts, attending to reputation (for himself or his clients), socializing, and naturally adding a positive spin. Others laud his incredible saves of executives in trouble with the media, the stunning speeches he writes for them, his alacrity under fire. However, as she describes his abilities—or her own, for that matter—it is with more objectivity and neutrality than I've ever heard. Ellen sounds nearly clinical as she gives her observations on how her partner does what he does for their marriage. Knowers, with less access to emotions, can easily be interpreted as uncaring. The best poker players, they don't give away much that most other *brainstyles* show. Knowing this, I know that whether she describes them or not, her actions show how deep her feelings are for her husband.

> *BRAINSTYLE CLUE:* A Knower spending time and making someone or something a priority = love and caring.

I ask about the relationship. "I am the hunter. He is the gatherer," Ellen says, naming the fact that they have flipped the gender stereotypes. Her gifts have taken her to leadership and executive positions in the same way Knower men take charge, set goals, and make changes. Her successes contradict expectations for women, whether executives or homemakers. "If I married another hunter, it would be boring." Boring is a punishment worse than fire ants, it would seem. Ellen is more than fascinated by differences; she is quite aware she needs them at home, just as at the office. She sees the world in contrasts.

Ironically (to a non-Knower), she also names herself as the caretaker, the nurturer. How? "I enable the adventure, he provides the stability." Ellen gives direction, solves problems, sets boundaries, and applies her skills, for example, by engineering and getting a second home built and furnished on schedule and within budget. If you are surprised at this definition of nurturing, you can see just how much *brainstyle* impacts the way we define the world.

> *BRAINSTYLE CLUE:* A Knower "nurtures" by applying her gifts to solving problems.

Their relationship can be characterized by the recent major project mentioned above: building a second home. Carl's concern about the project, she says, was expressed as a concern for the reactions of others: "What do I tell people?" "You tell them your wife is building a house for you." This settled the matter, she says, and ended the discussion.

Carl is startled by her comment, which, read from another point of view (his) could be seen as embarrassing. Naturally, his recollection of the conversation might just have a different scenario. However, he ignores it, just as he does in social conversations and at other times where her flat, conclusive statements tend to terminate (or potentially detonate) the topic, and makes a joke about something else. He picks his fights. Carefully.

He is proud of her abilities, she says. Having met them both, I can verify the observation, listening to him brag about her and her success. They take turns as breadwinners, he reveals. No small thing, when he has had a six-figure career income.

The differences in a Knower's processing are profound. If you look closely, this is the real reason to envy and malign folks with this gift: *Life is truly simple for her.* Her partner and husband has a life like most of the rest of the planet: infinitely complex when it comes time to decide, as he must think through his own and others' sensitivities and potential impact on reputation, memories of similar topics, and, at times, significant emotions about an upcoming event. She says, "When I'm quiet, I'm just quiet. When he's quiet, it *means something.*" You can almost hear the dialogue scripted by their *brainstyle* gifts:

Carl: "Is anything the matter?"
Ellen: "No."
Carl: "You're being very quiet."
Ellen: "I'm quiet."

Carl: "Are you unhappy?"

Ellen: "No."

Carl: "You sure?"

Ellen: "Yes."

And so it would go until, as she describes it, he has enough experiences to "get it."[12] This, she appreciates, is just his way. She is patient with his (and all those others') need to have an explanation, be given specific examples, and often, look at the same lesson more than a couple of times. "I get the lesson and apply it." Boom. It's over for her.

Ellen has always known she gets answers faster than others, which has always meant "smarter" to her. She is now aware it's her *brainstyle* timing that's fast.

If you're a Knower, the term "smart" can take on a whole new set of definitions if you read the next few chapters.

If you translate her descriptions and detachment as "arrogant," that's your interpretation. To her, it is a reflection of what she sees: the *Reader's Digest* version.

I ask about love between her and her husband. Ellen does not address that intimate word; we're not close enough for such private revelations. Instead, she talks about being "bonded" to people. He is; she isn't. His e-mail talks to family, colleagues, and friends every day are a must; she is "happy with five minutes a week or a month." She doesn't "bond"; she remains unattached, ready to move, change jobs, or homes at any time. This, she says, is a result of her upbringing, which required continual relocating. Knowing others who grew up in this situation with a different set of gifts, I have not seen the same detachment in relationships develop. I believe it is primarily a result of her *brainstyle*, acted upon by that environment.

She, as I have observed, demonstrates her care for others with a quick loyalty, solid backup, focusing all her problem-solving abilities on their problems, and generous time and attention. You know she cares by what she does for you—and doesn't ask of you.

CHARACTER. PHILOSOPHY.

➤ Because you mean what you say and say what you mean, compliments from you are a Big Deal because they are so clear, well thought out, and possibly rare. Don't milk this (withhold a compliment because you know they're valued and you don't do it much) or you'll be resented hugely. You

---

12. In *BrainStyles* terms, this equates to convincing his left-brained logic that his right-brained sensitivities are about his own feelings, not hers.

are credible because of your direct and factual style. Don't hold back. Remember Coach Vince Lombardi: Motivate. Celebrate. Point out what they do well. Build character.

➤ If you have a faith or philosophy you will most likely relate best to something more structured and traditional. If religion doesn't appeal to you, nature or sports, which take you there, may bring you peace. Since your identity is so tied up with the results you produce and the things you know, there will come a time when you must confront the real value you bring without doing or performing at all. You are more than a provider, more than a problem-solver. Your wisdom comes from the lessons gained by solving the jillions of problems you've solved with the principles you've applied, to show the rest of us clearly and simply how to get through the day. You will confront, ultimately, your character. As philosopher James Hillman puts it in *The Force of Character: And The Lasting Life,*[14]

> "The soul is concerned with goodness and beauty, with justice and courage, with friendship and loyalty....Qualities [such as these] are the ultimate infrastructure, giving purpose and shape to what happens to the body. They are the force in character....Your mental capacities and physical vitality may decline in old age, as might your mobility weaken, yet your character shows ever more energy..."

Invest in your future by building your own character. Lead from your strengths. Apply your principles clearly and lovingly. Take a lesson from Fran.

How Can You Be a Lover When You're Dying? A Knower Woman Deals with Death. Others Grow. If you're a Knower, how might you face the ultimate confrontation? When dealing with life-threatening illness or the death of a relationship[13] we have only and ever two life choices: love or fear; with illness, an impending deadline looms to spotlight what is valued. Character is in the crosshairs. Decisions matter hugely. Choosing love gives broader options for health, clearer decision-making, and creates previously unimagined intimacy with your frightened lover, family, and friends. You can enrich others where there is loss and change. The truth of who you are emerges and expands your soul while enriching the souls of everyone you know.

---

13. A death in a relationship is an ending/beginning. It can occur when your beloved son or daughter leaves home, a parent dies, you leave a career, or you consider divorce, and so on.
14. Random House, 1999.

Fran has just gotten her hair cut off, almost to the scalp. "It's my bed-haircut," she says, laughing. She's going in for surgery. It's her *tenth* time through two death-defying bouts of cancer with "someone else's hands in my guts," she says, and she's decided to make a "guest register" for all the surgical visitors. Her husband isn't laughing. Nor are her friends. Only the surgeon finds this funny. As a Knower, she *stares unflinchingly at the facts without emotion.* The character she exhibits by "minimizing the whining," as she puts it, is invisible unless you think about it: keeping pain and fear to oneself, as Knowers are wont to do, minimizes the burden for others. Fran will give you the facts of her illness when asked, so this is not the self-pitying ploy of sigh, -I'll-struggle-on-alone phony bravado. No, this is consistent with her Need to Know policy for the essentials. This is an expression of closely held values for self-direction and love of others.

An interesting interchange that puts her gifts into bold relief took place when she was telling me about the findings that were sending her under the knife this time. Her approach mirrored her conversations with her husband.

WHAT CRISIS? "Well, the tumor was fuzzy at first, but now it looks like it's in the colon. I guess I fall in the 2–5 year population [of ovarian cancer survivors] and I've had my time." Pessimistic? Factual? She confronts the worst outcome and gets ready to act, without emotion or sentimentality. Her *brain-style in situ.* What other choice is there, she asks?

I recall my own Conciliator mother's tears and terror when confronted with cancer, her emotional appeals to friends, minister, bogus cures, doctor, books, and me. Emotions were front and center, belying the strength with which she ultimately dealt with death. My mom's Conciliator *brainstyle* needed structure first, logic came later. Fran is the opposite: first logic; later, far more privately, the fear and sadness.

In contrast, as a Conciliator, I have been full of hope. I replied with my feelings. "But what if they find out you're fine? They don't know what they'll find just yet. . . ." "Hope is an unruly emotion," as Gloria Steinem said; it is the native land of the right-brained. I was aware of the quiet on the other end of the line, as the Knower patiently attended to my rebuttal. I felt like a Pollyanna in the face of the calm confrontation with which my Knower friend prepared for her possible death. In stark contrast, I, the right-brained one, felt like shrieking. Hanging up the phone, I wept at my helplessness.

Fran's Deliberator husband continues to be deeply emotional, yet much more analytical in the face of the continuing diagnoses of side effects and peaking cancer numbers. Fear and emotion come later for him as they do for Fran; they have a well-established rhythm together. He listens and takes notes for hours, spends time on and attention to every detail, and intends to "make every day I have the very best day of my life," Fran reports. His character is expressed through his *brainstyle* gifts as never before. Business moves way down the list. The Deliberator loves by doing: cooking, running errands, following up with doctors, and attending to endless details on her behalf. They are closer partners than ever before.

The Knower doesn't hope, she plans, and then gets things in order. Her only statement of fear or depression was, "Yes, I got a bit down, you know, anxious a bit, but I got busy, listened to tapes, and was fine." This Knower goes forward, not down.

As a Conciliator buddy, I fretted, got anxious, called frequently, argued with her about the idea of meditation being of help ("No way," said Fran), and finally figured out that the very best thing I could do was to pray, putting my right-brained gifts to work for my friend. (This activity put me back on my own turf, rather than floundering in the logical arena of the Knower.) The research[14] that prayer can impact healing has meant a great deal to me, especially as a Conciliator who can't generate proof so easily. If it has any relevance to the Knower, she didn't let on. Her faith is private and closely held. She seems to continue to put her faith in things she can see and understand, which doesn't mean that she doesn't have her own deep beliefs. Her conversation, however, is about provable, observable medicine (in this case) and the next hurdle to overcome. Matter of fact. One foot in front of the other. There is no drama for the Knower, especially when compared to other *brainstyles*. This is the crux of the difference between the way these opposite *brainstyles* initially face the future: the Knower looks for the worst that can happen in order to prepare for it; the Conciliator looks for the best, with emotional attachment to the outcome, and hopes for it.

> BRAINSTYLE CLUE: The more left-brained, the more "negative" the view of the future can be; the more right-brained, the more hopeful. The logical ones prepare, the emotional ones despair—and then can leap to a rainbow. Motivations are vastly different. Only your spirit can transcend the facts to bring peace. Each *brainstyle* accesses truth uniquely, in its own time, with its own requirements for evidence and structure.

15. Larry Dossey, MD, *Be Careful What You Pray For* (HarperCollins, 1997).

Consequently, I often interpret my left-brained friend's conversation as pessimistic, yet brave, strong, and tough. The Knower sees her own illness as a series of unfortunate obstacles that she has to deal with as long as she can. "Flowery" descriptions are left to other *brainstyles*. Looking me in the eye over a dinner, Fran says, "Cancer's going to win, you know. I'm just keeping it at bay. My husband talks about buying another home, and I have to remind him that I don't know if I'll be there to see it." Emotional Conciliators find these pronouncements heartbreaking. In fact, I have never wanted to imagine the loss of my sick friend at all; I feared my very thoughts would make it true. (This, Knowers, is why we Conciliators need to talk: to find our own logic, to hear yours, and to get through overwhelming, fearful emotions.)

When I couldn't keep myself from imagining that loss, I was paralyzed. I then got very bossy with the need to take control again—to *fix* something, to tell someone what to do. But there was nothing in the world to do but seek my own inner peace, wait, and offer support in the face of my friend's self-control, calmly peering out of the poodle haircut, ready for the indefinite stay in the hospital.

Realizing this, I set aside time for meditation and prayer. My prayers shifted focus to my own healing, my own release of what can only be God's job with Fran. I then realized a shift, a shift in my perception of Fran and her illness that transformed me. My ability to be present, to be a friend, was renewed. Our communications opened. I moved to a more neutral position when discussing her traumatic and invasive treatments in our conversations (I was terrified and tearful previously). My insight was to simply reframe the way I saw her. I gave up my fear. I realized I'd been seeing her merely as a woman with cancer, rather than the strong, steadfast person she is, a loving friend with intellectual and artistic gifts, a woman I've admired always and whom I admire right now, a woman who is going through some very rough times. I then realized I have the ability to simply be a loving friend who supports her treatments, offers my time or assistance, fudge, or seeks out new research. I cannot help at all when feeling afraid, sad, or helpless. I cannot cure her; I can pray for and love her.

> LIFESTYLE CLUE: When feeling helpless or inept in any situation, shifting your focus from one of incompetence, suffering, or loss to one of love as expressed in strengths and health is to transform a situation into unexpected blessings.

Fran's survival has continued to beat the odds. Her suffering has been extreme more times than she can count. She doesn't count. She doesn't focus on the pain. She moves on. For her, it's been the only logical thing to do: to create her future by accepting the worst and dealing with it, issue by issue. Her discoveries have been of the ordinary, of the gift of one more day, of more time to discover the depth of her love for her husband and sons, friends, the true fun of life. Her character reveals itself in her increasingly gentle, yet clear, dealings with everyone, her patience with those who talk of their stress and daily frustrations, without ever lecturing or comparing. She has found a way to deal with her illness by writing a book[16] on the comic side of chemotherapy when she must stay in bed. She laughs a lot more—looks for excuses to laugh, her friends say.

She no longer postpones saying things she needs to say to others. She tells, she says, only a few people her most important message. She comes to my office one day to say, "I love you," catching me off guard. No more Need to Know. No more Close to the Vest. The most private of all the information she has is out in the open. The impact of this expression, so profound for me, is instantly visible in the tears that spring from my eyes. I fear that the words mean goodbye. I realize later that no, every day is a potential goodbye, and she is just saying what she means and doesn't want left unsaid.

She teaches me to look at my life, what unnecessary fears I have, and what has been left unsaid for me. She shows me what real living is.

~~~~~~~~~~~~~~~~

Knowers, the force of your *brainstyle* when conveying love seems especially powerful to others. You are who you say you are, you mean what you say, and say what you mean. Your joining with another is a spiritual act that carries with it all the logic and practicality of this world to open you and your lover—or any partner—to go beyond this world.

> ## DON'T FORGET YOUR
> # FREE READER'S BONUS
> ### Define your *BrainStyle* and your Ideal Lover
> ### See page xiii for more information

---

16. Watch for *I'd Rather Do Chemo Than Clean Out the Garage: Choosing Laughter Over Tears,* by Fran Di Giacomo, Brown Books, 2003.

CHAPTER 5

THE CONCILIATOR

BRAINSTYLE

L R

~~~~~~~~~~~~~~~

*Q: How do you balance your spiritual self with the
decisions you have to make as a businesswoman?
A: I don't think of myself as a good businesswoman. I am a person who
is aware of what my purpose is and what my gifts are. And what I teach
is that if you are strong enough and bold enough to follow your dreams,
then you will be led in the path that is best for you. The voices of the
world will drown out the voice of God and your intuition if you let it* [sic].
And most people are directed by voices outside themselves.
—Oprah Winfrey, *Newsweek,* January 8, 2001, a Conciliator

~~~~~~~~~~~~~~~

If you're like most of the Conciliators I've met over the last decade, you are fairly clueless about the real depth, breadth, and impact of your gifts. Worse, you may be hiding them, trying not to show what is really being generated by that Big Dream Machine & Hardwired Right-Brain Engine you have access to all the time. Oprah accessed hers, and look what happened to her.

BRAINSTYLE CLUE: The BrainStyles database shows that Conciliators make up about 33 percent of the population, with approximately 37 percent male, 63 percent female. (Note the nearly 40 percent of this group who are men, supposedly from "Mars," who culturally are expected to be logical and unemotional.)

Take a breath. And then consider giving up the endless chase outside yourself for direction and deadlines. Stop being so afraid of being different. You are different. You draw your wisdom from inner sources, and the messages don't always come out so logically or in a straight line. SO? People love you for who you are, not for how you try to please them.

No, this is not going to give you permission to be undisciplined and irresponsible. Just because your primary gifts derive from the part of your brain that has no voice (depicted in the graphic on the previous page) doesn't mean you now have permission to impose in some new way upon others. You may already know that doesn't work. It does mean that you can set up your life to leverage those precious, often emotional or inarticulate, gifts to do what you do best and, with the support of others, do it even better. You bring Spirit into the world; Love in all its forms. You support, encourage, and express your feelings, and by doing so, allow others to know their own. You explore the unexplained and unquantified, the mysteries of people and ideas. You are able to connect with others in a way that no other *brainstyle* can, and you do it every day with professional competence, speed, and touching results. You have a working right-brain window on cosmic intelligence, on the unexpressed sensitivities of everyone you know, and you touch their lives every day with your caring acceptance of their foibles, and your willingness to overlook their silliness or gruffness. You have the capacity to be a healer in *whatever* field you're in just by applying your natural gifts, expressed lovingly.

It's as simple as this: One Conciliator's husband couldn't fall asleep for the third night in a row, worrying about his lack of work and the mounting bills they faced. This night she turned inside and asked, "What can I do to support him?" and allowed these wise words to spill out, "You're not afraid that you won't get more work, or that we won't get a bank loan; you're afraid of your brilliance in taking care of our new future. That's what I'm here to remind you of. You've always come through, even when you weren't sure you could." She went on to list how they had worked together over the years to overcome similar scary, overwhelming obstacles. They fell asleep together in each other's arms.

However, Conciliators, this does not mean those logical ones want to hear you at *Time Zero,* accept you or take you seriously at first. Your biggest challenge in life is to honor your own gifts so well that you are clear on your contribution, and then offer that contribution lovingly (which is always appropriate) and with timing to others. The operative word here is to OFFER, not argue, persuade, passionately convince, or yell, sulk, or withdraw until they give in. They may never really hear or understand you. Go for approval and you lose yourself. Avoiding conflict at all costs can cost you your happiness. Avoiding conflict in order to time your response, reach clarity, speak responsibly and more neutrally is better. Being your best self is your goal, your challenge and your mission.

> BrainStyle Clue: Stick to your principles, NOT your positions and feelings. Your gifts allow tolerance, forgiveness, and empathy to trump your closely held, adamant opinions, grudges, and hurts.

Let us be clear: The right hemisphere of the brain is every human being's access to the soul and what lies beyond it. At the very core of you—the Source of you—is Love, not your fleeting emotions, fears, worries, or judgments. Your access to the loving essence that you are is substantial, continual, and hardwired. Deny it if you will, but there it is. Use it for a grand and loving purpose, and there is no end to the lives you will touch and repair, no end to the contribution you can make. Use it to meet your ego's needs and there is no end to the drama and suffering you can create and have to endure.

Too (fill in the blank) *sensitive, reactive, emotional, selfish. Egotistical. Outrageous. An airhead. Ballistic. Hysterical. High Maintenance. You wear your heart on your sleeve. You talk the talk, but don't walk the talk.* You may secretly subscribe to the labels slung at you to dismiss and demean, even though you get insulted and think up nastier names for the labeler. Have other "wiser" (left-brained) folks attempted to shut you up, get you organized, asked you to plan ahead, or to think before you speak? Are they helpfully and impatiently waiting for you to get a life or get focused, giving you oh-so-well-meaning advice to get you to change who you are naturally?

Why is this?

Neither of you understands what your strengths are and how to take advantage of them. Instead, they just react to them while you evaluate, focus on what you're missing, and spend lots of time trying to improve. Think Dave Barry,[1] Robin

---

1. Pulitzer Prize-winning humorist, author, syndicated columnist for *The Miami Herald,* and my personal writing guru.

Williams: Fun. Off-the-wall. Sally Field, Diane Sawyer, Oprah Winfrey: Passionate. Intense. Former President Bill Clinton: Personally persuasive. Openly feeling.

With your own self-criticism and second-guessing, how much time do you spend revisiting the decisions you've made or regretting things you've blurted unintentionally? Is "sorry" one of your most common words? Or "get over it" your defense?

Can we talk? You don't really appreciate yourself. Oh, there's the bragging and self-promotion you use to make those clods aware of just how misunderstood you are or how wonderfully you've performed, yes. But in the wee hours, you may also review your projects and tally others' assessments to define your worth. Of course, those measures do NOT reflect your real worth. When asked, do you spend too much time defending and justifying yourself? You may be wonderfully skilled, talented, creative, or athletic, but those publicly accepted abilities are your bottom line, aren't they? Not you, unadorned, without props. You're probably more sensitized to those who are more skilled, talented, earn more, or have a better wardrobe than you are to your own blessings and impact on others. Or you may have decided you're better than they are—those insensitive, hard-nosed, cold, domineering bullies. You may have cloaked yourself righteously in your ability to care more openly than others and use that openness to make others wrong. Stop it, you're denying who you really are. If you tend to turn your natural gift for introspection and emotional understanding (empathy) into self-doubt, you can lock onto the position that "everything is my fault." This is just another way of hiding. By feeling sorry for yourself and playing victim, you become unassailable to correction, connection, and ultimately, affection.

> *BrainStyle Clue:* Conciliators can conclude that either they are so innately caring, they couldn't possibly ever say anything mean or nasty, or conversely, they are always saying the wrong thing.
> Conciliator, if you have critical thoughts, you have critical words and deeds. Accepting your gifts, you can move to a loving presentation with no effort.

~~~~~~~~~~~~~~~

I was lost in my own goodness.
—A Conciliator's insight after learning about her *brainstyle*

~~~~~~~~~~~~~~~

You are a natural partner. You create plans that inspire, include, and instruct. Your right-brained ability to visualize and empathize promotes your language of idealism and oft-times unattainable perfection. You "talk the talk" before you can "walk the talk" as a way of motivating and inspiring yourself to a grander purpose. Perhaps the results you achieve over time are neither as grandiose as you can imagine nor as disastrous as you fear, but where would the world be without Don Quixote? Martin Luther King? You?

Yet can you honestly say that you are able to objectively evaluate how well you are doing? How well the relationships in your life are going? Consider what might happen if you let go of hoping and wishing that others would be who you imagine they could be instead of who they are, of trusting too much and too soon to wind up disappointed. Imagine putting more trust into what you can honestly deliver instead of waiting for the other to make your wish come true. Your inner critic does NOT know the truth of you.

Without a doubt, you are the best of friends and the most difficult to deal with on the planet, all at the same time, sometimes within the same sentence. You get lost in your own insights and feelings and shut others out. Am I ringing any bells here?

The very people you seek out ("Oh, she is so much smarter!") or resist ("I cannot stand being bossed around!") are there, not to approve or attack or wound but to teach you what you have to offer. The idol has gifts you overlook in yourself. The boss you could never work for, because of the way he says things, is the very boss who can provide what you're missing. The mate you rate as unsupportive can be precisely the one to set the boundaries you cannot, ground your schemes, and give heft to your plans once you get past the different way she shows love.

Now is the time for you to not only understand your strengths but also use the information to begin the most powerful process in life, forgiveness. Forgiveness is more than letting old hurts or resentments go. Forgiveness includes seeing that another who has hurt you is either a valuable teacher or a person who needs the love and gifts you have to offer him/her. Forgiveness is complete when you realize there was nothing there to forgive in the first place, that both you and the other person are perfect just the way you are—and the way you are not. Forgiving as your daily practice is the basis for a partnership that is a learning laboratory, an adventure, a romance, a place of healing. And you, more than any other *brainstyle*, have the gifts to create this kind of partnership.

You are hardwired to see your life with the right brain: personally, emotively, experientially in living color and sound. Can you start now to store those mental movies with a constructive voice-over?

Knowing about your strengths allows you to make a choice about how you want to live your life as a whole. Do you want to enjoy yourself for who you are? Or do you want to keep searching elsewhere for your answers and suffering with your comparisons? Do you want to use the magnificent hardware you were born with only to serve yourself? Or to expand and serve the world? This is a moment-by-moment choice, which will be apparent in every conversation and every negotiation, every interaction and relationship, as you realize how your strengths are the gift you offer to others.

~~~~~~~~~~~~~~~

Over time I learned that my world moved from the inside out. I created my own reality by my self-talk. I substituted Conciliator positive self-talk and my life improved—or more accurately, how I felt about my life improved.
—Yvonne Charnesky, Florida

~~~~~~~~~~~~~~~

"Go within, or go without," is a saying that applies to you and your gifts more than any other *brainstyle*. Your answers lie within you. Oddly enough, your extraordinary ability with others is where to find those answers, for it is in relationships that the universe opens to you.

YOUR BASIC STRENGTHS AS A CONCILIATOR derive from the fact that you first access the right side of the brain and later use the strengths of the left side to assess and analyze what you have just considered. (See diagram of your *brainstyle* access on page 77.) Brain research has proven that, surprise, the right side of the brain is the hardware that sees things exactly as they are. Because there is a delay in your access to the critical left brain, you are the one most apt to access spontaneous feelings, images, and intuition first and then later change your mind as you have time to think over and add interpretation and analysis to the equation. Your gifts mean you are the sparkler, the supporter, the natural friend. You put a little pizzazz into things, add passion, and excite others to action as a rapport-builder who doesn't have to work at it (except when you don't want to, of course). Did I mention "moody"? Your strengths are always apparent, and you often get the label "moody" because your feelings show in your body and spoken foot-in-mouth language more than with other *brainstyles*.

NOTES TO NON-CONCILIATORS.

- Identify, acknowledge, and praise a Conciliator's strengths to win his heart and focus her mind on what is true.
- When in doubt, ask and listen. Conciliators think out loud.
- Hold the image of your Conciliator partner at his best and remind him of it.

- Stop expecting him to think and act as you do (rationally, methodically, with quiet focus, and so on). I know you know this, but you actually have to do it.
- Don't give credibility to her emotions based on the intensity of the presentation. Use timing to allow the first storm to pass. Review the topic until you can both reach a clear-eyed decision.
- Include her.
- When in doubt about what to do to make him happy, what best to reply, or what gift he would love, just give back to him what he gives to others. Much of the time Conciliators give what they most want to receive.
- Love them. You can say almost anything to Conciliators if they know you love them.

DON'T FORGET YOUR
FREE READER'S BONUS
See page xiii for more information

~~~~~~~~~~~~~~~~

A *BRAINSTYLE* SUMMARY OF DISTINCTIONS: RIGHT BRAIN ACCESS

Most Delayed   Most Rapid

The Knower	The Left-Sided Deliberator	The Balanced Deliberator	The Conceptor	The Right-Sided Deliberator	**The Conciliator**

~~~~~~~~~~~~~~~~

RIGHT-BRAINED DISTINCTIONS. Many Conciliators confuse their *brainstyle* with that of the Conceptor. Both get tremendous ideas about possibilities in the future. Conciliators can imagine things far outside the box. Both *brainstyles* get a mere sweeping summary of lots of data, and both can get impatient with—because neither can process it—too much detail. The distinction between the Conciliator and the Conceptor is what is done with the information soon *after* it is received. Conciliators, think about how you envision, dream, paint possibilities, and get excited about what can be created in the future. You may have been criticized for getting too excited too early about things. Picking up the phone too soon. Coming up with too many neat alternatives to try. Wanting to *do,* when the Conceptors want to see and review and talk through it one more time. Conceptors can talk up their ideas, but they have a different, more rapid access to the left side of the brain, which quickly integrates the glaring realities of risk and reward and an analysis of practicalities that usually end up generating one whole concept, one doable, reasonable, often money-making strategy or direction, which can quickly generate new, complete, and distinct directions that clearly spell out a practical end result.

> *BRAINSTYLE CLUE:* Conceptors create a whole new game and a couple of ways to play it. Conciliators create brand new ways, places, and methods to play that new game.

Think about it, is your vision as quick to define clearly analyzed, whole answers? Aren't you even better at generating alternatives and wild-eyed possibilities? Brainstorming new and imaginative ways, with the people who could deliver them, to realize the goal? To see how all the parts will work together all at once? Aren't you better at seeing an idea, once the arena has been named and the new ballpark defined, as whole and complete *in action,* with real people, lights, camera, action? Don't you instantly know and trust that everything will work together, relying on your native ability to wing it at the moment? This is distinct from the Conceptor, who thinks in paradoxes, and solemnly considers the risks and numbers to come up with a vision, which may or may not include the lights, camera, and action, but probably will define why and how to go into the movie business.

THE CONCILIATOR AND THE RIGHT-SIDED DELIBERATOR. Many Conciliators also confuse their *brainstyle* with the right-sided Deliberator's. However, the basic gift of the right-sided Deliberator is steadiness overall, as a result of greater access to the sequential and analytical left brain. As a Conciliator, you may have been at the same job or in the same partnership for decades, but your natural emotional steadiness does not equal your look-alike, because of your greater right-brain access. For instance:

THE CONCILIATOR	THE RIGHT-SIDED DELIBERATOR
• Emotional and *internally* aware	• Emotional and *externally* aware
• Faster, more emotional language, and dramatic non-verbal reactions	• Quick sensitivities that aren't always expressed or shown at the time
• Unpredictable at *Time Zero*	• More steady and controlled at *Time Zero*
• Less aware of consequences, more apt to blurt or embarrass	• Often acutely aware of what and how things are said; more diplomatic and indirect

- Intellectually more practical

- Creates emotional bonds
  that are central to the
  relationship, but can end, boom
- More willing to confront another
- More likely to complete a project

- Intellectually more abstract and
  complex
- Creates emotional alliances and
  loyalties based on values and respect
  that are difficult to end completely
- Less willing to confront another
- More likely to start lots of projects

Both of these *brainstyles* take things personally, react empathetically and with feeling, are naturally intuitive, and spiritually sensitive. Both love new ideas and images, meet and befriend people easily, and are socially adept. Both love starting things; overall, the Conciliator makes it to the finish line more often. The Deliberator, however, is much less likely to confront than the Conciliator.

Because of the stronger right-brained access of Conciliators, relationships have closer bonds sooner and create fewer emotional boundaries between themselves and others (no distance, no ability to say no, and often the feeling of "being lost in the other") in the personal connections they make. Conciliators fall in love; Deliberators stroll. This doesn't mean that the Deliberator cousins do not feel just as deeply or get just as drowned in a love relationship. For the steadier, more literal and loyal Deliberator, relationships can rely on a heartfelt, yet more external identification with a lifestyle, its structures, and defined roles. Mutual values are prized more highly, nurtured, and deepened for Deliberators. Marriage can bring attachment to things they do with and for their partners; divorce requires mourning for and adjustment to too many new decisions, and so can take a long time to forgive and release to move on. Wounds (that don't show) can take a lifetime to heal. Finding new ways to love and teach others to love shortens the process for both.

Conciliators, on the other hand, can get lost in their own feelings and ideals about the other, along with a wordless attachment to having a partner to love. They tend to prize the relationship above all, and so either they are devastated by personal loss or make a change—when they feel secure in their partnership and have time to reconstruct why there is a need for change. New mental images must replace old ones over time for each *brainstyle*. Conciliators deal with change more emotionally at first; Deliberators can take smaller steps and keep their stride. When Conciliator feelings get hurt or are not reciprocated in the way they expect over time, they can declare "it's over," and walk away with a lifetime of non-verbal pain and angst that can be hard to heal—acting first, analyzing later. Healing requires revisiting the experiences to review and sort emotions from blame to shame, to reclaim personal responsibility, esteem, and self-worth over time, often by talking the memories through with another who can help reframe the lessons with love and allow forgiveness. Teaching others how to heal is another way a Conciliator—the natural teacher—heals.

STRESS. One of the most common defensive reactions for the right-brainer trying to survive in a left-brained world is to try to look like the factual, structured, fast-with-the-right-answer left-brainer: buttoned-up, buttoned-down, stressed out. Temporary fixes. You have the ability to let your passion inform your words to move dramatically between *charismatic* and *tough.* You (more than others) alternate from harsh to tender, technical/professional to fun/fancy-free, sometimes on the same issue. Ever feel just the tiniest bit schizophrenic? Compartmentalized? Overwhelmed? Trying to be equally skilled in areas that are not your natural gifts does it, especially at home where things are sooo personal. No one is fooled. The harder you try to be it all and do it all perfectly while pleasing everyone along the way, the more fault they find with what you provide (you may have noticed) or the higher the expectations for more of the left-brained delivery, which ultimately you can't deliver. You get resentful. Feel put-upon. Unappreciated. Unloved. Taken for granted. A real snit is in the works. In this state, you can explode, get drunk and disorderly, or maybe just walk off the job or out of the house, a steaming hunk of righteous resentment.

If your problem is that you have too many things you want to do and experience and your lists are endless like mine, you are being driven by an aptitude called ideaphoria, or the ability to self-generate ideas. Keeps you awake nights, doesn't it? Celebrating your strengths means steering them, not being driven nuts by them. Keep a journal, draw, tell stories to kids, entertain your friends, meet new people, but make sure you celebrate your lists and your ability to make them.

> *BRAINSTYLE CLUE:* Owning your strengths and accepting your non-strengths is the first step to a more peaceful, easier life. Next you must make your gifts and limitations public to those who matter in order to have workable agreements for what you can actually, lovingly deliver.

THE CONCILIATOR: A SUMMARY OF STRENGTHS[2]

TIME ZERO →	SOON AFTER →	WITH PRACTICE →	EXPERT →
Seeks harmony.	Revises initial reactions with logic.	Coordinates, plans, manages the project.	Uses intuitive or spiritual abilities as inner resource.
Imagines alternatives.	Criticizes, doubts, second-guesses.	Creates meaningful plans and projects.	Teaches, leads from experience; shows how.
	Includes others, brings people together.	Inspires others. Stands up for own values.	Guides, mentors, inspires with ideals. Heals.
Reacts spontaneously.	Takes action. Seeks reactions from others.	Is a persuasive organizer.	Releases need for others' approval.
Shows emotion.	Talks about the experience.	Generates options.	Finds joy in *others'* successes.
Feels.	**Is demonstrative.**	**Sells.**	**Mentors. Teaches.**

- The Conciliator is greatly influenced at *Time Zero* by what is said, seen, and felt. The initial reaction is with the right brain, which knows but cannot speak. Feelings and images are processed fastest to give an overall "hunch." Later, logic and language clarify or revise the initial reaction. Decisions are often changed because of this process.

- The Conciliator reacts quickly and spontaneously, usually conveying how he feels. Most are quick to trust others, that is, to form an image of the possibilities and hope for reliability or return of similar feelings. Using these abilities, they can be pioneers and risk-takers. When high-energy (extroverts), they can use the spotlight for great things. When lower energy (introverts), they can be marvelous moms, dads, nurturers, sponsors, mentors, and coaches, giving passionate support to those they care about.

- The Conciliator's main strength is in building relationships, bringing harmony to different elements, people, or things—and so does especially well in sales, education, advertising, public relations, retail, project coordination, drama, the arts, or administration, among other service or interactive fields.

- Conciliators are excellent mediators of conflict with a natural ability to "read" and empathize with people, and so are naturals at counseling, teaching, consulting, or humanizing a more technical or structured field.

---

2. All Charts© 1997, 2003 *BrainStyles*, Inc. No reproduction without permission. *www.brainstyles.com*

CONCILIATORS LOOK FOR OPPORTUNITIES TO:

- bring people together, help them, make them comfortable
- start things, make things happen
- support others
- inspire others
- add the sizzle, the smile, the ambiance, the mood or tone, and address the unseen
- bring personal meaning to events, objects, and ideas
- try a new way, imagine options, dream of what might be, fantasize
- make friends and make relationships count by being special and making others special
- participate, get included
- communicate by talking, writing, drawing
- see it and tell it as it *could* be, look for possibilities

A GUIDE TO LEVERAGING YOUR STRENGTHS AND MANAGING YOUR NON-STRENGTHS

You're fastest at sensing what's going on with others and quickly interpreting how you're coming across to them. Your natural strength is to instantly process nonverbal cues from the immediate environment with the powerful access you have to your right brain. Remember, the right side of the brain registers similarities, thus *bonds* with others. You are the one most likely to look for commonalities with others to appreciate them and see past their exterior. You're the first to love them, tolerate them, and then, when they don't live up to your often unstated expectations, to try to fix them or make amends and martyr yourself. If you have not yet clarified your values, you will "love 'em and leave 'em."

However, you have the capacity to make any relationship work—even with the jerks. You give loyalty an emotional dimension that is unparalleled in attracting others.

The biggest challenge for your *brainstyle* is how you create your reality from the moment-to-moment interpretations you make about what you see and hear. Your left-brained interpretations are based on one of two feelings, love or fear. Once you decide to respect yourself for who you are *and for who you are not,* all incoming information can be interpreted as helpful or as a signal that the other needs help from you. You can personalize less and become more neutral. You can give up resisting others by competing with them, and so start learning from them. Everyone can be your teacher to help you accomplish your goals.

> Q: How can you interpret what someone else says about you as a helpful or useful input?
> Linda Bush, a mature Conciliator, offers these answers:
> A: Others' criticisms now become my "Ah-ha's!"
> A: I use the mantra, "It's not personal," especially when I am tired or stressed, when I might choose to relate from my non-strengths instead of what is natural . . .
> A: I work with the concept of projection* too: If I spot it, maybe I've got it. I continually own my projections as often as I can become aware of them.

You're excellent at imagining and exploring possibilities and alternatives to a goal or idea. Brainstorming is fun, isn't it? It's your gift, that's why. Sometimes this shows up as being the devil's advocate, asking "What if?" about every idea or problem. Others may find this especially annoying, get impatient, and tell you to change this behavior for two reasons: 1) It is not on the straight path to the goal; 2) they can't do it nearly as well or as fast as you can; and 3) it interrupts their timing. The latter issue is what you can manage and be considerate about.

You're gifted in bringing harmony to any situation and in a variety of ways: with feelings, humor, in color or design, or with sounds, depending on your particular brain specialization. You draw primarily from the ability that resides in the right brain to see whole things, rather than bits or pieces, which is why you "get a sense" of what to do or what the problem is in a situation without knowing how you know. The Japanese, it has been reported, use their sense of *wa,* or harmony and agreement among people, to reach a true, committed consensus. This is what the right brain specializes in, the sense of union, a quick read, a hunch, unencumbered by logic or analysis. Thus your blurting, quick-witted, off-the-wall comments which, with your awareness and focus on them, can increase in accuracy, articulation, and loving impact to increase harmony. Your strength is derived from a right-brained perception of patterns to see and then openly join commonalities, in groups, families, or with a partner. Because of this, a specialty

---

* Reminder: A *projection* is a psychological term coined by Sigmund Freud to mean a defensive mechanism where we seek to disown our feelings. Doing this, we see in others the sins that we don't wish to acknowledge or take responsibility for in ourselves. To ensure that the projection stays outside us, we literally forget the projection, which allows us to feel hurt or justifiably angry over how others treat us unfairly.

of yours is empathizing with others, adding warmth, making things beautiful, coordinating projects, and bringing people together.

Your erratic timing can drive others up a wall. Your need to translate words into images or connect them with your previous experience (what you know to be true) can get you called stubborn or especially slow to change. On the other hand, your right-brain access supplies instant associations and conceptual leaps based on that experience, so you constantly interrupt or go too fast and leave others behind.

Passionate, charismatic, entertaining, and persuasive are descriptors for you when you're in a good mood and clear about your gifts.

You're most likely a communicator and enjoy talking, telling stories or jokes, giving examples, illustrating a point, or reading and learning from others who do these things. Putting ideas into words, or taking in words and making ideas and pictures from them, mirrors the process your brain uses all the time. You learn best by experience, and next best with an example you can understand.

Time can slip away, schedules and promises disappear as you respond to others' needs, share your empathy and experience, process the information, and experiment. Working in the home is challenging, because there is no structure except that which you create. Routines and structures are necessities for you to feel like you're accomplishing something. Even your lists can't provide the boundaries and direction that other *brainstyles* can offer to ensure you're heading in the right direction. Time management is a Band-Aid that does not suit your gifts, takes more work, and one you will probably give up soon after you try to apply it. Since overview is not your strength, you need to seek out others who can provide direction and help you regroup. If you still fail to take assessment time to review your limits, your priorities and direction, you can end up giving away your independence to the endless demands of others.

You're best at spotting problems quickly—especially where people are concerned—not at solving them. You can "feel" what's wrong, or so quickly intuit problems in a group that people may wonder how you came up with your "analysis." The strength that underlies this ability is your experience-based, nonverbal sensing of the environment. When you leverage this ability with a supportive, open communication style, you can offer insights to others who cannot sense or articulate what is second nature to you. Allowing time for more left-brained input (either your own or from others) can start you on the path to better and more successful problem-solving.

You're happiest in situations where spontaneous reactions count. When you are operating fully from your right brain, you are the most capable of all the *brainstyles* of living "in the thin moment of the present," according to Dr. Michael

Gazzaniga, Harvard/Dartmouth neuroscientist. Known also as "the zone," you achieve a flow[3] where you glide along, operating with your skills but without self-consciousness. It happens when you allow yourself to override the left-brain connection that keeps you analyzing and correcting and asking why. You may have called these times just "being yourself," or they may have meant more to you than just an event. Keep this in mind as you do your job or interact with family members. Many Conciliators channel this ability into making things more fun or meaningful so they can be applauded. This means you may expect others to appreciate you in ways they cannot. No other *brainstyle* offers the artless, natural warmth and open support that your *brainstyle* can. Don't expect those with other gifts to do so.

Q: When with others and you sense that your quick reactions are not appreciated, do you react defensively? Are you making your own feelings more important at the expense of another's feelings or ideas?

A: Think how you can make things work for both of you by quickly showing you care for the other. Point out how he or she is right about something. Use your humor or fast thinking in a dance with their *brainstyle* strengths and timing. Your secret is simply timing, not changing who you are.

You're quick to personalize the meaning of things or events. You add quick left-brain interpretations to right-brain experiences. These can be extraordinary insights, or when you are fearful and draw only from your own subjective experience, very inaccurate projections of your own feelings. Reconsider your conclusions about others whom you dislike or distrust and evaluate what parts of their actions are *brainstyle*-based.

Depending on your energy level, you either prefer doing or being still and meditating or dreaming. Taking action, getting involved with a project, or keeping busy are easier than planning, studying, or researching, for the extrovert. This can translate to continual high-wired action to do things *now*. Your ability to dream (active meditation) takes more quiet time and can be an inner resource for writing, teaching, consulting, or supporting others.

---

3. The whole notion of "flow" has been studied and documented in the book *Flow: The Psychology of Optimal Experience* by Mihaly Csikszentmihalyi (Harper & Row, 1990) as a state of elevated attention where strengths drive a vitality and interest that overrides emotional problems and produces deep satisfaction.

If you are more introverted (quiet, lower energy), your strength draws from an ability to empathize deeply, to put others in the spotlight, realize joy when they succeed, and make the impossible occur by your loving support for them.

You trust easily. Your gifts include showing your feelings and creating an open give-and-take with others. You establish trust with others by disclosing how you feel and think more easily than other *brainstyles*. You tend to trust first, ask questions later. You do so because your non-strength is analysis. All you need is timing and an intention to stay neutral for a longer time. Your optimism and openness, however, are your gifts and are what give you more chances to win in all of life. Don't give these away because of a couple of strike-outs.

> Q: Do you tend to trust quickly? Do you look for times when others disclose personal information or drop names of people you know? Do you have to get "burned" before you are cautious?
>
> A: The key to trust lies in trusting yourself: You need to be conscious of how you first look and hope for the best in another. Seek counsel. Allow time for logic to fully study what lies ahead.
>
> Q: Are you aware of how other *brainstyles* establish trust?
>
> A: It's critical for you to read about other *brainstyles* in order to know what to expect from their strengths and so expand how you can deal with others more reliably and neutrally.

You have the highest of ideals for yourself and others. You create the dreams, the quests, the Magic Kingdoms. This is perfectionism that can only be served by learning how to love. When your ideals are merely for your own ambition, they are gained at the expense of others, lack integrity, and have a limited shelf life.

You are, however, the most likely to rely on an inner spiritual or philosophical understanding of life to get you through the highs and lows. This is the gift you can draw from to sustain yourself and give to others. You are a natural lover and healer. Your right brain provides the ability to store experience, create symbols from it, and believe something (you just know it) without facts or data. This is both good news and bad news. You may seek and articulate broad principles that serve as comprehensive philosophies, inspiring teaching and spiritual or personal leadership, or you can stubbornly defend your beliefs in the face of logical contradictions and new information in order to be *right*—and not be able to broaden or discuss your point of view because your feelings block further understanding, *and* you have no language in your right brain to expand your ideas. This is why you are called stubborn. Forgive yourself. Your stubbornness is merely a fearful reflection of your gifts and timing which can transform with your own loving acceptance.

SOME SELF-MANAGEMENT EXERCISES UP TO THIS POINT:

- Think of one of your personal "if-onlies" (example: if only I had the money, I'd . . .). Extract the substance of the dream (travel, adventure), and see how you can make it a plan that is actually doable. Don't be surprised if you have to experience it to some extent to find out whether you really want that dream or not. The motto of the right brain is: *I wouldn't have seen it if I hadn't believed it.*

- Name an area of discomfort in your life where you feel overwhelmed or resentful. Think of ways (or ask a left-brained friend) how to structure it with a deadline, time limit, and focus. Notice if you feel freer.

- Notice how you add the "sizzle" to events or things. Give yourself at least three examples of how your gift made the day a little brighter, more fun, or more exciting for you and others.

A SUMMARY OF THE CONCILIATOR'S NON-STRENGTHS, WHICH TAKE LONGER AND REQUIRE MORE EFFORT.

If you don't appreciate yourself for your limitations as well as your abilities, you will find yourself, as many Conciliators have, victimized, "maxed out," sacrificing, unappreciated, depressed, alone, vengeful, and most certainly, unsuccessful in life.

NON-STRENGTHS FOR CONCILIATORS.

- You do not FOCUS on one thing, priority, or project, because your strength is to associate ideas, not eliminate them.

- You do not SET BOUNDARIES WELL. Your strengths are to harmonize and expand, dream, and open to new possibilities. Saying no, putting a limit on eating, smoking, or friendships are all challenges in boundary setting. Conciliators need to learn to set limits—and do so in a neutral way that doesn't reject the other person. Prepare ahead. Give yourself time.

- You do not DECIDE just once. After you get more input, you tend to change your mind. This is because your gift is to react spontaneously, often emotionally ("sparkle"), with incomplete information. You can learn to manage your timing, but your real gift is spontaneity.

- You do not ASSESS information in an objective way. You're best at being subjective, or personal, by adding emotionally-based images and experiences quickly.

- You do not ORDER things into a linear or rational sequence that can be measured or repeated easily. You use your own internal organization that is not a straight line, which is why you can't find things. You don't do things the same way twice unless you have learned discipline, which requires substantial left-brain access and never feels totally comfortable, yet allows you to perform very well in business. Staying centered in a measurable world is an endless challenge.

- You do not STAY EVEN or METHODICAL for great lengths of time. Your gift is to express the inexpressible, access the emotive, see the invisible, and explore the illogical. If you persevere, it will be for a dream, but the path will not be a straight one to the end.

- You do not ACHIEVE for the sake of the achievement but for what that achievement brings: "Worship," as one Conciliator put it, or stardom, fame, or more truly, love, connectedness, and strokes. This can mean that no matter how hard you work, it's never good enough because the reward is not in the work, it's in the intangible parts of the job, and when you try to make those rewards measurable (money, recognition, status, fame), they never satisfy.

- You do not BALANCE your perspective most of the time: You take care of others too long and feel neglected, or you focus on your own needs too much at the expense of others.

- You do not CREATE THE WHOLE PICTURE in the future. You're best at generating future possibilities that do not integrate factual analysis and bottom-line assessments. Don't expect yourself to have the whole thing. On the other hand, Martin Luther King's "dream" was exactly the kind of inspiration that generations have followed. Look at how you can use your dreams to inspire and heal.

- You do not generate SEVERAL COMPLETE, WHOLE ANSWERS to a problem. You do generate several alternatives to one answer. If you can stay with the problem for a while, you can generate wonderful options and innovative and fun formats, parties, business ideas, and fallback plans. Most Conciliators rely on their spontaneity to "wing it" when plans fall through.

- You do not HANDLE CONFRONTATION well. Rebelling and reacting are high art forms in the mouth of the Conciliator, and those who have leveraged the quick response to the delight of others are on the stage or writing for the stage. Those who just react because they feel like it are continually going *through* stages, all of them stormy and self-serving, designed to protect their images rather than their principles or relationships. You can confront others when you feel strongly, with passion and righteous indignation. You know you don't receive confrontation nearly as well as you can give it, so you may resort to defending with personal attacks that complicate things very quickly. Since the right brain has no language, left-brainers get to the name-calling first, and you may take it seriously and escalate the conflict with things that are hard to take back. In these cases you'll say things you regret and end relationships needlessly. Manage your timing, use your gifts lovingly, and redirect the conflict into learning, or another "Ah-ha!" for your own effectiveness.

- You do not naturally follow through and KEEP AGREEMENTS. Your first response may be "Oh, yes! I want to." Later you discover you're overcommitted, have no idea how to get to the goal, or need more of a plan. Promises, promises. Don't make ones you can't keep. Have a plan that includes collaborating to cover your non-strengths or allows extra time to deliver.

To leverage your natural strengths, use coalition-building and a service orientation to inspire and lead others. Select a situation where rigid structure and straight-line thinking are only *some*, not most, of the requirements for job success.

A REVIEW: HOW TO LEVERAGE YOUR STRENGTHS

1. Decide to be your own biggest fan and appreciate the things you do that can't be measured. Don't wait for the "thank you" or paycheck; it'll never be adequate.

2. Practice some discipline to help you achieve an inner focus, such as meditation, affirmations, routines in exercise, music, or art, to give yourself time to reflect on all your ideas and to-do's.

3. Revise your ideals into doable goals, in line with your strengths and non-strengths.

4. Develop your intuition into a reliable strength by tracking your results until you can predict accurately most of the time.

5. Do not accept your first decision, but don't overanalyze it to death. Get trusted input. Don't over-rely on one source because you feel comfortable with her or him. Experiment and learn.

6. Continually monitor taking things personally or making things personally meaningful only for yourself. Make things personal (beneficial) for others.

7. Define a life vision or purpose for living that articulates the contribution you want to make to others. This is essential for managing your personal ups and downs. A vision is a vivid mental picture or symbol for you that inspires you and moves you to action. When your actions match your vision, everything

flows; you automatically draw from your strengths and offer them to others. Life is a workshop and you experiment to learn how to better deliver what you have to give. When your actions are incongruent with your vision, you experience tension and conflict.

~~~~~~~~~~~~~~~~

There is no guilt warranted in the process of discovery.
—Judy Kyle, PhD, psychotherapist, Dallas

~~~~~~~~~~~~~~~~

> Here is a formula for stating a Life Vision:
>
> [Being] I am a _____
>
> _____
>
> [Doing] who is here to _____
>
> _____
>
> [Having] so that I may contribute _____ to others.
>
> > A true vision is something for which you will take a stand.

My first attempt at completing the above exercise took about two years. It was something like "I am a communicator." Often it is the most private and intimate thing about you, gathering as it does your dreams and experience into an actual statement. The revisions come easier as you grow. The exercise is crucial for expressing and focusing your character, or inner you. Your statement may not make sense to others, but if it does to you, that is what matters.

Today my vision is to be a teacher of love. The formula above helped me write the longer version over the years that translates to this simple phrase.

~~~~~~~~~~~~~~~~

8. Partner with other *brainstyles*.

> ➤ CONCILIATORS NEED THE KNOWER IN ORDER TO:
- provide focus on one or two goals
- bring in the cold, hard facts so trust for another includes the downsides
- prepare for the pitfalls to their dreams
- reduce the complex personal problems to simpler objective, measurable choices
- state the limit and outline its boundaries in order to finish, let go, and move on

> ➤ CONCILIATORS NEED THE CONCEPTOR IN ORDER TO:
- define their philosophy, goals, or activities more broadly as an overview first

- see where to go in the future
- work on things that will be practical, expect the unforeseen
- plan for more than one outcome (rather than several ways of achieving a single goal)

➤ **CONCILIATORS NEED THE DELIBERATOR IN ORDER TO:**
- get organized and get realistic and stay grounded
- carry out the plan thoroughly
- analyze the numbers, the steps, and the timetable
- lend accuracy to their ideas
- provide calm or reassurance without the emotion, allow detachment

Knowing your strengths and taking advantage of them means acting on them, growing them, using them for the good of the whole. Knowing your non-strengths means ensuring someone else covers them and giving that person the responsibility to put decisions into effect in those areas. You must get out of the way. Take direction. Admit, "I don't know how as well as you do."

> *BRAINSTYLE CLUE:* Friends and supporters mean survival for the right-brained who measure self-worth with 1) another's approval or 2) inclusion, rather than focusing on their own ability to care for, approve, and include others.

COMMON CHALLENGES FOR THE CONCILIATOR.

1. **JUDGING AND COMPARING.** A consistent source of pain for this *brainstyle* is looking out at the environment with the right-brained ability to see things as they are, and leaping to the best and brightest image of the possibilities, only to add the criticisms and comparisons learned by the left brain over the years. These criticisms and comparisons are spirit-killers.

Low self-esteem is the result, a measure of how much time is spent attending to non-strengths: worrying, comparing, measuring—yet never measuring up.

2. **BEING MANIPULATIVE.** Being sensitive to others' "vibes" means bonding to build relationships, most often without words. It includes being indirect, and avoiding conflict. It is the norm in the Far East; it is suspect in the West. You will be avoided or judged as manipulative when you use feelings to get what you want ("I'll be hurt if you say that again") or work through others indirectly to get what you actually want ("Don't you want to do this?"). Say it. Request it. Be willing to work things out. You deserve it.

> *BRAINSTYLE CLUE:* The Ego always goes for what it wants, using any tactics it can; the grander, mature Self goes for what includes and expands. Conciliators, you have the gifts to do just that when drawing from love rather than fear.

3. **INTEGRITY VERSUS TRYING TO PLEASE.** Integrity is a touchy subject. Many Conciliators give examples of learning to keep their word by watching others fail to do so. A personal decision must be made by Conciliators that "words must match actions," that a promise made is an unbreakable bond, that getting somewhere on time is a caring promise for another.

> *BRAINSTYLE CLUE:* Keeping your word, honoring agreements, and making sure your words match your actions are decisions and commitments you must make as a Conciliator. Your hardwired *brainstyle* strengths do not support these actions.

Keeping your word is not letting someone down. Guilt is the gift that keeps on giving when you fail (unless you take responsibility and tell them what you plan to do to clean up any mess or upset that your failure caused).

4. **PERSONALIZING.** A lifelong issue for a Conciliator is taking things personally, meaning interpreting another's acts or words as directed toward one's self rather than reflecting the other's *brainstyle* reality. We've all been there. Neutrality and detachment become impossible, defending one's survival the only response. Fear rules the day: lying, striking back, blaming, crying, and yelling are mere justifiable tactics.

> *BRAINSTYLE CLUE:* Given that the right brain learns from experience, right-brainers listen to and observe others and instantly introspect to see what the action or event means to them personally. Maturity comes from asking the question, "What can this teach me?"

Conciliators are natural gossips. They are on their way to sorting out the experience by putting words to it. They live what they know how to do best: learn from their own experience. Gossip is a heat-seeking missile locked on to the negative. Is this what you want to contribute?

> *BRAINSTYLE CLUE:* Conciliators, the introspective ones, talk about themselves and their feelings a lot in order to put words to and make sense of their non-verbal, right-brain experiences. Talking about others to seek clarity about how to bring out their best is respectful and purposeful.

Combine the ability to examine another's success or misstep with the notion of *projection,* or displacing feelings onto another, and you crank up the learning several notches. Knowing when you are projecting your feelings of envy, resentment, anger, even caring, to see them in another (rather than realizing you actually feel them yourself) is a way to reclaim power and self-esteem.

CONCILIATOR SOLUTIONS:

1. **TIMING.** Learning to wait before the initial impulse becomes an edict, a decision, or a commitment is the simplest way to manage the quick responsiveness of the right brain.

2. **ALLOW ANOTHER TO GIVE LANGUAGE TO AN EXPERIENCE OR EMOTION IN ORDER TO MAKE A DECISION.** The right brain needs language. Other *brainstyles,* lovers, and friends are vital for you to talk things through to realize your own wisdom on a subject.

> *BRAINSTYLE CLUE:* Conciliators need to talk or keep a journal as an introspective discovery process, unearthing the wisdom of their experience and the insight available from their right brains. Writing, a left-brained activity, can actually promote healing and the ability to move ahead.[4] The solution is so easy and so obvious, it gets lost in the Hurry Up and Do It world of action so many Conciliators live in.

3. **DECIDE TO BE DIRECT. USE FEELINGS TO CLARIFY YOUR INTENTION.** "I had to confront my boss. I realized he was doing the wrong thing and I was the one lying awake thinking about it. I geared up to face him by getting mad first so I could let go of [my] fear. I was very calm when I went into his office. I had a plan," said a Conciliator of a former boss at IBM.

4. **USE THE LEFT BRAIN TO INFLUENCE THE RIGHT BRAIN.** In the book *You're Smarter Than You Think,* cognitive psychologist and author Seymour Epstein suggests three approaches for managing what is stored in the experiential, nonverbal right brain. By now, you might know exactly what this means for you. a) Use your rational mind (the verbal learning stored in the left brain) to train your experiential mind (right brain). b) Provide your experiential mind with corrective experiences. (Create new, loving outcomes by accepting *brainstyle* gifts and practicing forgiveness—daily.)

To provide the experiential mind with corrective experiences means storing the lessons your adult, more left-brained abilities have assessed and provided over

---

4. "Scribbling My Way to Spiritual Wellness" by Musa Mayer, from the magazine *Mamm,* April, 2000.

the years. It means taking in the wisdom from others who have tried and failed. Even though books provide this information, your gifts will store this information most readily when you try it for yourself.

c) Learn from your experiential mind. (This means creating and using the most loving answer you can think of.)

Paying attention means continuous learning from the right brain. "Once I found what I was good at [being with people], it just goes so easily. All my old ideas of who I was and what I was afraid of just fell away," says a mature Conciliator.

~~~~~~~~~~~~~~~~

Taking responsibility for *how* you feel starts with the self-awareness of *what* you feel. And that starts with giving yourself permission to have the feelings you have. Seeing them as a gift allows the next step: using them to grow and contribute to the world.

THE CONCILIATOR AS LOVER

Because your gifts are largely immeasurable, dear Conciliator, you of all the *brainstyles* have the hardest time honoring your own gifts. For this single reason, you seem to choose the roller-coaster life of passionate ecstasies that bullet in a twinkling to the agonies of defeat. How?

Here is the story of a Conciliator man, typical of the cultural stereotypes common in most cultures today, who based his marriage on his non-strengths, only to lose everything for a time: himself, his marriage, his children. Learning from the experience was painful, but it resulted in a complete career and lifestyle change. Today he is a productive, happy, successful manager, developing individuals and teams, leveraging all his gifts with his kids, his new wife, and his colleagues.

A MARRIAGE GONE WRONG. This is a cautionary tale about a Conciliator man and the marriage created from unrealistic expectations of his strengths. His partnership became based on promises he could never deliver; his partner focused on his non-strengths, comparing him to a model of "manliness" that is the stereotype too many Conciliator men still believe in.

"Oh, if I had only known then what I know now." Words can't capture the years of stress, and ultimately pain and loss, this husband and his very left-brained wife went through in their 18 years of marriage. It's of some comfort that he can now go into the rest of his life knowing how to offer, up front, his *brainstyle* strengths and admit to his non-strengths so that he can create a partnership where no one is expected to change who they are. But that knowledge came too late to save his marriage and continue living with his two children. No, he has to endure the pain of visitation and return his beloved son and daughter to his ex-wife on a regular basis.

Paul is a handsome, GQ kind of man; six feet or so, with brown hair and dark eyes, a smile that says *wow* when he feels it, and eyes that still tear when he feels the loss of his family.

MISTAKE #1: COMMON INTERESTS WERE CRITICAL. Oh, it's always so easy with hindsight to sort out the problems; in real life it is so much easier to just drift into decisions that create those problems, and then *wham,* suddenly it all blows apart.

Paul dated Natalie in high school and for several years thereafter. Their families were close and lived nearby. It was all so comfortable, right, and traditional: they all got along so well, you see. The young couple both loved the outdoors and enjoyed sports and camping together. Then each, for different reasons, decided college wasn't in their future. They had fun together. So how could they miss? Surely they could make a go of it because they had such similar interests.

A NEW AND UNFAMILIAR SITUATION. After high school Paul went right to work. Great with his hands, mechanically able, savvy when it came to figuring out technical and mechanical things, he was a natural in construction. She went to secretarial school, and they were off and running, planning a marriage that looked just as they expected it to look, until way too soon, Natalie, the smart and able secretary, was promoted. It seems she was outstanding at analyzing and summarizing reams of data[5]. She was offered an excellent job 1,500 miles away. Wow!

They thought, "No problem." They'd remain near home for the wedding, go on their honeymoon, return home, and take off for their exciting new lives together. A dream ticket!

DECISION TIME, ALL THE TIME. They moved. Paul got a job right away that he loved—he fit right in. Natalie, not able to make friends so easily outside of work, was very lonely, he says now. There was little time for the outdoors, no time really for any common interests at all when Paul thought about it. Why? They both worked, and his schedule quickly prohibited any social life during the week. In describing this time in their marriage, he made an interesting observation: "I realized I *loved* working, and ten to twelve hours a day were no problem for me. Time didn't matter. I loved learning new things, and there were so many things to learn. I could see the results so quickly.[6] It was tremendously satisfying." His job satisfied his need to do and be active, he says. Although he hated to sit still in a classroom, he loved the action and quick results he could achieve. He started going to night school and loved that even more. Possibilities were opening and life was exciting for him, the imaginative, high-energy, friendly one. Paul did not mention that being at home with Natalie or playing tennis on weekends wasn't nearly as

---

5. Clue #1.

6. Conciliators love to see and hear their impact on the tangible world. Talking, doing, measuring results gives the ego proof you're alive (see chapter 9).

exciting or nurturing as his work. His omission is noticeable, especially for a warm, relationship-oriented man who bonds so easily with others.

MISTAKE #2: REAL DIFFERENCES ARE OVERLOOKED IN FAVOR OF BEHAVIORAL CHANGE. OK, so there were some problems in these early years, he noticed, but nothing that couldn't be fixed. His schedule from 5 AM–7 PM meant no real time with his wife in this new city where they had no real social life or family support. "She was on the phone with her mother a lot in those days," he recalls. "We played tennis on weekends and spent some time together then, but not really enough to get close." Paul was not offering his *brainstyle* strenghts to his partner. So, a year and a half into the marriage, they went to see a marriage counselor. Since it was the '70s, we can forgive the counselor now[7]. The advice, it turns out, was the worst possible for a Conciliator—and double that for a Conciliator man.

THE WRONG ANSWER. Paul says he'll never forget what he was told, because he made it his priority for the rest of his marriage. After eliciting each of their dissatisfactions with the marriage, the counselor turned to Paul and said, "Do you hear what your wife is telling you? YOU HAVE TO CHANGE!" And of course there was a more explicit description of just what changes he was to make: "We had a program then. How well were we meeting each other's needs?" So what were the needs he was to meet? His wife wanted a strong, decisive, assertive, highly controlling husband.[8] In fact, these descriptors *were exactly what Paul loved about Natalie.*[9] Oh my. And Paul? He just wanted a softer version of her decisive, controlled (left-brained) strengths. "I wanted her to be warmer," he says, "but I loved her strength."

Do you get the stereotypes they each had in mind? Do planets come to mind?

THE SHAKY FOUNDATION. Paul was never certain, even when they married, that she loved him for who he was. In fact, she told him later in one of those dental-drilling "honesty" sessions they were encouraged by the counselor to unload upon one another, she had had serious doubts (assessments) about Paul even before their marriage. However, her mother told her it was just normal, premarital jitters, and she was encouraged to go forward with the wedding. The message: Paul was definitely not the man of her dreams. Even in retrospect, Conciliator Paul, the more accepting inclusive *brainstyle*, does not say the same about Natalie: Paul says he loved her for the strengths she had, including her rather introverted, aloof, and abrupt ways. She was highly analytical, he said. She planned their vacations and he went along. They settled into a "married pattern: [with] separate interests and few

---

7. If your counselor gives you this advice, I would suggest you reconsider your choice of counselors.
8. Clue #2.
9. Clue #3.

common friends." Paul thought everything was fine as long as he was a good provider, working hard; and, well, the cost was just what you paid to build a nice life together. He worked harder. They worked on their communications. He tried to be stronger. Since that didn't really ever work at home, he was more aggressive at work and applied for a job in a whole new field: sales. This time the new job would require another move from their current Houston base to Los Angeles. Paul was busy being strong and professional. Competing. Achieving.[10]

BAND-AIDS DON'T WORK: *TIME ZERO* REVEALS ALL. What he now knows were his gifts became clear when they had their son, eight years into the Doing Married Activities Program that they called their relationship. "I knew we were different when my son was born,"[11] he says. "I cried when he was born, felt instantly nurturing and tender. Told myself to get a grip but I couldn't help it; I felt so much I just couldn't contain it. On the other hand, she was much less emotional than I. Then, with the addition of my son, it meant [we had] even less time for one another. He was so active, so restless—he never slept more than 45 minutes at a time for the first nine or ten months. He was highly sensitive to everything. Years later we were to find out that he had Attention Deficit Disorder, and maybe, so do I—just not to the same extent."

ANOTHER SET OF NEW DECISIONS. Paul's idea of how to advance his career through sales was great for him, but terribly timed. The couple took on a whole new layer of stress to the already demanding family situation: They had moved to California, with fewer friends to rely on for help. Paul sees now that during this time, "I was into my new career in sales, so was gone a lot, again, and she was alone, managing our son mostly by herself, until I would return home to help. I can see now that my real joy was in my work, where I loved the challenges, the changes, the people, the learning, the feeling of accomplishment, and that's where I spent my time. I wasn't reliable, I know. I'd say one thing and do another, like I'd say I'd be home at seven, and *whoops!* it was ten before I knew it. I felt very conflicted about where to spend my time: home or work?"

Two years later, their daughter was born, adding more joy for Paul but more stress and distance to the marriage.

---

10. Many high-energy Conciliator men have done exactly what Paul did to launch their careers. One example is the high-profile chef, Emeril Lagasse, whose family suffered greatly in his absence; he divorced his first wife after a few years. Paul Prudhomme, another Conciliator, married a woman who ran his restaurant with him and so was married far longer.

11. This would be a *"Time Zero"* event in *BrainStyles* parlance, or clearly a new and unfamiliar event in which natural *brainstyle* is exhibited most clearly. Note how his lack of awareness of what this timing means for him allows Paul to pile up the stresses on himself, the family, and work ever harder to do what he thinks he *should* do to fulfill his expectations for his wife and his role as a father and provider.

MARRIAGE DEATH-THROES. "She said I'd abandoned her, that I was a wimp, that I wasn't strong enough when a situation called for it. I know that I was totally involved in my work and not nearly the fun-loving person I once was. My friend told me 'You're trying to be super-everything: -dad, -husband, -business partner, -sales guy . . . and it's impossible.' I thought I was really trying to support my family, sacrificing for them by working hard and trying to be strong—the breadwinner—in the best way I knew how. I was not meeting her needs as a husband, I knew. She wanted safety and security, steadiness and predictability. That just wasn't me. I found it hard to laugh when I was under so much pressure to be all things, all the time. We seldom played anymore. Our travel consisted mainly of flying off to visit family, or, if Natalie and I did arrange a trip, it was like starting our relationship all over; we were suddenly uncomfortable with one another, with all the time we had to spend together.[12]

"She warned me she was going to do something about our situation, probably told me several times. I was so caught up in my work and its immediate issues, I couldn't think of anything or anyone else. She, however, found what she needed in another man she met at the gym. When she told me, I knew the marriage was over, just like that.

"She'd assumed I was having an affair since I was gone so much. My business partner's statement was, yes, I was having an affair and her name was my new company. Short of the physical relationship, everything I needed involved my work; it consumed and satisfied me. If we had had a true partnership, I believe now that we would have found time to assess not only our marriage, but also how achieving the goals of the business would provide for the family and our future. We might have gotten a clearer picture with a realistic time frame for getting a return on our monetary and personal investment."

Now, some five years after the divorce, Paul has gingerly entered another relationship that he spends a great deal of time attending to. He still has to wipe the tears away when he takes the kids back to their mom and stepfather.

LESSONS. What can you take away if you are a Conciliator (especially a husband/father)? This is what Paul would tell you:

---

12. Vacations are classic *Time Zero* situations. Think of all the new decisions you must make. For this couple, just having a change in their schedules was disconcertingly, newly intimate.

"First, and most importantly, never feel guilty expressing your feelings openly. I was most miserable when I thought it was 'unmanly' for me to express myself, either verbally or emotionally.

"After people get to know me, they realize I am energized by being around people. They kid me and tell me I sure am touchy-feely. Before becoming aware of my *brainstyle*, the only place I ever felt comfortable being myself was with my family. I'm fortunate. I had a mom and dad who openly showed their emotion and affection, and still do.

"I remember shortly after my divorce, when I had to return the kids to their mom's house, trying to keep from crying as I said goodbye. As I drove away, I couldn't do it; I broke down. My ex-wife told me, "You have to stop crying around the kids, it sends the wrong message." Well, it's been nearly five years since our divorce, [and now I know] the nurturing, caring side of me has to express itself so I just let it happen. The kids have seen it so often, they just take it in stride, they know that's the way I am.

"I now realize I have become a great parent on my own without the stress of having to act a certain way or be a certain type of dad, as I felt compelled to when I was married. I now believe my parenting is balanced very well with their mother's. They know they can come to me and talk about emotional issues, and I can relate very easily, especially now that they're both teenagers.

"My son is very much like me emotionally, very compassionate, and we have some of the best conversations because of the bond we share. My daughter shares some of her mother's restraint and is less open emotionally; yet when she and I do talk or she writes me a note, I know it is directed straight from her heart, and it just floors me.

"Secondly, as I continue in my new relationship, I am much more aware of what I can bring to it. And, just as importantly, I am able to explain those areas where I need support [my non-strengths]. I know I can be the eternal optimist, the big idea person, and sometimes wildly spontaneous. Fortunately, I've found a partner who is caring, compassionate, expresses what she thinks and feels, yet is organized and detail-driven.

"In this relationship there is no pretense; there is a respect for each other's strengths and a mutual understanding of what each of us can provide. I know she needs order and a schedule, something not natural for me; yet knowing she needs this, I call upon my learned behavior generated from years of business deadlines to create, at least, a schedule we can discuss. I know I can ask more of her to help me plan, to set schedules, and get specific, to supply the rudder to my wild and erratic course. She does so willingly because it's so natural.

"With my greater understanding of my gifts, I realize that being a man—and specifically a Conciliator man—has nothing to do with being 'manly.' What is important is to let your emotions show, to express yourself in such a way that you let your inner self out. This will not only benefit you and keep your life less stressful, it will also allow you to bring compassion for—and provide a far greater contribution to—others with whom you share your world."

Paul's insights and the wisdom they provided gave him the confidence to try again. He is now very happily married to his Deliberator bride, with mutual, open regard for one another's gifts.

~~~~~~~~~~~~~~~~

A MARRIAGE THAT WORKS DESPITE ALL ODDS. In any marriage of opposites, the strengths of each partner are in bold relief. Here is a brief introduction to one such marriage, which showcases how your gifts as a Conciliator can make a relationship work with a Knower, who is vastly different on any scale you use to measure it.

First, this is how the Conciliator bride-to-be describes what she really fell in love with in this man a decade younger, far shyer, a man who worked with his hands instead of his mind—someone completely unlike herself. If you're reading other stories of couples who fall in love, note how it's the common values she names and emphasizes that provide the foundation, rather than the common interests. Note also how the Conciliator uses all her empathy and openness to lovingly look for his gifts—so natural as we fall in love—so possible any time we choose.

"On the back porch that evening, over a couple of Dr Peppers, we talked for hours about our mutual love of families, children, dogs and horses, sports, home improvement. We discussed our business approaches of respect, honesty, and integrity. His manner was unassuming, non-boastful, charmingly witty, yet careful about disclosure. I'd never known a man to be obviously strong as an ox yet sweet as a puppy. I was aware he spoke less than I, but I always laughed or agreed when he spoke. He said he worried that his shyness would be interpreted as conceit. I assured him that I worked with a load of conceited people, and he didn't fit that character. . . .

"He didn't talk about goals, but he sure accomplished many. I asked why he appeared so wise, and he said he'd made all his mistakes by the time he was 18. . . . I tell friends and family, it makes no sense on paper, our differences are enormous. . . .But I've never felt so safe, so loved for who I am versus what a man idealizes."

TIME PASSES. When married or partnering with someone very left-brained, the relationship must be managed continually by the Conciliator. The solution this couple finally reached, not without a great deal of angst on the Conciliator wife's part, I might add, was not to partner in the traditionally Conciliator-defined sense of that word. A hard lesson learned, so don't say you weren't warned. The Conciliator wife calls this partnership strategy "divide and conquer," meaning split the turf into separate project arenas. This means the Conciliator had to give up her image of the Mythical Perfect Partner Hubby, the one who would spend hours alongside her, listening, sharing, acknowledging her for her brilliant ideas, disclosing his intimate thoughts and insights, and reveling in the bond they would openly acknowledge. Nope. Didn't happen.

Because they each work, when they carry out projects, they are partners on the goals. They each take separate parts of the plan and agree on the dates for completion. She celebrates their "wins"; he shows her the completed job without much comment.

When things go awry, Conciliator tactics can be indirect and stormy, Knowers brutally judgmental and autocratic. Fights can be messy, with differences in *brainstyle* blamed as the cause for problems instead of used to resolve differences. Time-outs can help. Even better, fights can be prevented by the Conciliator who focuses on strengths rather than reacts to "inflammatory" Knower word-bombs.

A CONCILIATOR'S GIFTS TWELVE YEARS LATER. As a couple, they are now in a stressful time. They have sold their home and had to move out immediately. It's transition time—always difficult with the routine gone—all the structure and familiarity of the known nest replaced by boxes and temporary everything. She uses her Conciliator gifts to keep upbeat, keep moving, and keep the family together while she stays in a hotel with her son so he can finish out the term at his grammar school. They are a commuter family in the worst sense of the term.

There are many boring, frustrating tasks to do to get their new home underway on the property purchased for this purpose. Her Knower husband will help build it when she gets an architect and contractor for him to work with. To make an enormous understatement, she's been busy with the hectic time of maintaining a full-time consulting business and a semblance of a home life for their son.

Her husband drives in from his makeshift digs on their property one morning early, about 5:30 AM. He is quiet. She offers a perky idea. "I have an idea for a project the boys could do this weekend . . ." which her husband glaringly interrupts. He is tense, aggressive. "Like what, build a house?"

The options for retorts flash through her mind. Sure, she'd fallen behind in their agreed timetable, but she'd spent whole DAYS trying to get phone service; and YES, she'd volunteered for her son's school, which she knew her husband thought a waste of time, unfocused on the needed task as that time had been, but it was so necessary for her son and her to be together . . . the list went on in her mind, including all the blaming accusations of HIS lack of progress on HIS agreed goals to remodel the old house on their property while she was still in town.

Then, she said, there was a mental pause. Unnoticeable to the naked eye, she decided to "shift her vision," and look for his *brainstyle* strengths instead of react to his words or defend herself as she always had in the past. Just shift her vision and find his strengths in this situation.

"What's on your mind?" she said.

"I want the foundation poured in 30 days," he replied.

Her response transformed the morning and the day:

"Thirty days. Sounds like a goal. I like that."

He relaxed, she said. Their conversation took an easy turn; they went on to decisions and action items they could divvy up and actually accomplish.

Partners again.

She realized that her old reactions would have created a three-day, icy standoff.

She liked this better. Easier. More loving. More common ground. A partnership once again.

~~~~~~~~~~~~~~~

DON'T FORGET YOUR

FREE READER'S BONUS

Define your *BrainStyle* and your Ideal Lover

See page xiii for more information

CHAPTER 6

THE CONCEPTOR BRAINSTYLE

The following description is the best available for this *brainstyle*:

> *Visionaries are, typically, driven people. In the vernacular, they see things that others don't see, march to a different drummer, play by new rules. In work, they tend to be strange and difficult to get along with. Their strangeness or differentness is easy to understand, for by definition, they have perceived . . . some difference that makes a difference (to them). Where others see only ending (destruction), or nothing at all, those possessed by the vision see some difference, small or large, that renders futurity a possibility, and marks the first step toward a new version of reality. If visionaries are compulsive, they are also frustrating, for they tend to talk in repetitive circles, struggling to bring their object of awareness into focus. Their compulsion gives them the appearance of certainty. Their lack of clarity will often make them an object of scorn. It is very difficult to be convinced of something that nobody else can see, and it is as hard to live with one who suffers from such a conviction. But all of that comes with the territory.*
> —Harrison Owen, *Leadership Is* (Abbott Publishing, 1990)

CONCEPTOR GIFTS. You have the *brainstyle* gifts to set the direction, make things clear and simple, less scary, and, well, make the impossible *possible* by seeing things others cannot see. The service this provides is incalculable. It is the basis for your label as a *visionary*, which is either a rush for your ego or a responsibility you take into relationships with respect and caring. Your passion grounded in the logic you access quickly is a powerful force for creating, uplifting, and moving people and ideas to greater understandings and broader horizons. You can envision the unseen potential in someone, instill her with belief in her own possibilities, and set her free to reach them. When you focus all that intensity on a partnership, you are well nigh irresistible.

> BRAINSTYLE CLUE: The BrainStyles database predicts that Conceptors are not quite 10% of the population, with approximately 65% male, 35% female.

The hardest time in a Conceptor's life, it seems, is being young and inexperienced with visionary hardware that has no track record, no credibility. This lasts until enough has been learned, tested, and put into a discipline that translates to some real results. Conceptor Michael Dell was precocious with his ideas of portable, mail-order computers at age 16, born at just the right time after Conceptor Steven Jobs and the breakthroughs of Bill Gates and Microsoft, to be the wunderkind and huge success that he's become. Einstein and Edison, the most famous of this *brainstyle*, defined the twentieth century's living and thinking. Neither was a model husband nor a flashy dresser, certainly not into hairstyles nor celebrated by colleagues. Ted Turner, the "mouth of the south," called obnoxious by many, was drowning in red ink when he had the outrageous concept of live news, 24/7, on television. His personal rocket to the unbelievable success of CNN as an international television staple began when the fledgling network was available to give up-close and personal Gulf War coverage in 1991. Entrepreneur: A+. Social maven and husband: D-.

> BRAINSTYLE CLUE: Stop waiting for the world to appreciate you. It can't. It won't. Your job is to appreciate your own gifts and do what it takes to establish your credibility.
> It takes inner strength and outward confidence to be yourself as a Conceptor. The only things you have to rely on are your inner resources and your self-created track record.

CONCEPTORS INVENT. How? The term "conceptor" refers to a person who quickly forms global ideas, or hypotheses for decisions to come, by mentally combining left-brained facts and right-brained insights into several complete solutions.[1] In the *brainstyle* diagram of the Conceptor, an attempt is made to depict

---

1. All solutions do not necessarily come at once, but Conceptors seem to be unique in being able to generate several answers that each address the problem quite differently.

the rapid use of both left and right hemispheres to tackle an issue. The only way I've found to describe this mental process is with the term "thought balls," formed from analysis, experience, random facts, and associated images that are simultaneously held, not just as alternatives, but whole, complete resolutions.[2] Another way to name this process is "creative abrasion,"[3] where contradictory ideas are mentally (and sometimes verbally) pitted against one another until something new is ground out to create breakthroughs. Breakthroughs make leaps, which means there is a great deal of right-brained access which has no words. This takes time. Daydreaming and pondering are part of the process, but not all. Logic and analysis play a very strong role to assess and eliminate many possibilities. Other right-brainers just don't use the same process to focus and set priorities.

Conceptors create directions by seeing patterns invisible to others. For example, Roger is shown pages of numbers. He says two or three just "jump out at him," and he sees instantly where to go and how to focus the future. Erik looks at a blueprint for his new home, gets a pen, draws new lines, and X's out parts that "won't work." His wife says the builder confirmed with amazement that Erik's three-dimensional plan needed no revisions.

These declarations, or hypotheses, have little if any proof initially, while the Conceptor declares implausible possibilities inevitable. They sound like hunches or hot air to other *brainstyles*. They are overwhelming in scope or timing or both, especially when the Conceptor knows a field well. Others' reactions can cause the Conceptor to conclude she's all alone, "weird," and has no real contribution to make. It takes inner strength, often a strong faith or set of sustaining principles, and outward confidence to be yourself as a Conceptor. The only thing to rely on is a self-created track record. Here is a self-description from a young woman who is articulate and introspective enough to describe how her gifts work.

> *My whole life in an invention. I don't mean that pretentiously. Because of my rural setting, I have had to create my occupation(s) from nothing. No jobs exist for what I do, so I find them or make them for myself. I create consulting jobs by finding problems and then approaching the right people for money to solve them. . . . The process for me is as follows: Instant COMPLETE vision of the executed idea or concept; e.g., I see the completed painting very clearly in my mind before I even look at the paper*

---

2. The process of mentally working with all these variables slows down the response process somewhat, contrary to the high-energy idea machine of the Conciliator who has fast, intuitive answers, which also leap ahead. Conciliators, however, are better at generating HOW to do it and far quicker to take action and get excited about untested ideas. Conceptors seem to focus more on the WHAT to do, with comparatively more caution and analysis.

3. This term was created by Marilyn W. Norris, editor of *Strategy & Leadership* magazine, when I explained what this *brainstyle* could do.

or board. I see myself with the completed new enterprise before I even take the first step. This is like a slide/snapshot that appears in my brain before I even am cognizant of any inner workings that have prompted it.

—Cheryl Williams-Cosner, rancher, mother, entrepreneur, MBA, Washington

WEIRDNESS. What is distinctive about your gifts, Conceptor, is your comfort in living ahead of yourself and most others, not to just anticipate, but to live and play as a maestro of the future. This strength allows you to be a standout, or—for many—isolated from the majority, who build more easily and articulately on what is already known. To make things worse, you are most at home with spontaneous change, willingly take chances with something new, and find it easy to look beyond what is to what could actually work in the future. Your gifts propel you into being the one most at ease with change, and we all know how everyone feels about change, don't we? They talk a good game, but when it gets right down to it, they don't really want to move or spend all that money or make over the old den. When toying with new ideas, you are not what others consider cooperative: You tend to be confrontational, often socially strange, with an automatic bumper-sticker sorting and reductionism. You can see nuggets within a muddle that have huge potential—but only to you. Others are astounded. "How'd you see that?" Your vision is apparent when taking one little piece of another's complexity and making it into a whole new direction.

SELECTIVE LISTENING. Not what they teach in Communications Class. This is what sets your *brainstyle* apart from others': taking an idea to a new and unheard-of place and seeing how it will work in the measurable, competitive world. Thus, getting along socially or demonstrating you are a loving partner can be one of your biggest challenges—*unless* you use timing and show appreciation for your partner's strengths. Double those challenges if you have a lot of energy. Multiply them if you have little personal support from family or someone in business.

> *BrainStyle Clue:* The terrible irony of your *brainstyle*, Conceptor, is that of all the *brainstyles,* you are the most dependent on partnerships to live and achieve in the world.

People are attracted to your ideas. You know, however, that you throw in lots of assertions about what ideas you can deliver before you actually know they can happen. Your sales mode is always on, right? This is where Conceptors get knocked out of the box. All Show, No Go, as my Deliberator dad used to say. Galvanize the vision. Go ahead, make it palpable and inevitable. And then seek out the partners who can make it real. No Conceptor ever got there alone, even Einstein; he just chose a perfect field for his gifts as a theoretical physicist.

> *BrainStyle Clue:* You can use your hardware to be right, or you can use it to propose a future that can be challenged and engaged with by others. You lose in the first case, you learn how to join up with others and win big time in the second case.

Did I mention "moody"? If you get intense about your concepts and take time to move from your inner world to the outer world of performance and relationships, you can act very inconsistently—and so can be described by others as alternately passionate and controlling, then preoccupied and distant. What they are overlooking is your consistency of thought.

> *BrainStyle Clue:* Stick to your principles, NOT your positions. Be gentle.

Your gifts allow the most mobility between a closely held, adamant opinion and openness to other completely contrary conclusions and points of view. You know others cannot do the same. They need time and care for what can be a gut-wrenching shift to make in their thinking.

AVOIDING TROUBLE. You clarify priorities. This is your contribution and your curse. Never assume the same goal with someone dear, else you be rebuffed as merely insensitive and uncaring. You know how it goes: "What do you mean, that isn't important? It's important to ME!" Others get testy if you don't listen and include their ideas, so you must explain that your ability to eliminate information and boil things down is your gift, and add respectfully that you want to use their ideas when you can see how they fit. Apply the *Strengths Contract*[4] where you each contribute to the common goal from your strengths. If necessary handle different turf in parts of the project.

---

4. See Chapter 14.

Many Conceptors work hard on getting along with others—with those I've interviewed, mostly after they've reached their thirties and had their share of rejections. Although these attempts to grease the wheels of the social engine or be an attentive partner are usually transparent and short-lived, especially after some communications seminar, others recognize the attempt. Stop auditioning for Perfect Partner. Go for Loving Partner instead. You just can't compare with the natural gifts of the Conciliator or right-sided Deliberator as an empathizer and romancer over the long pull. You'll naturally become more at ease and easier to deal with by being authentic and naturally loving, in the way you are truly tender and show your caring—especially about the things that you know really matter.

If you have a bit more access to the right brain, you may tend to trust others readily and invest in risky deals. Of all the *brainstyles*, you test highest on taking the biggest chances.[5] Conceptors learn early and well the principles of investing by losing it all or most of it. If you don't partner with a savvy Deliberator or Knower to "keep some powder dry" when you're investing, don't say I didn't warn you. However, it takes a lot of confidence to make the big score, and you have what it takes to see the whole picture. To really expand, you need a team or partner who is trustworthy (now there's a mouthful) in order to take your best shot. Caution: In selecting a partner or a colleague, you can create a sunny forecast of their potential and trust them to join your risk-taking with integrity. You may be assuming they can keep up with and support your *brainstyle* gift, when they can't.

> *BRAINSTYLE CLUE:* When your partner has a plan, expect his/her strengths every step of the way. You must let go of control to do this. You, of all the *brainstyles*, can do so. One Conceptor puts it like this, "People will never do what you want them to do. [Stay in control by] Get[ting] them to do what they were going to do anyway."[6]

Expect different goals, strengths and timing, all the time. Or, as someone put it, if you ride the horse in the direction it's going, you might be able to turn its head. The key is to be clear on your own priorities and your own self-interests and disarm everyone by openly sharing them. Other *brainstyles* won't do this necessarily, especially when they lack the foresight to see the overall benefit that integrity and openness provide—at home or in business. With your *brainstyle* strengths, consistent openness about what you're willing to give and take along with a dedi-

---

5. Comparative testing of *The BrainStyles Inventory*© with 25 standard psychological instruments was reported in *BrainStyles™: Change Your Life Without Changing Who You Are*℠, Appendix C.

6. David Cherry, inventor and developer of the concepts that became *The BrainStyles System*®.

cation to a mutual win can bring long-term personal and professional homeruns in negotiations. Believe it. I've seen it.

> BRAINSTYLE CLUE: The line is crossed from immaturity to maturity, from self-doubt to self-confidence, when you know not only what your gifts are, but also how to apply them with integrity and offer them respectfully in your partnerships.

Don't discount your feelings and your capacity to express caring for others. Billionaire Conceptor real estate developer Trammell Crow built an empire on an extraordinary ability to love and trust a lot of people. Mr. Crow told me that you win a lot more than you lose with this philosophy. In fact he went public during an appearance before a class of Harvard MBAs. When asked what "the key to executive success" was, his jaw-dropper response for the young and the restless success seekers was one word: "Love."

Your strengths demand achievement or the need to see your ideas put into reality. This means learning the discipline of a field of study with its procedures and systems so that you can track and measure your ideas and their impact. At home, you can't just promise and forget the promise, can't just expect everyone else to do the heavy lifting when it comes time to make things happen. Your caring is shown when you join in, not just initiate, and keep your agreements to show up and follow through responsibly. It's been said that keeping your agreements makes your life work. Take this statement seriously.

> BRAINSTYLE CLUE: Conceptors, in order to be effective in any relationship, you MUST explain what you can offer. Others can't read your mind or guess why you offer your thoughts in the way you do. They are baffled. They think differently. Address this openly. Don't isolate yourself by getting defensive, arrogant, or withdrawing.

YOUR TIMING VERSUS OTHERS' TIMING. If you have read about *brainstyle* timing, the start of things is where the most trouble occurs. This is where *brainstyle* kicks in. It is when considering new ideas that each *brainstyle* approaches the subject with its own *brainspeed* and need to consider information in its own unique way. Here you come, bursting in with an outlandish or seemingly preposterous future or a new way of identifying what's missing, what's not being said, what's needed, and why. You challenge. You contradict. Worse, you interrupt the timing of the methodical Deliberators who are fact-gathering, the imaginative Conciliators who are just filling their promotional balloons to get everyone pumped up, and the focused Knowers who are trying to figure out SOME way to quantify and make practical your wild-eyed off-the-wall speculations. This is only the first thing you do that gets others annoyed. To top it off, you BEGIN with conclusions and get to the proof later. Oh, dear.

One of the problems others have with your presentation is how you simplify ideas. *Stereotyping. Over-generalizing. Too simplistic.* Ever hear these labels used with the condescension, even revulsion, of those so good at delineating the shades of gray in a matter? Those who love a good argument over the fine points hate your punchline thinking. Getting to the end so quickly interrupts their analytical assembly process and takes the wind out of their thinking. Explain your gifts and manage your timing to solve the problem.

> *BRAINSTYLE CLUE:* Timing is the problem. Timing is the solution.

CONCEPTOR CHALLENGES. Since the Conceptor *brainstyle* plays in the future most of the time, you are both blessed and cursed. Fear can only be experienced about the future, so worry is a continual problem to manage. Early in the '80s, research done on outstanding achievers showed that they approached difficult situations by first imaging what could go wrong, and then continued by generating several images of potential resolutions. Mental rehearsal can be your main contribution to big decisions. As you know, getting those two or three resolutions can still keep you up nights, anticipating how to deal with their tactics and strategizing how to frame your approach to get to a real solution.

- The Conceptor's blessing is the joy of mental play when noodling an idea or doodling it on scrap paper, cocktail napkins, or whiteboards in unintelligible symbols about the new and untried. Problems can arise when you expect your lover to not only understand the scribbles, but also attend to your thinking out loud as long as you need an audience. Your best choice here is either a Conciliator or Deliberator who knows your subject. If that is not your partner, make new friends! Consider a mini-*Strengths Contract:* As you present your ideas, point out what his/her *brainstyle* contributes to your thinking. Make him/her an important contributor.

- To discuss it again and again seems necessary to look at the same thing from new angles with new depth. Repetitive review of an idea is often a Conceptor need. This is contrary to other *brainstyles*, who wish to move along from idea to idea, topic to topic. This may be an individual Conceptor idiosyncrasy, and if it fits you, it seems most common in new areas. You need the most time—

both internal and airtime—at the beginning. Other *brainstyles* are readily stimulated by the environment—books, seminars, research, synthesizing as they go. Conceptors minimize the quantity of others' ideas and input in order to delve and coalesce ideas with their own internal process.

- Be ready to take time-outs to allow others to put in their two cents. Acknowledge their contribution out loud and own up to the fact that your idea may be unsettling and need more thought and discussion. You are the one to bring up the uncomfortable, the unseen, and make conceptual connections in others' thinking. Conceptor Chris says, "I get in people's faces with uncomfortable reality, and they don't like it." You are dealing with *brainstyle* strengths and non-strengths in processing and sorting whole bundles of information as well as your timing. These are huge issues in interactions.

- Don't be afraid to take time to look and relook; your process is unique each time.

> *BRAINSTYLE CLUE:* Some Conceptors seem to get to the new vision by repeatedly focusing on the same topic with new and deeper insights each time.
>
> **NOTE TO NON-CONCEPTORS:** Yes, this is boring, boring, boring, *not* new, *not* inventive. This is their process, not yours. The value comes later, not always first thing out of the box.

Conceptors are unique in considering and holding contradictory ideas or thoughts. Other *brainstyles* must reconcile, or synthesize, things that don't go together into a single concept or idea in order to understand and act on them. "I can't store an idea until I am clear it fits with all my other ideas," says Conceptor David. This requires a great deal of repetition and re-examination of an idea until it emerges as comprehensive, a whole idea, replicable in the future, encompassing or expanding beyond the sum of the parts. He rails at those who cannot do this, a mistake on his part that leads to much frustration for him. "Other *brainstyles* don't seem to look at the overview to see that one system [of thinking or belief] completely contradicts another, so they can head in one direction on one topic one day, and then head in another on a parallel subject the next, because they're looking at the specifics of each situation instead of the consistency of their concepts."

INVENTION. CREATIVITY. Everyone in the family wants to be respected for his creativity and new ideas. Everyone *is* uniquely creative. To honor them all for their underlying gifts and how those gifts contribute is the point here, not putting anyone in a category. Having said this, different *brainstyles* get to the new and untried differently. The summary below offers some pointers on what to look for and acknowledge. The Conceptor and Conciliator are often best on the front end of a new change or initial idea, the Knower and Deliberator best at refining and making the idea workable.

BrainStyles Clues on Inventing

Conceptors like to work on one major idea to reach a break-through solution, or define the direction for a few projects, depending on their energy level and whom they have available to delegate the implementation to. They work best at the creative level where others add the refinements, assess the realities, and take it to the finish line; however, when learning about some new area, they can be extraordinary builders, caregivers, and imple-menters to see their ideas at work in the world.

Conciliators tend to explore *many* new ideas and goals, love brainstorming, and can find many new ways to initiate projects, invent a business, give a party, or design an outfit, once they see the direction to head toward. This *brainstyle,* however, tends to expand projects rather than focus them by including others and continuing to brainstorm. Called the most creative, a high-energy Conciliator can spin out the far-out. The sky is no limit to the imagination of the highly right-brained, fun, and playful sparkler.

Knowers can sort information and choose to give you new targets and new, more practical applications for your ideas, redirect or create a start-up project or moneymaking idea, and identify the trash to be taken out.[7] Practically inventive, the Knower looks for ways to make things work better, faster, and easier with a payoff. At home, however, Knowers tend to be more traditional and use their energies to save money and streamline the big projects to make the home more safe, practical, easy to maintain, livable, workable, and attractive without being wasteful.

---

7. Part of their gift is sorting and eliminating the extraneous to get to the end efficiently. If they have high energy and a value for hard work, they may even take the trash out too.

> **BRAINSTYLES CLUES ON INVENTING** (continued)
>
> **DELIBERATORS** can show you how, after some study, to take an idea and make it better, cheaper, or faster, more realistic, or doable. They collect and assemble, research in depth to create projects that take the odd, turn it upside down, and *voilá!* a new decor, career, or molecule appears. They love new applications and new theories. They fascinate with a synthesis of many disciplines and much reading/study to create a new approach, or visually and mentally stimulate with the dazzle of their memory and assessments. They like to work on several different things at once to keep the interest up, unless they are investigating. They'll also add why your idea might not work or where the pitfalls lie so that it will be done "right," meaning better and more accurately according to their standards.

When considering a new idea, upcoming negotiation, problem, or behavior of another, Conceptors sort for and focus on the assumptions, the fundamentals, or the basic premises behind what is being said or presented. The gift, based in the right brain, is to see and assemble the patterns within complexities. Conceptor Warning: Test your interpretations to separate them from speculations before sharing them with the skeptics. Your job is to know your gifts well enough to be able to tell the difference between an internal guess and a clear-eyed vision. That is a potential breakthrough. Your discipline in testing your ideas mentally or with a trusted partner will mandate the timing and strategy of your presentation. Be clear. You don't have to be sure.

> *BRAINSTYLE CLUE:* Conceptors need a nonjudgmental, supportive relationship in which to pose and test embryonic ideas. Trial and error is the preferred mode of testing to develop the idea. Picking a *brainstyle* partner who
> a) is patient,
> b) is open to risk, new and changing directions, and
> c) brings some discipline of his/her own will serve them well.

NOTES TO NON-CONCEPTORS.

- Conceptors can reduce the complex and chaotic to punchlines and stereotypes without compunction, which can either drive you to fury, competition, or inspiration. The way the Conceptor reduces information is the gift. Simplicity brought to chaos is actionable, empowering, and clarifying—once you know how to use it.

- Conceptors generate more than one solution and can change the direction of anything totally, switching sides in an argument, looking for and thinking from the Big Picture on the spot, at the beginning, and all the time. Other *brainstyles* arrive at an overview; the Conceptor starts there.

- Conceptors have clear priorities, usually no more than two or three. Data and goals are continually eliminated to maintain clarity. This may come across as arrogance, negativity, or lack of appreciation for a Conciliator's or Deliberator's brilliance,[8] and that's when they're in a good mood.

- Conceptors are most open to change, as in giving up completely on a treasured idea or project that they can see will not work and coming up with an entirely new direction, location, diet, or philosophical position. Go to them when you're stuck.

- What a great partner for a family project or enterprise!

- Immature Conceptors can get into thrill-seeking change for change's sake, overcommit, and drive everyone around them into overload and distrust. You will do them a service by confronting them directly about what can really be accomplished. After all, setting priorities is something they do well and can be reminded to return to.

- Conceptors are most at home with chaos and ambiguity in work and tasks, not nearly as comfortable with personal ambiguity where they have to figure out the day-to-day details (as in losing a job or ending a career). They need material to work on. You can supply ideas and support. However, this *brainstyle* is most equipped to simplify, invent, and try out new and exciting ideas to redirect their lives. To sort out the new and untried is Conceptor play; to be locked into routine is a sentence worse than death by peat bog. When patience comes with age, a Conceptor has a longer attention span to include and care for others more of the time, if they have paid attention to building character as well as ideas.

---

8. Both of these *brainstyles expand* ideas and options. This section can help you see why your spontaneous, critical, researched, or detailed ideas need to come later; otherwise you interrupt what the Conceptor does best.

- To invent something new, precedent and proven facts must be put aside. Facts are merely working hypotheses waiting to be disproven, is the song Conceptors sing. To challenge their conclusions, wait until after the initial melody is established in their thinking-out-loud/proposing/speculating song. They, of all the *brainstyles*, are most willing to listen and change their minds, given new and reliable information.

> *BrainStyle Clue* for Non-Conceptors: Generalizations prove the rule for Conceptors. Exceptions are irrelevant. This is VERY important to understand about their *brainstyle*.

- There will always be exceptions, the Conceptor says, but they are merely the beginnings of new universal principles to be discovered. It is in the mega- and the meta-views that Conceptors see the Truth, unproven yet encompassing; it is in the mini-view and the specifics that other *brainstyles* look for the unerring and accurate view that can be tracked and proven.[9]

- Seeing their ideas in reality becomes more important to Conceptors than nice prizes or acknowledgements. Having more influence over more things is also top of the list (bigger projects, job, more money to make things happen). However, never discount the word of praise or attention to their ideas that you offer. They care deeply. Achievement is first on the list; however, a well-timed acknowledgment is evidence that their gifts make a difference to you.

- Conceptors by definition are spiritual or philosophical beings, seeking universals, looking beyond, and most often surrendering to the unknown with a leap into faith or the metaphysics of the physical world. This wonder and curiosity is a tremendous gift for others, for as Conceptors challenge the universals and question assumptions that are overlooked, we all have an opportunity to clarify who we are and why we are here.

> *BrainStyle Clue* for Non-Conceptors: One of the ways to value a Conceptor's gifts at home is to seek him/her out at the start of a big decision/project/event, before you get locked onto your answer.

---

9. This is where most harsh words are heard in my house, at the beginning of things. If I interrupt the initial thinking of my Conceptor husband with my "Yes, but," or "What about this?" he can get quite ballistic in reacting to ideas that distract him from forming the new overview. Exceptions do not expand his thinking; he is building by connecting patterns—not synthesizing differences. Timing is the answer every time.

- The Conceptor's gift is *foresight,* which is a leap into the future to know what's coming without knowing how or where the certainty comes from. Foresight is the ability to look out ahead. Foresight is different from anticipation, which is the gift other *brainstyles* use to leap ahead, based on a hunch, an insight, or a trend. Foresight, in the Conceptor's case, is a combination of analysis, a very personal cause-effect logic, known facts and random insights, and gleanings from a variety of sources. People with foresight have long timelines built in for projects. That is, they can go a long time without others giving them feedback or approval. They often act as "closed-loop" systems. For example, when thinking through a new idea, they can think about it alone—mentally or verbally testing it over and over without any smart ideas from you, thank you. Others need to discuss and noodle over their ideas for input or confirmation to have some measure of how to rearrange their own thinking. Whether this is a way they have learned to cope or because the *brainstyle* innately cannot handle the amount of input and variety of information that the other whole-brained *brainstyle,* the Deliberator, can is not as important as their timing needs. However, one scientist who was testing creative scientists back in the '80s offered that the most creative of them literally shut down parts of their brains when at their most inventive.[10] This seems to describe the Conceptor's process.

I think concepts, never facts or details. Though I love poring through chaotic facts to find hidden patterns. . . . [O]nce I see the pattern I toss out the facts and try not to allow them to cloud the concepts anymore. My replacement in Dallas is a great Deliberator. He once said to me that his goal . . . was to know every number [for the department]. I know no numbers. Instead I know how we are doing and what needs to be done to do even better.
—Roger Parker, Director, Allstate Insurance, Chicago, Illinois

---

BRAINSTYLE CLUE: Anticipation is a linear peek into the future or a leap to a conclusion based on a current event.
FORESIGHT, for a Conceptor at his best, is a mental mastery of the future, confronting the worst case, the best case, and developing the answering strategies. Random associations, mental leaps, and implausible analyses require immersion in the problem while eliminating options, or as one put it, "thinking in multi-dimensional modalities," to play ahead of events and create something new for the future.

---

10. Dr. Terry Brandt, director of the Center for Staff Development in Houston, reported his research with neuroscientists in measuring and tracking brain processing of the inventive process. His anecdotes included an engineer who immersed himself so deeply in a problem that he literally visualized a holographic solution while watching TV one afternoon.

Note that it is NOT dressing or acting differently or addressing unusual topics that make Conceptors "different." It is how things are first put together differently to get someplace new and different before analysis or proof or being pleasant.

MAKING IT PERSONAL. *Driven. Different. Strange. Difficult. Seers. Blue-sky thinkers. Vague. Weird. Outrageous. Dreamer. Head in the clouds.*

You may be familiar with labels like these. One Conceptor executive was nicknamed "El Beyondo" by his employees for the way he talked and thought. They said it with great affection, however, for although they couldn't understand him, they led the country in sales. Each person who worked for him knew that he cared personally for them. He had, because of that caring, applied his natural strengths by looking for *their* gifts to take them new places. Those places were out in front of all the other regional offices. Those places were also life-altering for those involved.

If you are a Conceptor, you may have had to put up with people all your life who have attempted to change you, tried to get you to file things, asked you to prove what you're saying, to stop being so moody or intense or distant, to fit in better and, well, to change who you are naturally. You may have adopted any number of social behaviors so you can walk among us, yet talk and think your own thoughts. At the same time, you join in, have some friends, and not feel so different. Why have you worked so hard? Because neither you nor others understand your strengths and how to take advantage of them.

And what about your own self-criticism and defensiveness? How much time do you spend feeling sorry for yourself, different, or alone? Do you then belittle the petty thinkers, the morons with whom you have to deal? How often do you get impatient with the slow and methodical ones or the people-pleasers with their fuzzy thinking and emotional hi-jinks? Do you see that speaking softly and simply so that the slow ones can understand you only gets you told that you are too arrogant to work with? Too weird to date? Would you be willing to give up hiding the way you think and the puzzled looks you get when you think out loud?

Most[11] of the population thinks either in a linear fashion (the Deliberators who write and teach and set the standards with a clear sequence or process) or randomly, emotionally, and illogically (the Conciliators). You can do either to some extent, but not nearly as well as they can. If you don't know how to define, value, and explain your strengths, your chances of selling your ideas or making a partnership work will be a never-ending struggle, as many Conceptors bemoan.

---

11. Nearly 80 percent of the *BrainStyles*® database is made up of Deliberator and Conciliator *brainstyles.*

To apply your ability to see and strategize with integrity is a moment-by-moment choice that will show up in every conversation, interaction, relationship, and negotiation that you move from win-lose to win-win. A caring, respectful approach for others will come naturally with a thorough regard for why you're different and why your gifts are neither better nor worse than any other *brainstyle's*. Combine your own regard with a consistent set of ethics and you have a solid basis for your reputation as a partner, parent, son or daughter, sibling, and friend, not to mention as a leader. The magnificent hardware you were born with can expand and make the world a better place.

YOUR BASIC STRENGTHS AS A CONCEPTOR derive from the fact that you first access both sides of the brain in a rapid, random way to quickly combine analysis with images or intuition to relook and reconfigure what is in front of you. Because there is no delay in this kind of sorting and creating, you are the one most apt to see a bloom among the daily weeds of conversation. You may be the one to stop the chitchat to bring that bloom into the foreground of everyone's attention, and propose a whole new direction—at length—for some simple idea that your loving mate expected to discuss for five minutes. *Oh, no! Hold the phone,* we're hiring a horticulturist and starting a new business!

When you grab on to something that everyone else has taken for granted or overlooked, you're more than persistent; you're powerful, and, some might say, obnoxious.[12]

~~~~~~~~~~~~~~~~

Making the simple complicated is commonplace;
making the complicated simple, awesomely simple, that's creativity.
—Charles Mingus, jazz musician

~~~~~~~~~~~~~~~~

---

12. I can say that because I married a Conceptor and I mean "obnoxious" in a good way.

THE CONCEPTOR: A SUMMARY OF STRENGTHS[13]

TIME ZERO ➔	SOON AFTER ➔	WITH PRACTICE ➔	EXPERT ➔
• Sees patterns and assumptions. • Analyzes and eliminates info. • Gets and gives the overview. • Associates the idea randomly.	• States possibilities. • Generalizes for the long term. • Restates with a new approach. • Poses an unusual argument.	• Decides quickly. • Gives the global view. • Outlines a complete or new strategy. • Reinvents 2–3 goals and/or the approaches. • Explains in more detail. • Changes entire plan.	• Contributes as a visionary. • Articulates details. • Invents, creates, makes breakthroughs.

- The Conceptor takes in selected information at *Time Zero* with both the left and right brain. She is best at picking out the patterns, themes, or underlying concepts in what is said.

- Conceptors use rapid, random associations and are best at generating new possibilities in practical areas.

- All Conceptors may do both of these things but have more access to one side of the brain than another. *Right-Sided* Conceptors are more visual and less articulate; *Left-Sided* Conceptors read more and collect more information to inspire their new ideas.

- The **Right-Sided** Conceptor's main strength is inventing the new and untried—leaping to mental images or "thought balls" that redefine reality or a future possibility, regardless of what has gone before. In working with others, this flavor of Conceptor can be openly emotional, expressive, and inclusive. As a leader and lover he can be fiercely passionate.

- The **Left-Sided** Conceptor's gift of invention is more thoughtful, draws on more research, seeks what is not visible, unstated, and then jumps to a whole new solution or three that may also outline several plans on how to get there. This brand of Conceptor is more unemotional, more apt to be articulate, a tough negotiator and strategist, and pushes for bigger and bigger ends. As a leader and lover he can be dispassionate with deeply held feelings that aren't as openly expressed.

- The higher-energy Conceptor expresses her ideas with intensity and passion that initially sound final. Later (from minutes to days) she is able to reconsider and redirect the entire original concept, incorporating others' ideas and input.

---

13. All Charts ©1997, 2003 *BrainStyles*, Inc. No reproduction without permission. *www.brainstyles.com*

- Conceptors thrive on change and chaotic situations where they can sort out the principles and establish new directions.
- Many Conceptors describe thinking "multi-dimensionally," with 3D images, words, and symbols.
- Routine and repetition (except their own) drives them wild.
  CONCEPTORS SEEK OPPORTUNITIES TO:
- Start things with a vision of the future.
- Lead and love, nurturing and developing the best in others.
- Solve problems in new ways by combining contradictory information, and so often break the rules only to make up a new game.
- Achieve, be the best at something.
- Take risks by going beyond what is given or known.
- See and tell it as it never was before, to startle others with the new and attention-getting.

A CHALLENGE CHECKLIST TO PREVENT DEPRESSION AND MAXIMIZE YOUR SATISFACTION: APPLY STRENGTHS; MANAGE YOUR NON-STRENGTHS.

If you haven't done so, you might consider establishing a support system for your gifts that simultaneously builds your partnership.

1. As an inventor who combines contradictions, your excitement about new ideas is more than stimulating and inspiring for others: it's downright sexy for others to contribute to. As you generate and create new ideas, your attention to others' input can be a real spotlight for them. If, however, when the other is just trying to be smart or right to gain a piece of the idea, consider whether they are just excited or simply competing. Set limits kindly. Acknowledge their gifts. It works better in the long run.

2. Keep clarifying priorities. It is one of the greatest gifts you offer. Offer your clarity rather than imposing your goals. Allow for the timing of your partner to engage with and share in the process.

3. You are probably used to your unique ability to live and work in unstructured, chaotic situations. Your love for real change and stimulating situations is what attracts those who love you and repels those who don't. To support your abilities, you may consider creating a "playroom" (or an office, a corner) where you can have your mess with a whiteboard or computer for mental play. More portable is a journal that allows for drawings and words, or a handheld

electronic device. The important thing is that you have a place to germinate ideas, leave them, and return to them with your special timing.

4. Share with your partner what you think about achieving as a way to create the best vs. achieving to be the best. Plan together to support one another in personal needs for achievement.

5. Get beyond the ego-based need for your idea or your way to win. You can then inspire others to go beyond their own view of their capabilities. You are capable of helping others succeed by using your gifts of foresight and invention on their behalf. You can and will touch and change lives with your loving use of the hardware you have.

6. Since you need a challenging career or engaging hobby, you may create drama, fights, or problems if not enough of those exist around you. Watch out for this and seek out, or allow your partner to bring, new adventures, people, books, ideas, and problems for you to solve. When you are bored or under-stimulated, take charge rather than taking it out on someone else.

7. You're quick to interpret the meaning of things or events into general principles or axioms for the future that you test as you go. This creates problems for Deliberators and Knowers, who base their interpretations on analysis of facts. They bring you balance and are a blessing, not a curse. Remember what they have to offer to remain peaceful.

8. You're best when you are not doing anything for periods of time, just being still and thinking. Taking action, getting involved, or keeping busy are harder for you than planning, studying, or engaging in lengthy discussions of ideas. Tell your partner that this is what you are up to and make it easier for him or her to understand and plan around. Being sensitive to others' timing needs allows them to do their own thing rather than resent your "moods."

9. You have the ability to confront an issue or a problem with a balanced, win-win approach. Your strength is an ability to analyze the issues while factoring in the personal. You can maintain enough personal distance to detach from taking things personally while being aware of another's feelings as you seek the best resolution. Remember: other *brainstyles* require preparation and review for big decisions.

10. Develop and nurture your own inner spiritual or philosophical understanding of life as a buffer to the slings, arrows, and misfortunes of life.

A SUMMARY OF THE CONCEPTOR'S NON-STRENGTHS, WHICH TAKE LONGER AND REQUIRE MORE EFFORT.

- You do not naturally follow through on plans and implementation. Your integrity and credibility are at stake because of this. Clarify what is a Big Idea vs. something you are actually going to do. Make a lifelong decision to keep your promises.

- You do not communicate so that others can follow your thinking at your pace. It takes repetition and time for an idea to become tangible enough for you and others to understand how it will work the way you visualize it. Remember, communicating in sequence is your non-strength, not stupidity on the other's part.

- You do not assess information in a neutral way or in detail. You're best at being subjective, biased, and global. Your truth needs to be qualified by other *brainstyle* partners.

- You do not organize things into a linear or rational sequence that can be measured or repeated easily (you use your own internal organization, which is not a straight line). You are exciting first, understandable over time.

- You do not stay even or methodical for great lengths of time. If you persevere, it will be for a vision, but the path will not be a straight one to the end. Routine or repetition, needed for follow-through, is a tough discipline for you. Ask for help.

- You do not balance your lifestyle or activities easily: It's extremes for you often, wholly committed or sick of it all.

- Relationships with those who think very differently can be very difficult for you, so socializing just for the sake of it is a challenge, and verbal swordplay with a Deliberator at a party can get tense. Lighten up. Be careful about your "jokes": Are you being kind and playful? Your sarcasm can be devastating.

- You do not take action quickly. You'd rather think about it than do it. You need a partner here to start the action. You may also impose on others' time, workload, and be too demanding of others to carry out the ideas you generate. Make time.

- You do not play politics well, which can make or break your relationship with the larger family and in-laws. If your energy is high and you get impatient with slower, more fastidious folks, you can jeopardize relationships. If your energy is low, you may tend to resist others' attempts to involve you, and so put them off.

CONCEPTORS NEED OTHER *BRAINSTYLES.* You know this already. Do it.

CONCEPTORS NEED THE KNOWER IN ORDER TO:

- discuss the future downside of risks; test out and verbalize the logic of a new idea.
- confront others with clarity, but without the passion.
- focus communications to clear, concise goals.
- move to action or streamline the action after the overview is presented.

CONCEPTORS NEED THE CONCILIATOR IN ORDER TO:

- feel supported and cared for, while getting help in relationships.
- enjoy and get support for the intuitive and imaginative ideas.
- know who to include and how to approach them personally.
- get enthusiastic about their plans and ideas.
- keep the partnership as a priority; manage the social life.

CONCEPTORS NEED THE DELIBERATOR IN ORDER TO:

- fill in the specifics; make the ideas reality.
- deal with people more objectively and assess what they have to offer.
- balance ideas by making them realistic, with a timeframe, and without what has already been tried.
- organize a plan that has clear limits and steps to the end.
- translate their ideas to others, step by step.
- handle the politics of neighbors and family with diplomacy.

TO LEVERAGE YOUR STRENGTHS:

1. Use timing to take advantage of and appreciate the strengths of others. You'll build your own character as you develop patience and a loving support team at the same time. You know you need a team to make it happen. Your biggest trap is to get so wound up in your own brilliance that you alienate the very people who truly support you.

2. Laugh. Lighten up. It'll help the skeptics and critics deal with you more easily.

3. Practice some discipline or sport to help you achieve an inner focus and balance. Try meditation, exercise, music, or art to give yourself time to reflect and stay calm. Go out in nature.

4. Use a tracking system of some kind for ideas and projects. Edison kept a notebook with both drawings and notes. Consider a white-board for your home, where you can draw and doodle and outline and think in pictures.

5. Expand your intuition by tracking your results until you can predict more accurately.

6. Admit you're wrong if you're wrong. Because you are a natural delegator and need others to make things happen, appreciate your limitations out loud so that others can do the same, feel included, get over their discomfort, and give up the sniping critiques.

7. As a partner or parent, get the family to tell you the answers so you can show them how smart they are. Ask them to use their strengths to solve their problems.

8. Want control? Get others to tell you their plan and commit to it, with no excuses. It won't work if it was your idea in the first place. It takes the time and patience to coach them into managing their own full-fledged plan, when they work in ways so different from yours. Key: Forgiving the others' mistakes and uncertainties. Support their risk-taking and set them free.

9. Stuck? Ask for input from strengths different from your own.

10. Partner with a Conciliator to get crazy, invent wild new things, and know whom to contact; a Knower to make future plans practical, efficient, and realistic; and a Deliberator to look for problems, assess the idea and the people, bring in the resources, check the plan, and carry through on the projects.

11. You tend to take more and bigger risks more often than others, especially in business or major areas of your partnership. Big decisions require lots of preparation for other *brainstyles*, which in turn can limit your risks.

BRAINSTYLE CLUES ON RISK-TAKING

KNOWERS: The least likely to put all their (own) money on the line, Knowers look at all the downsides and all the risks first and then take action. When they know enough to be confident that they can maintain control, they'll go forward, within logical limits.

CONCILIATORS: Most likely to plunge based on a trusted referral or personal hunch. Once stung, most will not go there again. They'll go plunge somewhere else, though.

CONCEPTORS: The most likely to put everything on the line after considering more of the potential than the downside. Most are confident that they will handle whatever comes up, given the risks.

DELIBERATORS: Most likely to take personal risks (skydiving, skiing); less likely to take other risks where they cannot control the process or outcomes.

DISTINCTIONS BETWEEN CONCEPTORS AND OTHER *BrainStyles*.

- **CONCEPTORS ARE DISTINCT FROM CONCILIATORS** in that they create practical, applicable ideas, where Conciliators create imaginative possibilities and alternative ways to reach the future.

- **CONCEPTORS ARE DIFFERENT FROM KNOWERS** in getting to the future because of the blend of right-brain input they use, which is irrational, intuitive, broad, and undefined; and are more inclusive than Knowers of people, unrelated abstractions, or squirrelly ideas.

- **CONCEPTORS ARE DISTINCT FROM DELIBERATORS** in that they invent in the future, where Deliberators ensure consistency and improvement of the past, draw from analysis, and install systems and processes that a Conceptor cannot create nor implement. Deliberators are more sensitive to the environment, i.e., attend to how to say things, do the right thing, and be more diplomatic than a Conceptor. Right-sided Deliberators can also be quite visionary, abstract, and live in the future. Their ideas contribute a process or path to get to the end. They also build wonderful, abstract descriptive models to follow. Conceptors may build a model, but it is a hypothesis to be changed. Conceptors give more attention to the workability of the final idea, the right-sided Deliberators to the process of getting to the idea, the elegance of it, and the inclusiveness of other, parallel, or related thoughts or references.

An Illustrative and hopefully entertaining, stereotypical **example:** The four *brainstyles* are each considering buying a home.

- A Conceptor might think about how it can be changed, improved, opened up, and made simpler.

- A Conciliator might first ask, do I feel at home here? Do I like the neighbors? Is it pretty? Is this a proper neighborhood?

- A Knower will likely first consider cost and whether she can get it cheaper.

- A Deliberator, especially a left-sided Deliberator, will want the comparative market values and want to assess the value against the price. The neighborhood's prestige is a factor. Next might come a thorough look through the home for everything that might not be working or has a potential for breaking, along with the design and accessibility, and many other things that either meet or do not meet a well-prepared list of criteria. She will then negotiate price down to the dollar.

- A right-sided Deliberator might consider more of the intangibles involved before settling on the asking price (avoiding that uncomfortable bargaining):

the "feng-shui" of the home, the feeling within, the locale, the view, the comfort, neighbors, cultural activities in the area, schools, the previous owners, and the price, of course. But they'll go along with whatever you pick.

THE CONCEPTOR AS LOVER

MARRIAGE AND SOCIAL LIFE WITH A CONCEPTOR. Being social is not the strong suit for this *brainstyle*. "I can feel misunderstood, fragmented, and perplexed by others who can't understand me for what I am. Often when I choose to engage in social or civic groups, particularly with my own sex (female), I find myself losing interest and drifting away, because it feels artificial to me," says Cheryl, an introverted Conceptor who lives in a rural area with her Deliberator husband and three children. She hates making social arrangements and has gotten frustrated to the point of anger (i.e., acting from her discomfort with her non-strengths) that her husband hasn't made the calls. His reluctance stems from the fact that "he wasn't raised to be the one who calls for dates and parties." Getting used to the idea, he says, means getting comfortable with a non-traditional marriage where his wife often takes the lead and provides the direction, one where "lots of things we do fly in the face of social norms."

The Brave New World of the Conceptor can be quite challenging for other *brainstyles*.

> *BRAINSTYLE CLUE:* Making connections and meeting people just don't ring the chimes of most Conceptors; connecting ideas or finding something to ponder does. If you are a Conceptor, be aware of getting defensive or being offensive in social areas where your non-strengths are required. Challenge yourself at the next event to look for the *brainstyle* of the person you are talking with. Then think of a way to bring out her gifts. It's endless fun.

Robert, Cheryl's husband, says living with this lady Conceptor is "never dull," with all the understatement so typical of the wry and unemotional Deliberator. Being married to an unconventional thinker means fewer rules, more change. She is the "font of ideas"; he, the "devil's advocate." They not only live together on an isolated ranch that is the source of their financial support, but they work together to run it. "Having a Conceptor wife is like having a whole team of people to think up ideas. Her knack for seeing the end is really helpful. Getting there can be really interesting," he says, as I mentally substitute the words *darn near impossible,* given the way he says it.

> BRAINSTYLE CLUE: Although the Deliberator also meanders around the entire brain to think of new ideas, the Conceptor accesses fewer areas more quickly and randomly to be much less steady, more moody, more cyclical, and usually a person of extremes, regardless whether they are introverted or extroverted.

What initially attracted him is her way of thinking creatively; what he married her for and stays married for are her similar values of hard work, family, learning, and opening to new ideas. New ideas mean "a more positive way to live" for him: "I don't sit around with the other ranchers and complain about all the negatives," he says. He can't. He's too busy moving toward the future with her.

> BRAINSTYLE CLUE: Conceptors, now is the time to recognize and acknowledge the sacredness of another's willing support and ability to follow you. This gift conveys authority to you, which cannot exist otherwise. A loving partner creates a safe place for you to do what you do best: Invent. It is the basis for a *holy relationship* that extends beyond individual egos to expand the reach of both of you.

Although he is "more satisfied with the status quo" than she (naturally), he too has become a more conscious "lifelong learner" because of her, something he really appreciates. More than this, he deeply respects his wife for her abilities.

There have been some tough times, which he attributes to her view over the horizon and her drive to always have something new, better, or different in the way they live.[14] They found a way to stick it out in those times through a common faith (he joined her church) and some counseling to focus on what really mattered to "put first things first." He is aware that he brings stability, a "quieting," a closer look at things in their partnership. He keeps her tethered to the earth, to bring their differences to bear in offering a lot of love from very different points of view to their children, which is, I might add, a wonderful way to create a loving, mature family that can consider and appreciate different people and views.

---

14. Overall, Deliberators look for better, more enriched, more effective ways to live.

> *BRAINSTYLE CLUE:* Partnership begins with a synergy of strengths. It requires giving up myths, hopes for change, and a desire for the Ideal partner.

In another such pairing, the Deliberator husband is the sounding board who asks questions that help challenge and focus the Conceptor wife's new idea *du jour,* her musings on "Why am I here?" to gently move her to the next meal, set of bills, or routine thing that they must address. The Conceptor-Deliberator marriage is a terrific partnership of opposites where most of the bases can be covered; it is also one with a continual demand for one lover to adapt to the timing and topics of the other. As Bob, Cheryl's husband, said, "Things are never dull around her."

> *BRAINSTYLE CLUES* on Partnering:[15] Partner with a Conciliator for support of new ideas and yourself. You need someone in your corner who is accepting.
>
> Partner with a Deliberator for balance and execution at work and at home. This works best when you have similar energy levels and values.
>
> Partner with a Knower to get things done at work, and at home if you don't care so much about personal warmth and nurturing.

A CONCEPTOR AT WORK AND HOME. ONE *BRAINSTYLE*, ALL THE TIME. "Things that scare people in business, scare people in a partnership," Chris says from the vantage point of his 31 years, the overview his *brainstyle* creates, a lost company, and a lost marriage.

A highly extroverted Conceptor entrepreneur while still a teen, Chris spared his parents no amount of embarrassing situations. Funny now, his parents can laugh at the poker games Chris ran behind the scenes at Boy Scout camp, the wild games he'd invent to get all the neighborhood kids to play. School was way too structured for this particularly energetic, dyslexic[16] young Conceptor. He left a couple of schools to get in and out of trouble. He then started his own computing business at 19, which was substantial enough to attract the interest, and a personal telephone call, from Bill Gates.

Building his company took most of him. He dated one Deliberator girlfriend throughout his twenties. In nine years, he "had so much time invested," that even though they really hadn't achieved a successful partnership, they married anyway. They hoped they could work it out.

---

15. Given by a Conceptor.
16. If interested in more about dyslexia and the Conceptor's gifts, go to *www.brainstyles.com* for an article on the topic.

> *BRAINSTYLE CLUE:* Conceptors need long-term relationships to provide stability for their unwieldy hardware and a safe place to land. Their emotional sensitivities can be keen, and often overlooked in favor of their "differentness." In fact, Conceptors can be quite vulnerable in any relationship and very dependent on the other in the partnership to supply what they cannot (their non-strengths).

In this Conceptor's view, the marriage with that Deliberator was never meant to be. "Everything I do has an elevated level of risk, which terrified her. She was screamingly frightened when we went sailing. I think so fast and make decisions so easily; she took so long." His voice trails into the next thought. "If you don't enjoy the same risks, you run out of common things to do; those things become wearing by the sixth to tenth year. You can make things appear OK, but by then you'll have an affair with someone else or your job—same thing." The romance and the pretense at romance were over just about the same time that his company partnership ended. The Deliberator finance officer was finally just too scared by the risky, loose style of Chris, the Conceptor president (the Mardi Gras office with couch and bar), nor could he understand how the Conceptor's $100,000 entertainment expense for the year brought in $35 million in business. He overlooked how much the employees loved him for "treating them as partners" and maneuvered the investors to take control, ousting Chris.

It takes people time to see the possibilities a Conceptor can open for them. Those who remain in his former company, who couldn't identify the invisible concepts that just magically made things happen when he was there, tell him, "We didn't understand what you did business-wise, and [now] we're sorry." The Deliberator executive who won the company has called to apologize and admit his error. His ex-wife didn't understand the benefits his gifts might bring her either; nor perhaps did the younger Chris understand how to offer them to her in a way and at a pace she could handle.

Chris is thoroughly and happily remarried to another Deliberator—though higher energy—business executive who keeps up with his pace and shares his business. With all the astuteness of her *brainstyle*, Julie told Chris she was going to marry him on their very first date. She also told him she had described his curly hair, energy, intellect, and personal depth as her future mate to friends years before. It got his attention.

Julie adds a steadiness and grounding to her mercurial husband that is a wonderful synergy. Her deep faith, yet openness to the expression of that faith, meant a search by the couple for a new church. This brought Chris back to childhood values that were priceless—and lost in the rock and roll of starting and running a high-tech computer software firm in the booming '90s. They go to church twice a week now, once to teach and support teens in how to choose a positive environment, once to attend church and take Chris' new instant family of two girls, two and four years old, to their favorite Sunday school. They not only share their faith, they each apply it in their lives. "[Church] gives you an environment that brings you back together in a non-threatening context. You have tools to resolve things," he says.

As they move beyond the first-year honeymoon, they are learning how to partner. Chris reports that even though she acknowledges his description of her as a "high-end" follower and supporter, when it's decision time, she competes for leadership. Soon Julie will likely join with Chris' former employees in saying, "The one thing we love about Chris is that he can get people to perform way beyond what they thought they could do."

~~~~~~~~~~~~~~~~

"WHAT IF BIFF" was his nickname as the Conceptor kid in a family of four children. He was always making stuff up, according to his sister, writing poems, composing songs with lyrics, inventing standup comic routines that were so funny, he was constantly compared to Steve Martin, the brilliant comic actor and playwright. He designed elaborate naval vessels, just for fun, at age eight. His mom thought he was going to be a naval architect. It could have happened.

Very shy and introverted, with only one friend at a time, if that friend couldn't play, Erik had no problem entertaining himself with drawing, model building, or music. Erik, a.k.a. Biff, loved to play chess for the strategy of "thinking three moves ahead," his sister says. Harriet, his mother, says she saw from the time he was a boy the gifts he brought to any project or relationship. "He would take on just a few big things, and those he would pursue with tenacity." It is worth noting the loving environment Erik/Biff grew up within: Conceptors develop self-esteem early in a safe place to incubate their ideas. He not only had one, he had a mom who openly acknowledged his gifts.[17]

But Biff didn't have a real direction, just lots of talent, it seemed; so in college, he spent most of his time hanging out, playing and composing songs for the guitar. The Conceptor brother was not serious about much except golf and sailing, nor did the family take him seriously. College was easy, but then he didn't really try. After college, a short marriage to a Deliberator came to a halt quickly, followed by

---

17. This is not at all the case to develop gifts, insists Conceptor David. His home life was particularly unsupportive, which he insists just provided further opportunity to define and apply his abilities earlier.

the sudden and tragic loss of a brother. Overwhelmed with loss, Erik left a promising new job at IBM to return to the serenity of the guitar and home.

BrainStyle Clue: Conceptor sensitivities are keen, although like their whole-brained cousins the Deliberators, they don't always show just how much they feel or express their emotions directly. It will take awhile to learn their code; then you can read their moods clearly.

Then came the day when he met Beth, a waitress at the place where he was to perform some of his songs. Suddenly, sis says, a whole new person emerged. Motivated. Job-oriented. Had to make "at least $60K a year," he announced—and this was in 1981 when that was another social class and a galaxy far, far away. Daydreaming for play was over. Daydreaming for pay began. The focused, goal-oriented visualizer was front and center.

Today, as a Conceptor dad and husband, he is immensely caring, committed, and emotional, according to extrovert and Conciliator wife Beth after nineteen years of marriage. He also "likes to be needed." She is unabashedly candid about their different roles in raising their two children:

"He keeps me on track, opens my world, and lets me be. He's very disciplined; I'm not. I'm late all the time. He sees the best in people; I see through people. I tell him to get real; he hates to be fallible. He's very nurturing; I'm more headstrong and selfish. He'll drive all night to come home because he knows I don't want to be alone at night. He caters to me always, even to the point of leaving his [birth] family behind for the first years of our marriage. I am the wanderer; he's the home-body. We're both bad at details, so nobody gets it done [like insurance payments]. So . . . oh well."

She describes his sense of humor as "dumb"; that is, he laughs at simple, silly things.[18] But what he brings to the family is an overall acceptance. "He loves me for who I am, and because of this, I accept myself. . . . The kids really feel safe with him. I bark at them all the time, and they don't take me seriously; he follows through on what he says, but they pay serious attention to him."

And the basis for their marriage? "We agree on family goals, the way we raise the kids with discipline and limits," Beth reported, and one can't help observing that she keeps him "motivated" by setting a standard for their lifestyle, which is beautifully decorated, expensive, and socially active.

---

18. Conceptors are noted for their silly or offbeat sense of humor. Introverts of all *brainstyles* can also laugh at odd things, but Conceptors seem to have this characteristic consistently.

Her husband has been rapidly promoted over the years, and with a recent corporate acquisition, moved from a vice presidency at IBM to a new position as a chief operating officer. His mother asked him about his recent promotion, "What will you be doing?" He said, "I've got to get 6,500 people all looking and walking in the same new direction."

No problem. Even though they live in Atlanta, and he manages business from New York City, his ability to manage a large and complex business is relatively easy. Erik simplifies complexities to take what seems like simple information and turn it into Big Ideas, Big Risks, and Big Payoffs.

What If Biff still dreams and invents, making simple premises into management principles he lives by at home and at work. He is disciplined. Focused on a few priorities. He nurtures others. Attends to their needs. Keeps his eye on the long term, discards the irrelevancies. Loves his family.

This is a Conceptor using his gifts to serve. This is a sketch of a man at mastery.

And he's got his whole life and career ahead of him.

So do you.

CHAPTER 7

THE DELIBERATOR BRAINSTYLE

~~~~~~~~~~~~~~~

Duty, Honor, Country. Those three hallowed words reverently dictate what you ought to be, what you can be, what you will be. They are your rallying points: to build courage when courage seems to fail; to regain faith when there seems to be little cause for faith; to create hope when hope becomes forlorn.
—Deliberator leader from World War II, General Douglas MacArthur, who led U.S. troops to victory in the Pacific theatre, in his final speech at West Point in 1961. His commitment, persistence, and innovative strategy triumphed in the most complex of battlefields. His unwavering values inspired men to give their lives for their country in some of the bloodiest, fiercest battles in American history.

~~~~~~~~~~~~~~~

Oh, the difficulty in trying to discuss your gifts in only one chapter, you multi-talented person, you. If you had several tied scores on *The BrainStyle Inventory©*, your gifts are the cause. Look to the extraordinary leader, General MacArthur, to exhibit the gifts within you: an ability to form deep moral convictions, master complexity, draw from a personal discipline, and strategize to outmaneuver a daunting enemy, while inspiring by example.

The diagram above is an attempt to portray what is going on for your *brainstyle* in a new situation. The smaller, bolder arrows denote left and right brain processing; the larger arrows connote a whole-brained search through memory when presented with new information. The gifts of such a versatile *brainstyle* make it difficult to consider how all your abilities can be stuffed into just one category or how anyone could say you have just one central, brain-based strength. But stay with me; you may like the results.

~~~~~~~~~~~~~~~

There's Deliberators in general, and then there's ME.
I don't fit in a category. I'm just me: you know, unique.
—Two Deliberators grappling with the idea of a single *BrainStyle* strength

~~~~~~~~~~~~~~~

Many with your gifts have gotten insulted by the name for this *brainstyle*: "Sounds boring," and "Who wants to be a Deliberator? It sounds so slow." "The *arrows* are smaller than for the other *brainstyles*!" Guess what? These are all expressions of the very gifts that allow you to bring and set such high standards, to keep the ship on course, to steady down and lead with such certainty; and they can be turned against you in a heartbeat when you get into the comparison game. This chapter is to help you quit doing just that and move into the arena you were meant for: grand and small projects that make this planet a better, safer, kinder, gentler place to be.

> *BRAINSTYLE CLUE:* The *BrainStyles* database predicts that Deliberators are nearly 44% of the population, with approximately 60% male, 40% female.

Who you are at heart is shown by your willingness to take on a challenge while very often disregarding the personal cost. When you are at your best, you are the explorer, the crusader, the soldier who gives his life to serve his country without pay or fanfare. You do not need the spotlight; you want the best and truest outcome, which is your grandest reward—even though you may initially lust for the corner office or getting your name on the marquee. In the end, your heart is bigger than your intellect.

In the diagram of your hardware above, the smaller arrows denote decision-making activity, which is delayed compared to most other *brainstyles*. Why? The larger arrows describe and explain a much more thorough, whole-brained internal search in memory that takes place over time, especially when confronted by incoming information. Remember the tortoise and the hare? Claiming your more methodical pace, Mr. or Ms. Deliberator, will set you free to get about business more effectively and clearly. Because of this processing, a great deal of information can be taken in, assessed, and thought about (by comparing to what you already know), noting gaps, and formulating solutions as well as innovations. Deliberators' slower response is more thoughtful, more thorough and more apt to be step-by-step in new areas. No hip shooters in this crowd. If you're fast, it's because you already know the answer. Especially in things that count.

~~~~~~~~~~~~~~~~

All great masters are chiefly distinguished by the power of adding a second, a third, and perhaps a fourth step in a continuous line. Many a man has taken the first step. With every additional step you enhance immensely the value of your first.
—Ralph Waldo Emerson

~~~~~~~~~~~~~~~~

Solving problems with your hardware has led to Nobel prizes, gorgeous new home décor, executive positions, brilliant novels, diplomatic coups, and precise manicures, to name just a few things. Deliberators who develop their hardware-based strengths are noticers and perfectionists, and they become experts because of their natural sensitivities. Multi-faceted, Deliberators make diplomats, super-moms, loyal friends, and attentive lovers. Like the Energizer bunny, they just keep on going, persisting, tackling each new situation calmly, especially under pressure, with an answer tailored to fit each situation. Deliberators like former Vice President Al Gore, President George Bush Sr., current Vice President Dick Cheney, business mogul and home/entertainment guru Martha Stewart, most of the leading golf professionals including Tiger Woods, newscaster Barbara Walters, actors Clint Eastwood or Meryl Streep, and comedians Johnny Carson, Lucille Ball, and David Letterman, as well as most business leaders, belong to this versatile group. People who have these gifts keep perfecting what they do, what they contribute, and often try to perfect themselves and others they live and work with. That's where either leadership launches or trouble begins.

> *BrainStyle Clue:* Your genetically based, hardwired gifts are limited. It is your spirit (heart) that is *unlimited.* Your lifelong challenge is to distinguish the difference, then align one with the other to create wisdom, not perfection.

A DELIBERATOR IS a Sherlock Holmes, a Renaissance person and a chameleon, the genius who looks for and finds what is missing, then thinks it over to put all the known information into a new conclusion. Oh, and along the way, challenging, testing, questioning, searching for better options—pushing standards ever higher ("We can do this faster, better, cheaper"). How you get where you're going, what is said, and who is included along the way to get there is quite important to you, no?[1] Thank heavens, because the rest of the crowd is often in a big hurry about other things. For you, thoroughness or covering the most bases counts, and when you don't have time to do so, looking good and making a good presentation comes next. When you're conscientious, you want to go back and do it again, make it right.

B*rain*S*tyle* C*lue:* The Deliberator motto: Do the Right Thing.
The Conceptor motto: Do the New Thing.
The Conciliator motto: Do the Hot, New Thing.
The Knower motto: Just Do It.

Being good at many things, having a wide range of interests, hobbies, or job changes to make room for all your fascinations is true for many in your *brainstyle*. I have met Deliberator masseuses who were former accountants, intuitive counselors who were trained as engineers, and realtors who were moms trained as educators who had careers as fundraisers for multiple charities while raising families and giving killer parties. Because of this lifelong versatility, many Deliberators navigate career changes and sail into retirement with more ease than other *brainstyles*.

How **Y**ou **D**o **I**t: More than other *brainstyles*, you have an ability to notice distinctions, not only seeing the trees in the forest, but also seeing which tree is slightly different, which tree is missing that's supposed to be there, and how to restore the landscape. This is how you are innovative and bring forth new methods, inventions, dress designs, party themes, and abstract models to teach ideas.

Aloof. Perfectionist. Way too controlling. Too quiet or talks endlessly about one thing after another. Takes forever to make up her mind. Hard to read. Stubborn. Opinionated. Can't tell him anything. You may be familiar with labels like these. Have you had those helpful books and family members attempting to get you to share your feelings, stop getting distracted, grow, develop, learn more, try harder, get to the point faster? Change who you are naturally? Why? Because they don't understand what your strengths are and how to truly appreciate them. Instead, they just react to them. Worse, you agree. You think you really can change, don't you? Given enough time, there's nothing you cannot master, am I right?

How much time do you spend in your own prodding self-criticism and

---

1. Problems that your awareness creates arise when you expect or demand the same from others. Learning about *BrainStyles* will save you a lot of grief.

second-guessing? Your own headstrong attempts to master the If-You-Can-Name-It-I-Can-Do-It-Better game? How much time do you spend revisiting the decisions you've already made or regretting things you should have said better?

The reason you do so, of course, is based on your gifts.

While we're applying labels, do you also recognize these? She is SO mature for her age! So professional. So calm. So capable. How does he get so many things done?

Understanding how your gifts for breadth and depth of analysis, desire for challenges, and sensitivities to each piece of a puzzle mandates your ability to see the trees in the forest—even to the point of getting lost in the greenery at times—will explain how you can overcommit, get caught up in trying to please everyone no matter how much time it takes, to lose your sense of self (wander aimlessly within a topic at times) or even tally confusing scores on self-scoring inventories.[2] Your comparisons with others are most often with others in your same *brainstyle* group rather than the scarcer Knower or Conceptor *brainstyles,* and so you note behaviors and situations—ever in flux—to define yourself as a *Man for All Seasons* who adapts to the weather.

> *BRAINSTYLE CLUE:* Your drive to find the exceptions delays action and promotes doubt. Focus the search when seeking answers. Otherwise, return to your goal and see if you need to answer every question. This is where other *brainstyles* can help.

THE NOTICER. A Deliberator invented "situational analysis." Your motto might be *Exceptions prove the rule.* The reason is, you're more aware of the specifics and what doesn't fit . . . at least as you see it.[3]

Your use of specifics can either be to make you look good, be right, fit in, or get things more accurate and raise the bar of integrity.

Those with this *brainstyle* have a hardwired ability to monitor themselves and their environment (taking in all the specifics) so well that pleasing and trying to be it all, do it all (and therefore have it all) often comes with the program—unless you are aware of this ability and choose to manage it differently. This gift allows Deliberators to be virtuoso writers, brilliant marketers, artistic wonders, dedicated teachers, and

---

2. Yes, you can fill out self-assessment tests differently each time; you undoubtedly are thinking of a specific situation when you fill them out. You see situations as discrete, specific, and requiring a suitable customized answer each time. You also perpetuate your notion of "progress" and self-development with different answers: the ego's myth that there's somewhere for you to get to beyond where you are.

3. For the Conceptor *brainstyle,* the motto could be *Generalizations prove the rule; exceptions are irrelevant.*

public officials, as well as weasel politicians, pleasers, self-help junkies, and workaholics.

Leaders of the most extraordinary character who lived true to their principles, as well as real sleaze-balls who have fudged the numbers and used their knowledge to bilk others of their money, all draw from the same hardware to assess the situation, see what's missing, and identify the opportunity to provide what's needed—for selfish reasons or a larger purpose.

> BRAINSTYLE CLUE: Deliberators, you can quite easily define your identity by what you do and know. When no longer in your job or role, you can feel empty and worthless.
> Prevent problems. Become aware of your real gift, which is your approach to life. Create your life for all your life.

Now is the time for you not only to understand your strengths but also to use them to serve others. To begin, honor your limitations. This will allow you to let go of perfection and set some boundaries. In order to do so, you will need to employ the most powerful process available to you: forgiveness. Forgiveness is more than discussing old hurts or letting grudges go. Forgiveness, especially for a Deliberator, starts by not only accepting limitations but also seeing yourself as who you are instead of what you know. It includes seeing that another who has hurt you is either a valuable teacher or a person who needs what you have to offer them. It means transforming grudges into lessons. Forgiveness is complete when you realize there was nothing there to forgive in the first place, that both you and the other person are perfect just the way you are and the way you are not. You stop feeling guilty and have less "analysis paralysis," or procrastination. You can take feedback without personal devastation. You learn to trust your experience, your methodical approach, and your intuition; to listen to that small inner voice that guides you in the right direction—the direction of your deepest values. Forgiveness also allows you to appreciate and get the best from others who have values and lifestyles that contradict your own.

> BRAINSTYLE CLUE: The Deliberator chameleon is a specialist in responding to a situation; he is not a specialist in bringing all the answers to those situations.

More than any other *brainstyle*, you have the capacity to take in your surroundings, sort all the incoming information, and then choose to reframe what you take in. You can choose to put a loving or respectful interpretation on what is being said and how you respond. You are not driven as much by the emotive right brain as others, nor do you need to shortcut the time needed to get the whole story. Your willingness to listen and consider is one of the kindest, most caring acts there is. Your patience is why people often come to you and no one else. When you use your gifts with a caring purpose, your soul expands; when you do so to be right, better, or smarter, it doesn't.

Knowing about your strengths allows you to make a choice about how you want to live your life as a whole. Do you want to use the magnificent hardware you were born with only to complete and win at the expense of others? To interpret the world as merely a game of survival? Or, like other Deliberators, MacArther and philosopher Hillman, build your inner desire to expand and serve the world? This is ultimately a spiritual choice that requires conscious awareness of your long-term values and how you are committed to live from them.

~~~~~~~~~~~~~~

A word on Rules.
Simple, clear purpose and principles
give rise to complex and intelligent behavior.
Complex rules and regulations give rise to simple
and stupid behavior.
—Dee Hock[4] *(as quoted on the Internet by Inspirelist.com)*

~~~~~~~~~~~~~~

THE NOTICER SETS STANDARDS. Of all the *brainstyles*, you tend to believe in role models. Why? You tend to be one. You learn by observation, taking note of how others do things and deciding the right way to go. When you're in charge, you lead by example. You don't boast as much as you show how. You prefer a "model" or definition or roadmap to clarify the rules, so you know how best to play the game—or improve it or help it go more smoothly. You like to know what's expected. Another motto for your *brainstyle* could be No Surprises.

Given this, you can easily be a slave to fashion, a follower of the failed, and limited to what the other guy has done. Consider this: No one can teach you how to be yourself. Sure, they can open possibilities that you can take on as challenges, but can they really teach you what you need to learn? Okay, other Deliberators can teach you a profession or a career, but what about those dicey decisions? You have to fall back on your own principles and assessments, right? You learn by mistakes, as painful as that is, and as much as you detest making them. No guts, no glory.

---

4. Courtesy of David Allen, ©2002 Information Advantage Corporation, via *Inspirelist.com*.

DELIBERATORS AS PARTNERS. But enough about you alone. Because your *brainstyle* is the most numerous of the *brainstyles*, it makes sense that Deliberators are the most varied and distinctive of the personalities propelled by *brainstyle* who make the point in dress, lifestyle, discussion topics, or career changes. One commonality across all the different expressions of this *brainstyle* is that those who grow and move beyond their ego-based need to compete for personal status and recognition show they care by doing things for and paying attention to *others*. There is no more dedicated soldier or executive, no more faithful teacher or fanatical supporter, no more tireless parent, son, or relative, nor devoted lover or partner than the committed, stable Deliberator.

> B*RAIN*S*TYLE* C*LUE* for other *brainstyles:* Deliberators show their caring by paying attention—noticing the little things, taking care of and doing things for others. Cooking, cleaning, fixing things, knowing before he speaks what he's going to say are all expressions of love. Look behind the act for the intention, rather than demanding declarations or exhibitions of passion.

NON-STRENGTHS—YOU HAVE THEM! They are the strengths of other *brainstyles.* You will realize that when another criticizes or maligns you, not only is the criticism based on the perceptions created by his or her own (and different) *brainstyle*, but also you can actually turn the situation to your own advantage. Other *brainstyles'* gifts start at the boundaries of your own strengths. These are your non-strengths. Non-strengths are most clearly demonstrated when, say, you are hardwired to be right-handed. Sure, you can learn to use your left hand, but when you do, you don't perform as well, as effectively, as fast, or as comfortably.

BELIEVE IT OR NOT: DELIBERATORS NEED OTHER BRAINSTYLES. One of the hardest things for you to confront, dear Deliberator, is that you do not have all the gifts. I know, that's insulting to some of you. Perhaps in your late twenties, if you learn the things you should learn, you will realize the profundity of collaboration. More than this, you will feel the relief of sharing the burden that your perfectionism demands. You can release the guilt for the mistakes and boners that actually taught you how to be compassionate and become more open to others' thinking. Along with this will come some humility as you see how much better others can perform in an area you are struggling to handle when their natural strength is applied to a problem. It will be joyful.

DELIBERATORS, YOU NEED THE CONCEPTOR TO:

- Provide long-term direction that goes beyond your facts and linear reasoning. She'll think of things you never would have considered.
- Suggest broader, more comprehensive, new possibilities.
- Simplify your ideas from complexity to workability.
- Suggest new strategies for overcoming obstacles that are more comprehensive—or different—than your strategies.
- Challenge basic assumptions of the plan or project, which can illuminate the whole plan to make it simpler, newer, and more inclusive.
- Confront the big issues, make change a reasonable target, and strategize how to approach the people necessary.

DELIBERATORS, YOU NEED THE KNOWER TO:

- Give you focus through all the complexity and chaos by stating the target simply and clearly.
- Reduce the possible options. You can't do them all anyway, at least not in this lifetime.
- Sort the facts into a simple, doable, streamlined plan.
- Get it done, efficiently.
- Push, challenge, break through obstacles, no matter who or what they are.
- Say what needs saying directly; give you the words to confront the issue or person directly to get it resolved and over with.

DELIBERATORS, YOU NEED THE CONCILIATOR TO:

- Show or clarify the feelings involved, while inspiring others.
- Openly support and promote you or your idea, get excited, make it fun.
- Determine the personal self-interests of those involved. They know things, these Conciliators, from gossip and intuition. (If you are a right-sided Deliberator, you can forget this one.)
- Make things exciting, give them sizzle, personal meaning, pizzazz.
- Expand the possibilities for where you can go, and brainstorm alternatives for how to get there.
- Make things comfortable, warm, informal, and friendly.
- Wing it; get you out of a tough spot, on the spot.

YOUR BASIC STRENGTHS AS A DELIBERATOR come from the fact that you access both sides of the brain as you process and monitor incoming stimuli, seemingly in greater quantities than other *brainstyles*. This makes you the one who is first in line to seek the best and most reasonable answer to everything. Your most natural response to unfamiliar events and situations is to ask questions. You often cannot go forward until those unknowns are settled; you know what's at stake and plan what is likely to happen next. Your memory (which is stored throughout the brain) is actively involved when you do this, so you may also be looking for what you remember as the *right* answer.[5] You are a natural at assessment, critique, or noting what's missing or wrong. Thus your delay in making a decision, taking a guess, or reacting emotionally as quickly as other *brainstyles*.[6] Later, and to a somewhat lesser degree, you become aware of your feelings, your imagination, your conclusions, and then your goal or focus (which can change or expand with new information).

Your brain access demands time to understand others more fully, think things through, or evaluate a new direction before just leaping (emotionally) into things. It also allows more time for evaluation of everything, including yourself. You are most comfortable with time to study and learn something, rather than being pressed for a decision. This is especially true in a NEW area. You may have been criticized for being too slow and, conversely, you may have rejected others as too pushy. The solution—erasure of the friction and criticism—lies in timing and how you manage it.

Your timing allows for you to be the one who wants to learn more in order to improve things, who sees things as they might be and loves to raise the bar (make things better) and close the gap (see the problems or what could go wrong) all at the same time. You go into new events needing or demanding certainty before you'll play. These same abilities make you a natural critic, a nattering nabob of the negative. Knowing this, you can pose your "criticisms" (naming what is missing or could be improved) as a way to prevent problems or make things smoother for others who don't naturally look at things this way. And you can say so in a way that supports what others are trying to do. You should know; you're a natural diplomat—except when you are sulking or pontificating.

Offering your strengths to support others' goals rather than using them to make people wrong will prevent them telling you to "quit being so negative." When a Deliberator has to deal with a Conceptor boss or Conciliator friend, he tends to keep reviewing the facts and hammering at his own carefully crafted answer. Persistence,

---

5. Your memory is gone, you say? Age creeping up? Not according to the latest research. Your RAM (working memory) is full. Too much going on, too many priorities, too many books at the same time, etc. If you weren't able to forget, your brain would be paralyzed. Some of us just have better and faster access to complex memory items (like names) in specialized areas of the brain than others.

6. A special category within your group, the right-sided Deliberator, however, can be quickly emotional when his/her exquisite sensitivities perceive abruptness, or harsh behavior or events. A resource for managing those keen sensitivities is the text *The Highly Sensitive Person: How to Thrive When the World Overwhelms You*, by Elaine Aron (Bantam, Doubleday, Dell Publishing, 1997).

your gift, often wins the day. But you win a battle and lose the war: You get to be right in the short term, but lose another's ideas—or worse, his commitment.

> BRAINSTYLE CLUE: If you can't reach the end of something, you need to collaborate with someone who can assist you.

When dating or in a romantic relationship, your self-control can be seen at first as mysterious, later as withholding information or true feelings (especially so when you are more quiet and introverted and your partner has a different energy level and *brainstyle*). "Still water runs deep" may describe the depth of your ideas and feelings. As you know, your stillness does not mean you're not busy. Can you let another know early on that you are assessing and processing information inside and not as expressive outside, if this is true for you? It is important for you to discuss your ideas or feelings with those around you, because they cannot read your mind or guess your interpretations. You also may discover a clearer, more focused direction as you talk to other, more decisive thinkers (the pushy ones), who can help clarify your decisions, your feelings, and your direction.

At work, others will rely on you to keep your cool. Because you can do so (when you choose to), your *brainstyle* is the one most often found in executive positions.[7] You have a seemingly unlimited curiosity and ability to learn, store, and assess information in any number of fields, to bring a rational approach to a problem, a sport, the outdoors, or a lover.

> BRAINSTYLE CLUE: Your value is not based on being right as much as it is on how you make the right answers available to others.

Don't make the mistake other Deliberators have made when approaching retirement. If you start to feel less valuable because all the information that you have learned over the years is obsolete, you are looking at the wrong criterion. Your brain is a natural problem-analysis machine and will continue to approach life situations—like travel, family gatherings, community organizations, reading and exploring whole new fields—with wisdom gained by the same rational approach of assessing, planning, and ensuring a good, thorough job is done.

---

7. In an early *BrainStyles* study performed by professor Thomas Hurt, PhD, of the University of North Texas, it was found that the Deliberator *brainstyle* was the most numerous in senior management. Observations of government and business confirm the initial finding.

~~~~~~~~~~~~~~~~

A BRAINSTYLE SUMMARY OF DISTINCTIONS

Dominantly Left-Brained				Dominantly Right-Brained
The Knower	**The Left-Sided Deliberator**	The balanced Deliberator	**The Right-Sided Deliberator**	The Conciliator

~~~~~~~~~~~~~~~~

DIFFERENT FLAVORS. DIFFERENT DELIBERATORS. The biggest differences in processing for this *brainstyle* occur quickly after *Time Zero*. For one group, the left hemisphere is their gift and dominant strength. **Left-Sided** Deliberators are the focused ones, the competitive, knowledgeable "whiz kids" who find numbers, proof, facts, analysis, and logic part of the air they breathe. The biggest challenge for this group is including any others, especially those who have different gifts, in their decision-making process. Admitting they made a mistake ties for first place.

All are excellent networkers and have many friends and associates in their lives, especially when more extroverted. Some examples include corporate engineers, technical whizzes, promotional or publishing executives, both male and female, who wanted more control, and so became consultants or business owners. Or spouses whose home lives weren't challenging enough, and so became heads of charitable organizations to drive their causes to new focus and recognition. You may know someone who is "brilliant" and articulate and gets things done while keeping her fingers in many pies—social, travel, community—while exercising and entertaining, all at the same time. *Whew.* They take your breath away.

> *BRAINSTYLE CLUE:* The challenge in every personally loaded situation is to get unplugged from the electricity of personal survival. Connecting with the broader principles and values that bring people together means time for the right brain to add its wisdom so you may seek the best solution.

With observation, several things stand out that reveal the left-sided Deliberator's *brainstyle* gifts.

➤ The dominant left-brained access shows up in how ably they structure, organize, track, and recall volumes of complex information, often to support an established conclusion.

➤ Logical analysis is primarily relied upon. This means decisions are whittled down and assessed to be practical, factual, and based on data instead of speculation and emotion; *ergo,* they are correct.

➤ Deliberators seek to be right. The more left-brained they are, the more sensitive to an accusation of factual error, paralleling the sensitivity the right-brained have to personal slights. Answers can become positions defended as fortresses with armies of detail.

➤ The strength of the *brainstyle*, persistence—a methodical, step-by-step, controlled procedure—is the primary negotiating tactic used to establish a position. It is the same ability that allows this *brainstyle* to successfully take any project to conclusion.

➤ To change the direction of the proceedings, direct confrontation and supportive information for a new direction is a must. Time for analysis and discussion are essential. The more personal the issue, or the more opportunity for loss, the more time required.

➤ Other *brainstyles* are not nearly as successful in influencing the left-sided Deliberator's thinking. They just don't have the wealth of facts, the patience, and the reasoning. This creates a lack of trust by the other *brainstyles* for the Deliberator and is a major challenge for him in return.

➤ What others depict as competition is an intense desire to use natural strengths to reach a goal and be accurate in doing so. The ego seeks to be special by being best, first, most recognized, and having the biggest pile. For most in this *brainstyle*, winning is being right; focused, linear thinkers *hate* being wrong. For masters in this *brainstyle*, winning is furthering the field of study, contributing to the whole. Being right becomes a servant to the best and most comprehensive solution for all concerned.

> *BRAINSTYLE CLUE:* The biggest challenge for your *brainstyle* is to allow real influence by another *brainstyle*—not just in giving you an idea or two, but also bending your direction. This allows deeper trust and partnerships.

➤ Measurable specifics are real and true to the left-brained, in stark contrast with the right-brained who seek truth in universals. Thus, factual arguments are like hills hard won in battle; the goal is to make the world safe and comprehensible, and retreat to reassess can be a terrible defeat that undermines reality. Introspective analysis and examination of self-interests are delayed or unspoken. Other *brainstyles* must read between the lines to define personal motivations.

➤ The gift of rationality means a non-strength is a willingness to confront. Deliberators avoid emotional "scenes" at all cost.

THE LEFT-SIDED DELIBERATOR: A SUMMARY OF STRENGTHS

TIME ZERO ➡	SOON AFTER ➡	WITH PRACTICE ➡	EXPERT ➡
• Assesses the given information against standards, looks for gaps • Analyzes • Gets and gives a factual overview • Is thoughtful, shows no reaction, non-committal • Recalls what is known	• Is aware of others' reactions • Wants to streamline or clarify things into options • Wants more information • Challenges, questions, gives opinions • Calms things down • Settles on an answer	• Makes a decision, takes a stand • Organizes facts into a measurable system • Teaches • Maintains position or opinion based on experience • Influences one-one • Argues, debates	• Revises position with others' input • Breaks new ground, contributes to a chosen field • Mentors • Broadens areas of interest • Leads on a larger scale

All Charts© 1997, 2003 *BrainStyles*, Inc. No reproduction without permission. *www.brainstyles.com*

ANOTHER FLAVOR. Deliberator counterparts (who look sooo different, sooo opposite) are the **Right-Sided** Deliberators, who use more of the right hemisphere to influence their rational process very quickly after *Time Zero,* and so are gifted in visualizing a process or plan to go forward—not necessarily to finish it, mind you, but certainly to get it off the starting block. These folks rely much more on their internal ability to create images and intuit meanings. They rely more on spirituality and philosophy to influence how they think. They care deeply about people and their feelings and react personally, without showing it as often as Conciliators might. When a left-sided and right-sided Deliberator marry, they often focus on their differences, call themselves a Knower and Conciliator, only to lose their common ground.

Right-Sided Deliberators have a real challenge staying with something past their interest and challenge quotient, which is always high. Boundaries (saying no, keeping on the diet, quitting a job) are as much or more of an issue for this group as for Conciliators. Conflict is detested and creatively avoided, thus a necessary survival strategy for applying natural abilities is being exquisitely sensitive and diplomatic. Spontaneity is also a prized attribute of this intuitive, most spiritual of *brainstyles.* Calling at the last minute, letting things "fall through the cracks," or beginning many, many projects that are all of equal interest are trademarks of those who enjoy the playing of the game much more than finishing it.

These are the former accountants who become masseuses, ex-nurses who sell jewelry and counsel in astrology, mortgage bankers who are writing a novel, or realtors who are part-time yoga gurus. They are also, say, financial planners who care openly for clients, tender lovers, patient and loyal friends who listen.

Your specialties show up after your initial rational assessment of new situations, as you draw from the more emotive and intuitive side of the brain to experience a wonderful ability to react to and connect with others. You are the most sensitive of all the *brainstyles*. Don't expect others to be as verbally or visually sensitive: Look beyond the behavior to the gifts, the caring intention, the larger meaning. As you think through your responses to what you see and hear, you may find what you have in common, or you might linger on how you are distinct from the other person. Sometimes you'll mentally go back and forth. Don't worry about this. It's your incredible access to all those right-brained images and so many experiences that you have stored in your memory. That's why you need time to think, why you are slow to make up your mind and choose only a few close friends with whom you are compatible. You need to sort and organize a great many things. You get distracted by new and stimulating input. You have a lot going on mentally.

You can come up with unusual ideas when you want to get someplace quicker, better, or more elegantly. This means you can be more flexible and versatile than others without losing touch with the realities of life.

You may not have all the analytical abilities of more left-brained Deliberators who share your steadiness. In fact, they may appear to be your opposites, with their practical, harder-edged approach to life. Appearances are deceiving; you both have a basic sense of order and a love of challenge and learning, as well as deeply held values, to provide a core to the life you can share.

Your boredom with things comes from a need for challenge and the desire to have new things to learn. Your mastery, however, comes from plumbing the depths of a thing using your analytical abilities; allow your sensitivities to support those abilities.*

---

* See chapter 7 to distinguish your gifts of invention and from those of the Conceptor's forecasting.

THE RIGHT-SIDED DELIBERATOR: A SUMMARY OF STRENGTHS

TIME ZERO ➤	SOON AFTER ➤	WITH PRACTICE ➤	EXPERT ➤
• Assesses the given information against standards, looks for gaps. • Analyzes. • Is thoughtful, but may react emotionally. • Recalls what is known.	• Is keenly aware of others' reactions; cares deeply. • Wants to create options, usually in a step-by-step manner, that fit with precedent but go somewhere "interesting". • Wants more infor-mation. • Questions, seeks to understand why/how/what. • Reacts emotionally, then calms things down. • Says the right thing.	• Sets boundaries. • Includes others. • Makes a tentative decision with others. • Explores many areas and disciplines. • Leads by building consensus. • Politically astute. • Teaches or counsels. • Changes career or interests combining the practical with the artistic or spiritual.	• Becomes a repository of information and source material. • Mentors. • Deepens areas of interest, often adding a spiritual dimension. • Leads on a larger scale.

All Charts ©1997, 2003 *BrainStyles*, Inc. No reproduction without permission. *www.brainstyles.com*

THE EXPLORER. Right-sided Deliberators are often explorers of ideas, places, people, literature, and themselves.[8] Using all their abilities to process, sort, share, and explore ideas creates "flow" for this *brainstyle* specialty. Often people with this *brainstyle* have very stimulating careers and lifestyles.

One famous example is Michael Crichton, a pre-med student at Harvard who left medical school, impatient with the ethics and structure, traveled the world, and invented an entire career in literature, film, and television based on his love of research *(Jurassic Park and ER* come readily to mind); strength to create and describe his own visual imagery; and an ability to create an exciting sequence (plot and storyline) and describe people with the keen sensitivities and observational skills of this *brainstyle*.

When you combine these gifts, you often get a very articulate intellectual. Watch out for retreating into abstractions, which in effect allows you to hide in

---

8. For those familiar with the Meyers-Briggs Temperament Inventory, the right-sided Deliberator would fall into the Perceiving category rather than the Judging area, where decisions and closure are sought. The left-sided Deliberator is the reverse, preferring closure and completion. The right-brained are the more Intuitive Thinkers; the left-brained, the more Sensory Thinkers.

your intellectual abilities and make others appear stupid. This use of language is a gift, and to use it to enlighten rather than obscure is a choice you make out of love and respect.

As a lover or business partner with such a person, you need not only to have the patience for their exploration, but also to leverage it for the gift that it is to make your own life richer. Stifling those journeys would be akin to cutting off one of his limbs. Men with these gifts are tender, loving—if distracted—husbands and fathers. In chapter 15 you'll be guided in how to negotiate a way to communicate that uses timing so that each partner can win in his or her own time.

> BrainStyle Clue: Use your vocabulary and understanding of abstract ideas to introduce possibilities and show others how smart they are, rather than focusing on your own brilliance and getting tangled up in jargon or complexities. Take the time to take it simple. Those who "just don't get it" are your allies to make your discoveries and insights more accessible and touch more lives.

MANY DELIBERATORS COME ACROSS AS ARROGANT INTELLECTUALS when they use their expertise, or stored knowledge, as the sole criterion for determining the value another brings. This is when they use this formula: Smart = Knows many facts = Value or Worth to me, therefore deserving of respect (meaning *admiration for* rather than *sensitivity to* or *empathy for* another). "Smart" then trumps personal liking as the criterion for a relationship—respect which rests largely upon the knowledge and similar values of the other[9].

> BrainStyle Clue: Values are reflections of former significant, often emotional, decisions made by *brainstyle* processing.

Having similar values can make or break a relationship for Deliberators. After considering things over time, all *brainstyles*—and especially Deliberators—develop both expertise and a right-brained, experiential, I-know-what's-right-I've-been-there belief in certain values that are no longer questioned. Depending on the energy level of the Deliberator, these values—when contradicted—are either openly debated or end the conversation. Those who believe differently are most difficult to be accepted as a friend or ally by this *brainstyle*.

---

9. In informal surveys with over 200 MBA students at Southern Methodist University in Dallas, Deliberators overwhelmingly wanted bosses to provide structure, goals, and expertise, to be an "ideal boss" for them. *BrainStyles* dictates more than preferences for a Deliberator: It defines the basis for respect.

If your choice of a mate or a business partner rests solely on his or her expertise and/or values, you might rethink this process of evaluation. Learning more about *brainstyles* means knowing how to take advantage of complementary gifts that will cover your non-strengths, even when the person has beliefs that differ from yours and is not an expert in your field.

> *BRAINSTYLE CLUE:* Accepting your limits can allow you the greatest freedom of all: unlimited growth in your strengths, forgiveness for imperfections and mistakes, and the joy of partnerships.

AS A DELIBERATOR,

1. You're fastest and clearest where you have experience—you don't often "wing it." You're at your best when you think about it first. This means you tend to be prepared, come across as organized, and proceed with things in a more methodical manner than others.

2. You tend to be more private the more you draw from your disciplined left brain, and you prefer to keep things to yourself. You don't need to gossip as much as more spontaneous right-brainers. This is especially true if you have a bit slower metabolism and are more introverted or introspective. Your selectivity comes from your high standards or the criteria you have stored over time to figure out what the best answer, best car, best outfit, or best bargain is. Sometimes your high standards make it hard to have a lot of friends. Most in your *brainstyle* only want a few close friends anyway, prizing loyalty highly. Are you limiting the potential teachers in your life?

3. You'd rather do it yourself to get it done right, thank you. Delegation is difficult. When you do give it away, you may give it all away with an I-don't-want-to-see-it-until-it's-done approach, or you may just give small assignments so you can stay on top of things. This is based on your strengths for assessing and deciding more thoroughly than others, to reach your own conclusions. This can mean overcommitting and underdelivering, being too busy to get anything done, feeling overwhelmed, and never having time to really enjoy family, friends, or experiences. Planning the whole project first with others—especially a mate—will help. Making decisions to focus on a few things at a time or share the doing with another are simple things. They really are. One requires saying No, one Yes. You can do this easily when you have made up your mind to do so. Help yourself by not giving a Yes when you really mean "I need time to think about it." It is easy for you to try to do it all and be it all, so that, just maybe, you can have it all. Ambition and

competition are empty without a goal that serves you *and* others. This means balance, something you are more than capable of.

Here are some questions for you to ponder.

- How can I take advantage of my ability to plan, attend to details, and establish a process for getting something done to include others?

  _____

- How many projects am I willing to do right now?

  _____

- What do I need to start doing to carry this out?

  _____

4. You're best at spotting problems first, not as quick at resolving them. (Telling your answer is not the resolution to the problem.) Your ability to assess situations rests on your gift to take in and process many specifics. Solutions come later and most usually one at a time. That's because your gift is in assessing the problem. After you've done this in one field for a long time, you can get to the answers faster. That's when you can draw from your intuition more frequently to come up with new ideas; that is, if you're willing to let go of the controls a bit. Otherwise you may be stuck on your own right answer and attempt to sell it.

- When did I have the right answer and another refused to buy it?

  _____

- Do I listen to others in such a way as to allow my intuition to work in reaching a new solution with them, instead of either saying nothing or telling them my opinions or conclusions?

  _____

5. You are excellent at observing people and monitoring your reactions to a situation. Your gifts allow you to come up with the diplomatic or "nice" thing to say, which you know will get a good response. This remarkable gift of paying attention can lead you away from your own agenda, self-care, and priorities. Your ability to get involved with the specifics and circumstances of another's life is a wonderful way of caring about him. You may need to tell her you are caring by paying attention. Release the expectation that others can attend to you in the same way you can attend to them. It may also allow you to return to a balance between your agenda and theirs.

- When have I paid attention to another and felt cheated in return?

- How can I release my expectation and allow them to show me they care for me in their own way?

~~~~~~~~~~~~~~~~~

"We promise according to our hopes and
perform according to our fears."
—Francois de la Rochefoucauld

~~~~~~~~~~~~~~~~~

A SUMMARY OF THE DELIBERATOR'S NON-STRENGTHS, WHICH TAKE MORE TIME OR EFFORT.

You do NOT naturally (or quickly) . . .

- Decide quickly or easily in new areas. (Don't get this confused with giving quick opinions or telling someone a quick answer you have already thought of ahead of time.)
- Set priorities easily. You tend to take on too many things, overpromise, get overloaded, and often still want to do all of it.
- Handle conflict, especially emotional conflict, well. You tend to avoid the situation.
- Delegate important things for others to take charge of.
- Frame new data or issues passionately, broadly, or simply at *first.* Things appear complex at first, especially new subjects.
- Pose several solutions. You tend to favor a single answer that is well thought-out, reasonable, and a compilation of your analysis and study of several alternatives.
- Include others in the final decision. Discussing isn't deciding. Informing others is not sharing the decision-making. Making up your mind on your own is your natural bent. However, when truly in a partnership, you allow the other to influence you, *even—and especially—when you know the right answer.* Others tend to feel left out or put down when you decide alone, even when you asked them for their ideas to get to your conclusion. Of course there are times when your taking a stand can speed things up. It's necessary to assess when your expertise is going to lead and when it's going to lessen another's commitment.
- Offer emotional support with emotional reactions or a quick show of enthusiasm or excitement. In new situations, you tend to be more neutral. If anything, you tend to show feelings with *loaded words* rather than hugs or

facial expressions or physical displays most of the time. You are perfectly capable of explaining to others what you actually feel so they will understand that you care.

• Show emotions readily. Those who use nonverbal cues as their most important language may find you hard to "read."

• Spend much time on the overview; you'd rather get to the action, doing things—either physically (acting) or mentally (thinking about actions, issues). You can get bogged down in the doing, sidetracked into investigating interesting pieces of the puzzle that pop up and connections that pique your interest.[10]

> *BRAINSTYLE CLUE:* Many Deliberators' career changes and divorces are simply a result of not being willing to confront a situation or a person directly which might require giving up a long-held position (decision).

THE DELIBERATOR: A SUMMARY OF STRENGTHS

TIME ZERO ➜	SOON AFTER ➜	WITH PRACTICE ➜	EXPERT ➜
• Assesses. • Analyzes. • Is thoughtful or shows no reaction. • Recalls.	• Is aware of intuition. • Wants to organize things. • Wants more information. • Challenges, questions, gives opinions. • Calms things down. • Makes a list.	• Plans, organizes. • Has an answer or opinion based on experience. • Sets up a system.	• Sets the standard. • Teaches, mentors. • Becomes the expert. • Argues, debates. • Explores areas of interest. • Travels, learns, reads widely.

All Charts ©1997, 2003 *BrainStyles*, Inc. No reproduction without permission. *www.brainstyles.com*

---

10. Ever find yourself reading something from a shelf in a room you went into for an entirely different purpose? And worse, generating a whole new list of Things To Do?

DELIBERATORS LIKE OPPORTUNITIES WHERE THEY CAN:

- collect information in their own way and in their own time.
- set up the plan.
- learn new things.
- be challenged with different situations or problems.
- do the right thing.
- make the world a more rational, understandable, often better place.
- see and tell it "like it is" accurately.
- compete, proving their knowledge, skill or expertise by mastering a subject.
- teach others.
- be the expert who is sought after and respected for what he knows.
- partner with those they respect.
- discuss ideas, get direction, and then act on their own.

> *BRAINSTYLE CLUE:* The consequences for including others are never what you fear. Given your *brainstyle,* it's simple to say, not so easy to do. Knowing it's a non-strength will make you a leader rather than a frustrated micro-manager trying to control another's life or plans. Consider this the art of living.

CHALLENGES YOUR STRENGTHS CREATE FOR YOU:

➤ Being so good at taking in and processing information over time; it is very hard to let it go or trust others to use it as capably as you can. Control becomes an issue. Teaching others is different: You are passing on your expertise. The same context can propel you forward on the job as you develop others' abilities.

➤ Since most jobs are never really perfect or complete enough for you, it is hard to really sit back and revel in your own accomplishments, let alone acknowledge others (like the effusive Conciliators). Giving credit to others is hard when your gifts involve seeing the flaws, trying to correct them, and continually making things better.

➤ Sharing credit is a challenge, especially when so much of your thinking is done alone. Mature Deliberators learn how to seek the best answer by taking in information from others and applauding them for it.

➤ One thing that everyone needs to learn—but is particularly true for one with your gifts—is to allow others to make mistakes. When you are aware of the process of growth in which you are engaged, you will also be tolerant of others and provide a safety net instead of a continual critique. Your sensitivity will allow you to say things in a diplomatic way.

➤ Hating conflict as you do, you will tend to be Mr. or Ms. Nice Guy, avoid making clear requests, setting limits, or asking for the money.

BRAINSTYLE CLUE: Perfection is for your spirit, excellence the goal for your brain-based abilities.

~~~~~~~~~~~~~~~~

Do not seek to follow in the footsteps of the wise.
Seek what they sought.
—Basho

~~~~~~~~~~~~~~~~

THE DELIBERATOR AS LOVER

DATING A DELIBERATOR. Remember the part about assessing information before deciding? About researching, then comparing and evaluating alternatives? Keep those strengths in mind as you read about Chad, the Deliberator.

He's movie-star handsome:[11] strong jaw and brow, hazel eyes, brown hair with just the odd sunstreak, and the body to match. He's a personal trainer with a good (wealthy) client list. Not a very good student when in school, he's now an outdoor sportsman and clearly a Deliberator who can track your progress, keep notes, count your leg lifts while something else is going on, and notice the fine points of your frame without showing emotion. His humor is subtle, his demeanor professionally cool. He is not there to make friends; he is doing a job. He's 29 and a catch. Does he break many hearts? Not the way a Conciliator would. He "dated around" during his twenties, he admits, and did not want to be kept from traveling with a client around the world or "giving up his independence" by committing to anyone quickly. He's been gracious about it most of the time and "can still talk to" most former dates as friends. Is it just a coincidence that he remains so independent, or is it his *brainstyle* dictating that he wants to make his own decisions, not be rushed, and needs time to find someone who meets his criteria—his carefully formed standards for "the right girl"? I'd bet on the latter, if I were you.

Conciliator women for this particular Deliberator guy (not all Deliberators) are way too much of an emotional handful. "I had to break up with one girl I dated, because she wanted to fight all the time, and I wouldn't fight. I won't fight. I never fight." (Remember the part about avoiding conflict? No? Consider it on your list of non-strengths, Deliberators.) Talking to her, the perspective is quite different. She tosses around phrases that are real clichés for women of today: "I just wanted him to 'open up,' tell me how he felt," she says. "I wanted to make a connection, feel something from him, have a relationship. *Oh, you know,*"

---

11. Go ahead, men, generalize to your heart's content. You might also mention Cary Grant, Brad Pitt, Julio Iglesias, Andy Garcia, and Denzel Washington as examples of the handsome in your *brainstyle*.

sigh. *"Men."* (Meaningful look here.) "He just kept his distance." But the female Conciliator's point of view is not all women's. His current girlfriend, another Deliberator, doesn't find him emotionally distant at all. She's too busy doing things with him that they both enjoy: swimming, working out, dancing, hiking, and sharing his values for food (healthy), booze (not healthy), and life (Christian). "She makes me laugh," he says, "and no one has ever done that before." She also is not beset by his looks, looking past his pretty face, to act and feel natural around him.[12] Comfortability promotes fun. It looks like "common interests" to him.

COMMON INTERESTS VERSUS VALUES. "We enjoy the same things," he says. A common belief and a common trap for the single. It isn't the love of the outdoors or sports that is the real attraction, because interests, health, responsibilities, and abilities can change over the years. It's the values that prompt those interests and the companionship your partner provides in sharing them—the spending of time together in a mutually satisfying way when interests differ—that bind. When interests aren't the same, many couples take separate vacations, have entirely different careers or fields of study, yet stay happily married for decades. As author Hugh Prather points out, what do you have in common with your children, especially before the age of ten? That doesn't prevent you from loving them deeply.

> *BrainStyle Reminder:* Values are reflections of significant, often emotional, former decisions made by *brainstyle* processing.

In this case, similar *brainstyles* reached a similar approach to life that is thoughtful and less emotional on the surface. Evenness attracts Deliberators to one another, even when it looks like it's all the specifics of family and history and hobbies. More than this, each must respect the values of the other and value how his partner can contribute to him. Values are "make or break" for a Deliberator relationship. When Deliberators fall for other *brainstyles*, they always mention first how they appreciate the gifts of their complementary partners *and* their similar values.

Chad is slow to form a relationship, the way he is slow to do anything important to him. Passing his thirtieth birthday, growing steadily more in love with his fun date, he makes his choice. Once he decides, Tradition with a capital letter takes center stage. His proposal of marriage is a romantic, staged production in the ski resort where they met. All his friends are there. *He* plans a great deal of the wed-

---

12 Handsome men have a blessing and a curse: They never know if they are loved for who they are inside. Worse, as one woman admitted, "I won't date a guy that's prettier than me." It matters not that the hunk may be attracted to her. Outer beauty is surely a blessing; it can also become a mask and create defensiveness in its owner.

ding—down to the last detail, of course, for beauty, family, and fun afterwards. Most Deliberators are either non-delegators or abdicators. Chad is the former, and so takes control in their marriage right from the start. Besides, as he is a great believer in tradition, the "model" in his family is one in which the man is in charge. Of course his bride's is, too.

> BRAINSTYLE CLUE: Precedent and tradition are often more important for Deliberators than for other *brainstyles*. Knowers tie for first in this category.

GIFTS REVEALED. OK so far, but what happens after the wedding? The couple has a "honeymoon baby" and become parents much sooner than the new husband had planned. The *Time Zero* situation brings out his gifts. In his case, his faith, his value for family, and his respect for his marriage vows are all supported by his gifts for stability, personal discipline, attention to a step-by-step plan for improvement (renovating an older home, making sure his pregnant wife is cared for and surrounded by family, making sure they have time alone together and—when he arrives—as a family with their new son), and ensuring he grows his business by learning more in his field and attending to clients. His gifts overwhelm the anxieties of new parenthood ("I thought we'd have more time to play . . .") along with his value for taking responsibility for his life and providing security for his family. Their church and common faith is the source for a larger context to their marriage for each of them. They have a place to go to besides caring parents, for inner sustenance. Chad, the hunk and former single guy, with his family as the center of his life, is an attentive dad and husband, and a happy man.

DELIBERATOR LOVERS. Both men and women with Deliberator gifts keep the challenge and interest in their romances by applying their sensitivities to the relationship, spending time, taking care. The book on the Sensitive Self-Improving Male was written by this *brainstyle*;[13] the book on the caring, tender, patient, yet rational over-achiever was written by the Sensitive Female Deliberator. Michael writes love poems. Alan goes to seminars on self-development, sex and relationships with his wife. Bill doesn't believe in any of that "self-help stuff," but knows exactly what his wife means by each reference and each problem; and he needs no seminars to teach him how to respond in a way that communicates best to her sensitivities. Shirley, his wife, also a Deliberator, is upbeat, supportive, very

---

13. This can be shown in a variety of ways: The more left-brained the Deliberator, the more the self-improvement is directed toward learning new subjects; the more right-sided, the more the improvement can be introspective, therapeutic, or philosophical. Learners all.

calm and down-to-earth. She knows by a look or a word, she says, when her husband is upset. Even though more right-brained than her counterpart, her central ability to remain steady—sensitively steady—to him, his moods, his health, is applied without the emotion of the Conciliator. She's the companion who doesn't argue, but steers, who shows through deeds that she cares. Anita, in her marriage since college, looks to the untrained eye like her husband's best friend. Mary Ann keeps the house spotless, entertains flawlessly, and ensures that the family holidays keep up the tradition of eating and being together, providing a steady, sure home for her family. She would be the one with the "Ask Me About My Grandbaby" bumper sticker. Phyllis doesn't entertain much at all, having realized, she says, that there is just too much pressure (self-imposed, she admits) to do everything just right. So she shows husband, family, and friends that she cares deeply by visiting, calling, spending time with them, and remembering what is going on in their lives ("How did you remember *that*?"). Yes, she gets bossy at times, knowing better what is best for her husband than he does. The problem is, she's often right. She's watched and counted and tracked him patiently over the years. That's how she loves him.

TWO DELIBERATOR MARRIAGES.[14] Both couples have been married, coincidentally, for thirty-six years. They both began as stable families for their children. Each husband has been successful in a very different career. Husband #1 is more right-brained than his wife, as is husband #2. Both wives are left-sided Deliberators. Both have been through some rough times over the last few years, since their children have left home and they have returned to being a couple rather than being parents of a family. This is a stressful time in the life of any couple, a true *Time Zero,* in *BrainStyles* Land. Neither couple knows the other. The first couple is not only going to divorce, but divorce viciously; the second couple is "on a second honeymoon." Here are some differences in their approaches to their marriages.

NUMBER ONE: "I gave him thirty-six years of my life," says the wife in an angry, heated tone, which barely covers her pain and hurt. "And after what he's done, if he thinks he's walking out of this thing fifty-fifty, he's got another think coming!" She pounds the table on the last phrase.

Her respect for him as a businessman, (assessment of results produced) maybe even as a partner, she admits, has long been over. When the recession hit and he tried some multilevel marketing, she was clearly skeptical, rolling her eyes when discussing his new "venture." He had a drinking problem, she says, and so joined Alcoholics Anonymous. She found it creepy. She couldn't relate to "those people,"

14. Overall, Deliberators are the most successful same-*brainstyle* pairs.

meaning the spouses of the members who were to attend the support group, Al-Anon. Neither was she interested in the philosophy, implying that she had a great deal more self-control and said she didn't need "crutches" as he did. As it turned out, Alcoholics Anonymous was where he met another woman with whom he had an affair. Confessing this, he entered marital counseling with his wife.

They went to marriage counseling together for a time, but he wouldn't stick it out. Nor, she found out, did he keep his promise to stop seeing That Woman.

She continued seeing the psychiatrist, however, and has learned a great deal about herself and her value as an individual. She preferred the privacy of the one-to-one counseling rather than the more public sharing her husband chose at A.A. She secretly thinks that he had the affair because the other woman is younger and more attractive than he finds her; their mutual respect and values have eroded to become invisible, unimportant to them. What is obvious is that she has lost a life that was clearly defined and predictable, a perfectly acceptable life for her— evidently not so for her "unstable" husband. Setting boundaries (telling him to leave) is easier for her than for some in other *brainstyles*; that doesn't mean it's any easier in this situation.

Dallas psychoanalyst and marital counselor Barbara Graham discusses the source of the anger the woman feels. "Of course she feels horribly betrayed, forgotten, and terribly hurt. I see in my clients the time when they are confronted with the next level of choice, which is to look at their own barrenness of purpose, their own interests and abilities. They discover that they have lived vicariously [through the other partner]." As a self-aware newlywed put it, "They expect the other person to be their own all-in-all, when he's just human. He can't be." That lesson is front and center for the fifty-something woman who is now bitter with rejection.

Within this trauma lies the opportunity for her future: to reclaim her worth by re-looking at her own deeper goals and values, reevaluating her gifts, achieving on her own to respect just what it takes, and learning from the past to establish a real partnership where she can offer love in the tangible way she does.

If we look at the foundation for a loving partnership, we see that when the wife lost respect for her husband as a provider, the bedrock of the marriage was gone. When she failed to join him in—or offer an alternative to—the values that Alcoholics Anonymous offered, she gave up her role as a partner. Her critical view of him as unstable and unfocused never saw his underlying strengths of exploring introspection and the need for more open and loving support.

NUMBER TWO: In the second case, another pair of Deliberators sorted things out differently. In this case, the more right-sided husband used personal insight to frankly admit that from the beginning his wife[15] never fit his expectations for a woman.

"In the '60s, [when they married] I thought women were supposed to be emotional. She never fit that model. She just wasn't the woman who'd cry in public or in private. She wouldn't react emotionally. She wouldn't confront me. When I blew up in the first year we were married, she laughed. It was really deflating. When we'd argue, she wouldn't react. If she cried, she'd go in the bathroom. If I came home with a new idea, she wouldn't say anything."

He doesn't add how that hurt at the time, nor how he resented it. No matter; they never discussed it. They just moved on. They lived the Marriage Model.

After all those years of raising a family, when the kids were gone their purpose for being together had seemingly come to an end. A *Time Zero* crisis—a whole new life, with new decisions—was evident in the marriage. He wanted out. He was "suppressing" his feelings; because, he learned, he (along with his wife) hated conflict and confrontation.[16] The tough things had gone unsaid over three decades. That is why indirect, sniping putdowns were hurled when they were in the safety of social settings—to leave him "feeling emasculated"—but he let them pass. The two were physically distant most of the time, if you get my drift. He wanted warmth and closeness, available only, it seemed, in fantasy or with someone else.

Four things happened:

- He learned about *BrainStyles* and discovered they were both Deliberators. But far more importantly, that he'd been expecting her to be a Conciliator all those years!

- They went to counseling and began to really open up, to discuss what was unsaid. Since he was the more introspective of the two, and the more dominant of the pair, he led the way. She followed, sharing her resentments of all those years when he put the job first, the kids next, and her, she felt, last. They learned about one another's deeper feelings, and more importantly, that sharing them didn't explode into emotional hysteria; it actually helped clear the air and promote healing. This openness allowed a return to, and new appreciation for, their real values of the structured and traditional family life they each held dear.

- She took a clear and unwavering look at whether she would like a life on her

---

15. As in the first case, a left-sided Deliberator.
16. He discovered this by learning about his *BrainStyle* strengths and non-strengths.

own and weighed staying versus leaving. Given her *brainstyle*, she looked at the matter unflinchingly, thoroughly, practically, and in terms of the relationship she would be leaving. She decided to commit to the marriage, on her own, in her own time, with no guarantees.

• He returned to his church and its principles after "letting [them] slide" for a number of years. She went, too, and enjoyed the social life, the sharing, and the mutual bond it created for them. Gradually she rediscovered her own faith.

After making her decision, she then truly committed to do whatever it would take to stay and make it work with him, including the marriage counseling and the conversations it provoked. She tried some of the things her husband valued, like more touching, more talking, a renewal of faith—and *liked* them. A lot.

A SIMPLE CHANGE IN PERCEPTION was the miracle that transformed their relationship into a partnership. With the new openness, they both were willing to look at what they valued in the other. Neither required the other to change; they each looked anew for what the other brought that demonstrated love for the other; i.e. her planning and organizing, that he had previously compared to his Conciliator ideal's and labeled as "anal," he now saw as the demonstration of love and commitment that it was.

Thus the happy ending. Thus the feeling of a "second honeymoon," where the wife says they communicate now as never before, where she actually stops cooking ("I always saw it as an interruption before") and *loves* the hugs and kisses she is greeted with. "It's really nice," she says in a voice still amazed—perhaps at what she'd missed for so long. They are closer than ever before, companions of long standing, tender lovers, and spiritual partners, who value their family and their faith as the true center of their lives. Can there be a greater treasure?

A DELIBERATOR COUPLE WHO REBUILT THEIR PARTNERSHIP FROM THE INSIDE. By years, they are mature. In partnering, they are beginners. They were friends who fell in love and married. She had been a single, working mom for a decade; he had never married. He was the successful restaurateur, the high roller with the big bankroll. In the heightened state of the new romance with all its attendant chemistry, they had, in addition to merging homes and creating a new family with two children, each started new businesses.

Although bumpy and busy, things seemed to be under control until, about eighteen months in, she looked up and saw that her beloved had become a couch potato, zoned out, using TV rather than her willing ear as his stress-reliever. The new family, especially the teenaged daughter, were left to their own devices while new Dad immersed himself in the History Channel. They all had more stress, and, worse yet, there was no real family to lean on. The first to express the strain was the teenaged daughter. Angry and rebellious, she was openly resentful of her stepdad. Mom was patting and patching. Dad, unbeknownst to everyone, was losing his new restaurant, a new and terrifying experience for him.

THE FOUNDATION. Looking back, there were some fundamentals handled prior to their marriage that were essential, that normally might be overlooked. This couple initially resolved issues which, had they not, would have surely split them apart with all the strain at the time.

1. They began their marriage with counseling that included a prenuptial agreement. The legal document is not nearly as important as how she defined it: the contract acted as a device requiring each partner to define and confront personal measures of fairness in sharing responsibilities. They allocated payments and duties based on their clear agreements about income and newly defined parental roles. Thus, these daily issues did not become a source of tension for them.

2. They went to church together and shared a faith. Couples who do this have a purpose greater than their own whims and comforts, which in turn gives a bigger context to their marriage when difficulties arise. (Some couples create their own discussions about the future, go to marriage retreats, or out into nature to accomplish this same vision.)

3. The parents shared a happy social life, enjoyed laughter together, and had a real friendship.

FIRST STEPS TO HEALING. Gazing at her beloved ensconced on the sofa, our heroine asked herself a very serious question: "Do I want this [marriage]?" Testing her commitment, she came up with a strong yes. This isn't always the answer. A Yes means you're in position to lead in healing the relationship. A No might just propel the same thing in a different way. She then asked herself another question: "Do I want to live like THIS for the next ten years?" Oh, no, she did not.

It is worthwhile to note those two questions she asked herself.

Given their *brainstyles*,[17] her strategy for addressing their problems was more than appropriate. She was sensitive, used timing, and incorporated key elements important to the Deliberator *brainstyle* the world over.[18]

ATTEND TO THE SETTING. Having learned that the very worst thing to do was to talk about big problems at bedtime, she used this guideline to make her

---

17. She is a right-sided Deliberator, he is a Deliberator.
18. Knowers, Conceptors, and Conciliators might only use elements of this approach, not being so keenly able to address all the specifics in the environment, and not caring as much about it as the Deliberator *brainstyle*. However, these other *brainstyles* might just take note.

request for a future discussion, NOT a current problem review. Nonetheless, she wanted an intimate, non-threatening setting in which to pose her problem-solving idea, one in which there was touching and privacy.

MAKING THE REQUEST. According to John Gottman of the University of Washington ("the love-lab doctor"), the key to successful resolution of conflict for women partners is the gentleness of the request for action. She made her request in the softness and intimacy of their bedroom, when she felt safest and he the most reassured. The setting itself, she said, prompted a loving idea.

"Honey, I want to go on a date next Saturday night to talk about how things are going in the family." They both knew things were stressed to the max.

"Oh?"

"Not now, but on our date."

"OK."

The "date" had romantic and private connotations. The advance notice, she said, allowed each of them to think ahead, and as issues arose during the week, allowed them to add them to what they'd "discuss on our date," creating an agenda without pressure of having to think of a solution right now.

THE PROBLEM-SOLVING CONVERSATION. Her approach to the potentially explosive issues between them was gentle, wise, and instructive. Here are the highlights.

- **PUT THE PROBLEM IN THE PAST:** "We didn't plan this last year very well, what with each of us starting a business along with a family."
- **CREATE A CONSTRUCTIVE CONTEXT:** "We both have a lot to learn from this."
- **ASK FOR SOLUTIONS IN THE FUTURE:** "How can we go forward and do it better?" She then listed some of the problem areas she thought they should address after this groundwork had set the stage for learning together, rather than blaming.

Because of their *brainstyles*, this gentle step-by-step process was the perfect way to look at their issues. Other *brainstyles* will use different, though no less effective, methods of raising issues that matter between the couple. Our heroine used several communications techniques that will matter especially to the *brainstyle* that is so aware and sensitive to how things are said.

- **NO I-YOU SENTENCES.** "I can really get a fight going when I start with 'You-this' and 'You-that.' 'We' makes all the difference *when I mean it*" [emphasis added]. She added that the "I-You" opening was clearly a blaming, attacking approach (to her and her husband).[19]
- **MAKE THE PROBLEM EXTERNAL.** To reduce the threat, move the problem outside the two of you, so you both can address it as partners.

USE TIMING. For two Deliberators who both need airtime, the timing within the conversation is as crucial as the timing used to raise the question. The airtime allows ease over time to reach a decision, rather than to feel the pressure of *Time Zero,* which can be very stressful for this *brainstyle.*

"When there's repetition and frustration in the conversation and you're just going over the same things again, I take it as a sign of not being heard, so I just stop. I might tell him what I heard him say at that point. Sometimes we just take a time out. What's most important is to not interrupt, no matter what. When we start interrupting, I know it's a 'hot button.' That's when it's even more important to listen . . . which I find difficult, but then I can demand my turn [to be listened to], too."

BRAINSTYLE CLUE: No matter the *brainstyle,* the *intention* to resolve an issue respectfully and caringly will create the words. The music of the conversation always trumps the words.

Interruptions and emotional explosions as well as verbal attacks are signals for you to use timing with the other: more listening, more questions, more rapid logic, or a time out, depending on your *brainstyle.*

THE RESOLUTION. Their decisions were collaborative in the way that the Deliberator *brainstyle* is collaborative: sharing elements of each part of the solution. Additionally, they used a third party, a marriage counselor, to follow through on their plan to work more effectively together. When open to this input, there are many advantages to the imaginative, analytical pair who can explore every story, every conversation, every reference, and detour to avoid the conflict and lose the point. A counselor or coach can provide a safe and focused setting that moves the couple forward by re-framing conflicts to neutral solutions they can live with. Any

---

19. Although this is true for most of the population of Deliberators and Conciliators, it should be noted that the more left-brained use this method to get at the cause of the problem and do not see it as blame.

couple with the same *brainstyle* can profit from having another *brainstyle* assist them in their thinking. Deliberators are especially able to get to a solution sensibly by learning, improving, and—at their best—ensuring they openly discuss thoughts and feelings.

THEIR RESOLUTION: GIVING UP PERFECTION, ACCEPTING *WHAT IS*. They reached some solutions that are also worth learning from, given the prevalence of the Venus-Mars thinking when it comes to partnerships today.

He realized that he had idealized the role each of his new family members should play *if everything worked the way it should,* especially his own role as the new stepdad, whose job was to install and maintain the perfect family. Perfectionism: The curse of the Deliberator. After discussing his killer fantasy openly, he was able to release it, and he became much more open, forgiving, less tense, more available as a dad and husband; he watched less TV, created a more caring relationship with his stepdaughter, and had a whole lot more fun with his wife.

She realized that she couldn't fix everything—as she had assumed she should do as a single mom, provider, business owner, and sensitive, organized Deliberator. Part of their solution was to work together to save her husband's ailing business. The intimacy they faced on the job was true firefighting in which he, the always successful financial whiz whose worth was reflected by the bottom line, had to admit vulnerability and (groan) the need for another. She had to learn to be a partner without trying to control the outcomes the way *she* would have done things; to be a supporter, without taking on all the problems; and to be a wife who needed to express her caring for an often-despondent husband overwhelmed, facing *Time Zero* situations minute by minute, day by day, without making him feel less or stupid. "I walked on eggshells a lot, afraid to say the wrong thing. I learned that his venting was not my problem. He was vulnerable, accountable, and confronting failure for the first time in his life. I told him; 'We're a team. We'll get through this together.'"

And they did. Today, only a few months later, she says, they have a "solid marriage," a happy, loving family, and are having great times as a couple exploring the true joys of traveling and growing together. Business is in perspective. They have new plans.

She says, "We never knew we could be this happy."

SECTION II:

TAKE *BrainStyles*® into Your Life

THE *BrainStyles* PARTNERSHIP PRINCIPLES

🍃 **YOU CAN'T CHANGE ANYONE,** including yourself.
Honor gifts above all; respect limitations.

🍃 **PARTNERSHIPS** are ones entered into to see what
can be given rather than gotten, from two who are
complete rather than two who seek completion.

🍃 Any relationship can be a **SPIRITUAL PARTNERSHIP**
when two minds join to seek a common, loving goal.

🍃 **NO RELATIONSHIP IS ACCIDENTAL;** its purpose
is to practice forgiveness. This is why all
relationships are precious.

🍃 **IT ONLY TAKES ONE TO HEAL A RELATIONSHIP**
and transform it into a partnership.

🍃 **A PARTNERSHIP BEGINS** as each seeks the best
within the other, rather than problems, mistakes, or
defeats, and then honors their best over time.

🍃 **EVERYONE,** with no exceptions, **IS CAPABLE OF**
creating loving **PARTNERSHIPS.**

🍃 In all situations, **LOVE IS THE ANSWER.**

CHAPTER 8

YOUR GIFTS ARE INVISIBLE TO YOU. YOUR LIMITATIONS ARE *IN YOUR FACE*

~~~~~~~~~~~~~~~~

Those who don't love themselves as they are, rarely love life as it is either. . . .
—Rachel Naomi Remen, MD, *Kitchen Table Wisdom,* 75

~~~~~~~~~~~~~~~~

YOUR CHOICE IN LIVING IS SIMPLE: love and joy by living from your gifts, or suffering.

Suffering stinks. You know this. Why not live as you were born to . . . instead of suffering by trying to be who you're supposed to be?

What follows is a way to get to real success at home and work and beyond. You start by defining, honoring, and being more yourself all the time, especially with others. Doing so will give you personal ease and a simpler, less angst-ridden life as you discover and consciously accept the Real You, the loving, wise you. Partnerships are a joy when entered from this powerful, accepting, inner place.

THE DESIRE TO BE SPECIAL. Using the left brain to measure and compare makes us human. Our humanity at times is defined by a feeling of isolation, of being better or less than, and an underlying conclusion that we're special. *Special,* when you think about it from this angle, is the same as *alone.* One of a kind. The one no one understands or can relate to. Add competition to the equation, and we want to be special by winning. If we can't be the best, then at the very least we want to be *better than her,* the apple of Mom's eye. The innocent one. The most humble. The winner with the most toys. The one with the most heartbreaking story.

This desire is always rooted in a feeling of being incomplete and not good enough. Its solution is found, without exception, in something or someone outside to fill the inner hollow. Parents are the first targets for meeting this need, which is why our relationships with our parents are often so central to other relationships. We make our first mistakes with them, and we tend to repeat them until we learn the lessons the relationship has to teach us. The ego drives a constant need for recognition of just how unique we are. Receiving attention for how we perform can build confidence as defined by left-brained measures, but it never completes us by filling our souls with love for who we are. No, it is the right brain that makes a spiritual connection with others and the universe, without words, that fills us and knows—yet doesn't know how it knows. That feeling, reduced to self-esteem in the vernacular, doesn't go away. The knowledge that we are whole and complete just as we are is the rock upon which we stand in families and as lovers, to face illness, death, and failure. It is what we take from this life.

The demand to be special breaks apart families with fights over money, control, or who said what to whom. We want to be special, and so we experience jealousy, competition, or rage. We cheat, fudge the numbers, or blame our sister for what we messed up. All these behaviors are grounded in fear, fear that we are inadequate. Our guilt over our mistakes propels blame and shame. Anger is merely the mechanism to temporarily put the monkey on someone else's back. The result is desolation; the winner is the ego.

THE INTEGRATION OF LEFT- AND RIGHT-BRAIN ABILITIES. To think with our natural abilities, our own genius and wisdom, and draw from those of our lovers requires the most powerful energy in the universe to unite internal and external contradictions, to expand our thinking in all situations and at all times. It is accessible every minute and lies but a decision away to direct our hardware to be at its most potent, transcending human limitations. Using it, we create miracles, health, scientific breakthroughs, and transformations.

The power of which I speak is love.

To use your hardware with love increases its power exponentially.

To be an "ordinary person doing extraordinary things" is to be willing to give up being special by claiming credit, to "say you're sorry when you know you're right" (according to a 78-year-old grandmother). It is showing up at your high school reunion and demonstrating just how much you care about everyone else and their lives by listening intently, and when asked what you do for a living by a successful attorney/former classmate, sharing just how much joy you get by being the manager of a mobile home park with no hint of self-deprecation.

Getting over trying to be special allows laughter. Closeness. It begins with forgiving yourself for not being who you were supposed to be, for not being better than someone else, for just being you, "fat thighs and all," as Leo Buscaglia once said.

In any given day we can move to and fro, from accepting to snarling, from wisdom to pettiness, from deeply wanting to be special to certainty in how perfect everything is just as it is. We forget that we are choosing where we go.

BEYOND THE BRAIN: WHO YOU TRULY ARE. Have you ever stopped to consider what it is that causes your thoughts? What it is that pays attention, engaging those specialized parts of the brain to light up the PET scans just as the arm is instructed to throw the ball?

The essence that is *you* is the author of your brain's presentation, the one making the choices to use the actions and words you do. You are not your hardware; you run it. You are not your emotions or thoughts; you are the initiator and thinker of them.

You live at the center of your being, where you are whole. The essence of you exists beyond logic, intuition, analysis, or emotion.

Your brain's job is to keep you alive. Survival and maintenance is the purpose of 80 percent of the brain, and—to be accurate—all brain activity, including thinking. Another term for the left-brained survival functions (both thinking and autonomic activity such as breathing) is Ego. The term that represents your boundless center, the right-brained part that intuits and imagines beyond your limitations, is Spirit. Ego is thus limited (as is your *brainstyle*); Spirit is limitless. Love is the language that can overcome the limitations of your *brainstyle*-based personality to allow the expression of the infinite loving Source of energy to which we have constant access.

In our daily lives, our expression of these two aspects often appear in these ways:

THE EGO	THE SPIRIT
Fears, gets angry, feels guilty, resents	Loves

THE EGO	THE SPIRIT
➤ Is arrogant, better than	• Knows its worth is the same as everyone's
➤ Is humble, self-effacing	• Is at peace, no better or lesser than another
➤ Is less than, dumber	• Is neutral
➤ Is worse than	• Is connected, joined with
➤ Is right	• Sees what is right in others
➤ Is wrong	• Learns how to be more effective
➤ Is ethical by effort	• Is loving, respectful, and ethical effortlessly
➤ Has the answer	• Knows beyond the answer
➤ Wants things	• Is filled with gratitude
➤ Gets angry	• Knows emotions are fleeting, allows them to pass
➤ Gets disappointed	• Sees an opportunity to release an expectation
➤ Fears pain	• Looks at pain as a teacher

~~~~~~~~~~~~~~~~

TAKING CHARGE. By definition, your strengths define your limitations, or "weaknesses." With *BrainStyles*, once you know your strengths, you automatically know your non-strengths:[1] They are everyone else's strengths.

Our egos want us to work in our non-strengths, motivated by fear. Earn your keep. Cover all the bases. Feel that strain. Get in control. Win.

It has been said that fear is a great motivator, especially in business. In the world of measures, fear gets us moving to survive, to avoid pain or loss. Fear works only in the short term and produces limited, ego-based thinking. Fear actually promotes inaction, a paralytic, debilitating brain-freeze before the adrenaline pumps in. Have we learned nothing by watching the motivation provided by Hitler? Stalin? Saddam Hussein? Many say that the one who can instill fear has the real power. Belief in this premise means believing that real power lies in the ego, and that we are nothing more than our survival instincts.

---

1. This term is purposely used to remind you that non-strengths are simply not your strengths, they are another's. Work in non-strengths leads to years of stress trying to improve abilities, which can never pay off as well as focusing on natural abilities.

Nonsense.

Love is the long-term, ultimate motivator: Love as joy in achieving, love as loyalty, commitment, faith, and service for others above self. Love lasts.

Our spirits know a life based on fear is unnecessary.

~~~~~~~~~~~~~~~

Well, he finally showed me his true colors.
Wow. I had no idea how he felt about me.
—A statement confided to me after a particularly big office blowup

~~~~~~~~~~~~~~~

WHAT WE FEAR. The above quote is what a client of mine said about his boss because that's what he believed: Your true self is the worst of you, your dark side, your emotional blowups, your fears expressed as labels and vicious put-downs. Have you ever felt that you didn't really know a person until you saw him at his worst?

Many of us define our "real" selves as who we fear we are: the mad, psychotic, out-of-control bitch; or the vengeful, tough winner who is left alone with the winnings, unloved. Or maybe, less dramatically, we just know we're not as good as we'd like others to think we are. We live waiting for the other shoe to drop. When it does, well, it's only our "true colors" revealing themselves at last. This is called the Imposter Syndrome, or the fear of living a lie. Think of that visible minority, the beautiful people among us—Marilyn Monroe comes to mind—who never seem to resolve their fear of being unmasked as ugly inside.

A DIFFERENT DEFINITION OF SELF. This particular client of mine was wrong. He was putting all his faith in illusions: the fleeting storms of emotions, the judgments that come and go based on those feelings. Instinctual, fearful reactions are NOT who we really are. All of us are wrong when we believe the worst about ourselves and one another. We are more than our limbic systems, which promote a fight-or-flight reaction. Our true colors are the best of ourselves as caring, problem-solving, evolved beings who invent, dream, inspire, and grow.

To love and be loved, you must start by being at peace with who you are and how you express *your* gifts.

You may gain something from others who have different strengths in order to try new things, but only if you can release expectations for perfection, only if you can release the envy that comes from a lack of self-respect for your own limitations. It is only our ego's supreme arrogance that demands we be good at everything.

CHALLENGE: RECLAIM YOUR STRENGTHS. In high school, a young girl adored her choral conductor. No one else compared, especially her mother. The girl, at fourteen, was unable to articulate why she so idolized the woman. If she could have, she would have listed the following: The teacher was definite, gave directions clearly, set a task that challenged everyone, and worked with unwavering commitment to get done a job that was clearly her life's passion. The teacher loved what she was doing so much that she wasn't afraid to take a stand for her principles, disciplining kids in the face of their anger, for example, to create fine music. Students worshipped her. Lives were touched.

The young girl had no way of knowing that her role model had no formal training. It was decades later that she found out the conductor was simply using her natural gifts to do what she loved.

The girl went through college and her twenties with the idea that if only she worked and studied hard enough, she could follow her role model. Ah, but circumstances prevented this. Her own mother told her she wasn't talented enough. A cruel blow, she felt; one that she wouldn't forgive.

In graduate school as an educator, she confided to friends that she had wasted her life and her education and would never be who she really wanted to be: a music educator and choral conductor.

Thirty-five years later, the girl, now a mature woman, who had indeed become a passionate, dedicated educator, though not in music, volunteered for a battery of tests. Included in the tests were two measures of musical ability. As she completed those musical aptitude tests, she felt smug. I've aced them, she thought to herself. I'll finally find out what I knew all along.

When given the results, she was stunned. Her results were, contrary to all the years of dreaming, blaming, and imagining, merely *average*. She cringed. *Her mother was right all along.* She thought of the courage it must have taken her musically-talented mother to tell her that she wasn't as gifted as she needed to be to pursue the field. Her adolescent reaction was not pleasant at the time, she recalled. She was left with the real challenge of forgiving herself for a lifetime of blame and regret.

Talking to a counselor about her "failure," not only in music but in her life as a whole, she began to describe her teenage idol who had such commitment, passion, and impact on so many students. Her counselor's response was even more stunning than the results of the test: "But those are all qualities *you* have, dear." The counselor then helped the former student reframe her perception of her life story of "pushiness" to the intensity it truly was; how the woman now showed her commitment to life out of a passion to give to others, and how many lives she had touched with that passion.

The woman just sat, speechless. Tears welled in her eyes. She believed the counselor. She knew it was a true and loving way to look at her life, instead of her own demeaning critical interpretation. "I never saw that before today," she said. As she allowed herself to see her gifts, she gave up one more pedestal, let go of labels she had used against herself for decades, released confusion about her career, and settled into clarity. She felt powerful. Free. Happy. And she did more and better things at home, at play, and at work. She was free to be a real partner, more confident, more whole.

The role model who has your own *brainstyle* may be your idol because you appreciate the living example of the best of *yourself* in action.[2] You can now reclaim your gifts and honor your own abilities rather than project your admiration on another. Honor gifts rather than creating role models. Stop giving another the credit or love that you deserve from yourself. Look, Ma! No therapy!

> BRAINSTYLE CLUE: Those in your own *brainstyle* can hold up a mirror to show you what you may have overlooked in yourself.
> Those in other *brainstyles* have lessons to teach you. Love them for who they are. Allow them to give you what you cannot give yourself.

MERCURY UNDER YOUR THUMB. If you're like me, you have also committed the Two Terrible Errors: first and foremost, you have overlooked your strengths, so that you could then lock on to Number Two, fixing your "weaknesses." You've listened to criticism and read books that inspired you to *change your ways!* You've sought out *role models* to show you those ways. You may have gotten so entwined in learning how to become that better person, you forgot who was doing the learning.

You may have believed those who told you that you were too much of a good thing—and that was a bad thing; that your strengths taken to extremes are your weaknesses. You've cut back. Reined in. Set goals. Gotten feedback. Tried harder. Especially in relationships that count.

You may just have lost sight of who you are. If so, your closest relationships have mysteriously blown apart or become struggles. People have disappointed you. Betrayed you. You may have walked away or failed others somehow.

---

2. Otherwise you wouldn't be able to even recognize their gifts when you see them; they would be foreign to you.

In the normal course of affairs, looking at your own life is a confusing adventure at best. "Who are you?" is a favorite question. Labels are slung at you like quarters at a slot machine. You name your gender, describe your work, your roles and responsibilities. But you can't discover your gifts until you know where to look for them.

Your gifts are like mercury under your thumb. No matter how much you try to squeeze or squish them down, shape them up, or square them off, they pop up again and again. To see them requires a new recipe, a willingness to peel away the sticky wrappers of all those books and great ideas from other people (including your family) that you've accumulated about who you *should* be.

MYSTERY . . . CHOICE . . . ADVENTURE. A very effective clue to determine whether you really have a gift or not is whether you go ahead for your own satisfaction, regardless of others' reactions, or work only for their applause.[3] Criticism is easiest to hear when you are performing in your strengths. You look forward to learning more. Criticism is hardest to take when doing something that you have taken great pains to learn and worked very hard to be good at— your non-strengths. Watch for those times when you get most defensive and argumentative. You may be arguing for something you've learned to do and want to continue to control. Or you may be unconsciously aware that you need to start applying your natural strengths instead and stop trying so hard.

Most of us are unaware that criticism, especially self-condemnation, is a pirates' map to a real treasure beneath.

For the last fifteen years, my professional work has been to research and write about people's natural gifts and how to take them into the world with care, confidence, and impact. In the process, I am beginning to uncover my own gifts and wrest them from the language of fear and criticism to the more accurate descriptions of strengths and non-strengths. I was the girl who idolized her music teacher. Now I am left with the belief that we all teach what we most need to learn, that we "fall into" careers and persist in seeking opportunities to be who we were born to be. Our natural gifts are waiting to be named as such, applied, and celebrated. Sometimes it isn't easy to make the shift, being the sensitive social animals that we are. Both Frank Lloyd Wright, the most famous architect of the twentieth century, and Buckminster Fuller, the inventor and philosopher, had to retreat from everyday life for years and live alone. Each man

---

3. Authors Dunn, Dunn, and Treffinger in *Bringing Out the Giftedness in Your Child* (©1992, Wiley & Sons) cite creativity, motivation to learn more, and sustained interests which stay important for weeks, months, or years as true indicators of natural gifts.

said that he sought to *think his own thoughts in his own way*. Their retreats led to continual breakthroughs for the rest of their careers in their chosen fields.

Have you ever noticed that people who prize their physical beauty work to maintain it all their lives? The "Bob Hope Generation" of movie stars, which may include Joan Rivers, keeps looking beautiful no matter how much surgery it takes. Sophia Loren, prizing her spirit, keeps beautiful by continually celebrating herself as she is. I believe that when you recognize your gifts, you want to maintain them. You are proud of them. When you name your gifts, you name a highway into the future on which you'll enjoy cruising. When you enjoy the ride, others want to join you.

~~~~~~~~~~~~~~~~

Mom had it right. Pretty is as pretty does.
Happiness and wealth are inside. If this weren't true, all the
beautiful people would be the happiest, and all the richest people
would be the wisest. Knowing about your inner
gifts will prevent feeling like you're an imposter,
worthless except for your looks.
Look past your outside to the magnificence inside.

~~~~~~~~~~~~~~~~

By owning your gifts, your uniqueness can express itself naturally, lovingly, to allow you to excel rather than protect or demean yourself. And that, of course, is the larger purpose for your existence, to put your *brainstyle* abilities in service of a Grander Design, a Life Mission based on love instead of fear, guilt, competition, or anxiety.

OWN YOUR STRENGTHS. Here are some challenges that may assist you to find your own way home.

GETTING TO KNOW YOU = GETTING TO KNOW ME. I was appalled. First she was late to class, and now here she was criticizing everything about my work. "What a bitch," I thought. "Who does she think she is? She's just embarrassed and taking it out on someone else." Before I could do anything about it, I was reliving my own little troublesome adventure of some days before. There I was, thoroughly disgusted with the efforts of a man who had just delivered his product to me. And I told him so. I must have sounded just like she sounds right now, I thought.

Ever have a flashback like this? Were you as uncomfortable as I was with the realization?

We all know just how difficult, annoying, and testy those *other* guys can be who think, act, and speak so differently. But what of those people that we instantly relate to . . . and later recoil from? What if, oh nightmare of nightmares, we have made friends, found things in common, verify that they have the same approach to so many things, until Something Important occurs and they do all the wrong things? Worse, you see that they do all the things you have forever told yourself not to do?

Your Evil Twin has manifested right before your eyes.

That other may be your twin because they have the same *brainstyle* you have.

The gift—and it is one—of living or working with the same *brainstyle* is to hear your own foibles, see your own fumbles, and experience the impact of your own living, breathing righteousness, fastidiousness, arrogance, or impulsiveness, or whatever lessons you have left to learn. Here you are, looking on aghast at how silly or ineffective or defensive that other person is. Then the showstopper: That's how *I* must look, how *I* must sound. EGADS. They say things that make you cringe. Echoes of your own words come clanging back, things you'd much prefer to forget that were said and felt. Like a reflex, you might think, "But I'm past that now." I don't know about you, but when I've heard someone say, "I'm past that now," I've had to blink hard to stop my eyes from rolling ceilingward. I now remind myself that I know better. I remind myself I can learn from the annoying or smug ones. I note that people who learn from those others rather than think they're better or worse are more mature, more self-confident. They are natural and wise teachers, loving partners. So are you.

Question: If the blaming tactics of the other, his demands for attention, his defensiveness were not still part of your own repertoire, would you have the stomach-churning reaction you have when you see it in him?

Question: Those resolutions you make to never, ever do _____ the way she just did, do they ever stick?

Question: Can you look in your own eyes in the mirror without blinking? Can you see below the surface?

Or what about this: What if you actually admire the other person who turns out to have your same gifts? What of that shining example in front of you, the Good Twin, the Role Model?

Can you meet him or her eye-to-eye without a twinge of envy? Can you work together side by side without backing off the expression of your own abilities just one bit? Or do you watch and take mental note of how to incorporate her moves into your own repertoire just as she does it, so that you can move one notch closer to perfection?

Can you look into your own soul with loving acceptance and forgiveness for not being who you idealize?

I work with someone who, with the same *brainstyle* gift as mine, is so spontaneously nurturing, so warm, so automatically open and inclusive that she continually turns potential messes into constructive events. I am awestruck at times to think that I, too, have similar gifts and cannot imagine that I express them as ably and lovingly as she does.

CHALLENGE: DEALING WITH YOUR MIRROR. You may have already realized that my feelings about both my Evil and Good Twins are remarkably similar. I lose in all cases with my comparisons.

Comparisons confuse. Comparisons cause suffering. Comparisons create conflict, interfere with relationships, and prevent intimacy.

After some reflection, the truth of the mirror images dawns. In those moments of feeling less or more, I am not at all able to be my best. It is only when I release my comparisons that the smallness of my position evaporates and I recapture my gifts and myself. I can just relax. I can face any companion with love and respect. The flaws I see in another and feel gut-wrenchingly guilty about can be reevaluated in the context of *brainstyle* gifts. "Mistakes" are learning opportunities, when using a loving acceptance to define the gifts that prompt them. Actions are easier, with less defensiveness. The love and mutual regard I seek are miraculously present everywhere I look.

Centering on my gifts (rather than my lacks), there have been fewer mistakes and more wins, more personal and professional clarity. I see Evil Twins (former enemies and people I'd avoid) as simply others who know not what they do, what they have, who they truly are, and so are being as mean to others as they are to themselves. They need love, not correction. Focusing on who I am at my best, I am far more able to be a true partner with those who might have been idols or role models. I am free to use all my intelligence in the moment without trying to please or say it right.

CHALLENGE: DEALING WITH "WEAKNESSES." I don't believe in weaknesses. They sound like things to strengthen. You can't. You have strengths and non-strengths. Startling, I know. But stay with me.

There are lots of ways of dealing with the things we're not good at doing. We put them off. We just plain don't do them. We defend and excuse why we don't do them as well as we do other things; we get mad about being corrected when we've tried so hard to get them right; we get frustrated and call ourselves morons and feel ashamed. We get stressed, work harder and longer, and begin to hate the job and whoever we are doing it for. (Thus the burnout, the tirades about not being APPRECIATED, the demands we make.) We do all these things and sometimes make ourselves ill with our stress.

In this state a loving relationship is nigh impossible.

A woman I'll call Marcy was pacing around my office, sometimes shouting, sometimes crying. She was trying to describe why she was so tied up in knots when dealing with her financially gifted brother. The details took hours to explain and are irrelevant here, but suffice it to say that the hard-charging, capable woman so used to problem-solving was reduced to pudding because she couldn't seem to apply any of her gifts in a tangle of family, lawyers, and financial advisors. Her strengths lay elsewhere, in the realm of the personal: the land of the free and the home of the troubled, whom she would counsel and advise. It was her turn to be counseled now, and she was terribly uncomfortable. Worse, her relationship with her brother was suffering badly. They had stopped speaking.

How could she turn this around? She had spent days reading about and trying to understand the sophisticated legal/financial tangle. Suddenly her brother's interests did not seem to coincide with hers. Where could she turn? Would this mean the end of a relationship with her family? How could they iron out differences when it took a flair with figures that was beyond her scope?

The act of admitting your non-strengths can slip around on the sliding scale of difficulty from frustration to depression depending upon your personal stake in the issue. Marcy had such a personal stake in her family relationships that it was a doozy of an admission for her. She feared that if she admitted she couldn't handle these matters, well, she would be left out of family decisions forevermore.

> *BRAINSTYLE CLUE:* Your non-strengths are merely the strengths of another *brainstyle*.

Her answers included getting clear on her strengths and how she could apply them in the most caring way to the situation (no small chore when she was as scared and frustrated as she was). She also had to forgive herself for not being as gifted as her brother financially, forgive him for using his gifts "against her," as she first saw it, and move to a *reframed* perception that saw him as someone doing his best to apply his gifts that supplemented her own. She admitted she needed help, which is often the very last refuge of the overachiever when confronting non-strengths. She hired the services of a financial consultant with considerable experience in legal matters to talk things over and often speak on her behalf so that she no longer had to deal with the toughest details in her non-strengths, but she still maintained a responsible, informed opinion on major decisions. Finally, she then applied, over the course of more than a year, a *BrainStyles Strengths Contract®* in which she came to value and act upon what each of the family members brought to the family. This was the foundation that was missing for her. She could use timing to build on the strengths of each of them.

~~~~~~~~~~~~~~~~

The real source of any conflict is within.
Upsets occur when there is a difference between who you know you truly are
and what you are doing.
This conflict is then projected out onto the world as a view of reality.
Expectations for self and others cannot be met until who you are and what you are
doing align.
Thus, no one at peace within can experience conflict without.[4]

~~~~~~~~~~~~~~~~

LIVING FROM LOVE. THE PAYOFFS. Our purpose in living is formed by our response to events, not determined by them, and that purpose is created moment by moment as we discover the joy of how to be who we truly are and share our loving selves with others.

Here is what the new scientists are saying, in contradiction to the behaviorists of the last fifty years:

> . . . understanding that it is innate seems to help to cure it. One trio of therapists reading about the new results emerging from genetics switched from trying to treat their clients' shyness to trying to make them content with whatever their innate predispositions were. They

---

4. Adapted from *A Course In Miracles,* Foundation for Inner Peace, ©1976.

found that it worked. The clients felt relieved to be told that their personality was a real, innate part of them and not just a bad habit they had got into . . . giving group members permission to be the way they are seemed to constitute the best insurance that their self-esteem and interpersonal effectiveness would improve. . . . . Far from being a sentence, the realization of innate personality is often a release.
—Matt Ridley, *Genome* (HarperCollins, 2000)

Just since the turn of the century, "progress has been brisk," according to a *Newsweek* cover article in 2002, "The Science of Happiness," on the latest psychological discipline that studies and elevates happiness. The following quote from the article is a maxim for lovers:

The happiest lovers are not the most realistic but the most positive.
They idealize their partners and expect their relationships to survive hard times.
—Martin P. Seligman, *Authentic Happiness,* ©2002, Free Press

A book featured in the article and written by University of Pennsylvania psychologist Martin Seligman declares, "The time has arrived for a science that seeks to understand positive emotion . . ." The article notes that Seligman is just one of many of the "new positive psychologists [who] have amassed a heap of data on what people who deem themselves happy have in common." Summarizing the research on happiness, the article notes what the latest research has proven: "Lesson one is that mood and temperament have a large genetic component." Our hardware determines "emotional set points" for our lives. "Even paraplegics and lottery winners typically return to their baselines once they've had six months to adjust to their sudden change of fortune."[5]

Lesson two, the article continues, "is that our circumstances in life have precious little to do with the satisfaction we experience. Married churchgoers tend to outscore single nonbelievers in happiness surveys, but health, wealth, good looks, and status have astonishingly little effect on what the researchers call 'subjective well-being'. . . [G]reater wealth stops making life richer. . . . In America," notes Hope College psychologist David Myers, "real income has doubled since 1960. We're twice as likely to own cars . . . eat out . . . yet our divorce rate has doubled, teen suicide has tripled, and depression has increased tenfold."[6]

---

5. Geoffrey Cowley, *Newsweek,* September 16, 2002, 46.
6. Ibid., 48.

So, since fixing your circumstances doesn't work, what does? Psychologist Seligman challenges us to outgrow "our obsessive concern with how we feel." Emotions, like the waves on the ocean, come and go, splash, and make waves. Seligman asks people to go beyond mere pleasure to "the enduring fulfillment that comes from developing one's strengths and putting them to positive use." As an example, he cites one of the widows of the 9/11 attack on the World Trade Centers, who restored "meaning and even some joy to her life." She raised money in her husband's name to sponsor a lifesaving heart operation for an infant whose family couldn't afford it. "When asked who had fixed the [infant] boy's heart, [her] beaming three-year-old answered, 'Everyone who loved Daddy.'"

The happiest among us are triumphing over their circumstances by doing something with a grander purpose than honoring their fleeting emotions. They are making a contribution with their strengths and love.

~~~~~~~~~~~~~~~~

A CHALLENGE, A PAYOFF. Recently in a *BrainStyles* seminar the leader presented the following quote from my second book:

> *Your job in life is not to learn how to be different [or better]; it's to spend more time realizing, and living from the best that's already within. The difference between people who "realize their potential" and those who don't is not the amount of the potential, but the amount of permission they give themselves to use it.*[7]

Linda[8] asked the class what their lives would be like if they were to live from that premise. Silence. Finally a woman said, "Scary." Why? A man, a very successful executive, answered, "What if you really did pull out all the stops? What if you could *really* succeed?" The look on his face told it all. He would find it very hard indeed to unbutton and stop working at being "professional"; i.e., his idea of what an executive should act like.

Then another woman spoke. "I think it would give you peace. I see living like that as living in peace."

You are making those same choices each day.

---

7. *BrainStyles™: Change Your Life Without Changing Who You Are*℠ (Simon & Schuster, 1997) p49.
8. Linda Bush, MA, Master Facilitator of *The BrainStyles System*.®

A reminder:

I don't have to be perfect,

I just have to be me.

CHAPTER

9

CREATING A PARTNERSHIP: THE FUNDAMENTALS

~~~~~~~~~~~~~~~

What the caterpillar calls the end of the world,
the master calls a butterfly.
—Richard Bach

~~~~~~~~~~~~~~~

WHERE TO START AND END: LOVE INSTEAD OF FEAR. A newly-wed commented on what she wanted to change in her new marriage: "We have similar energy, but our timing's way off. We have fights about nothing. We see negative qualities in one another that we hate in ourselves." In these simple, insightful sentences, she had defined the only thing she'll ever need to fix: her fears about herself, disowned and projected upon her partner. She just didn't know it then. The same goes for you. You don't look for your own wisdom, because you overlook your gifts; your attention is on what embarrasses, annoys, distracts, and should be changed and improved. You hate these things in yourself, but rather than own them, it's easier to attack your partner's flaws. You don't take time to see your partner except as someone whose job it is to make you feel better. You're on the Task Train, crossing off the To-Do's on your Fix or Improve List.

~~~~~~~~~~~~~~~

Marriage is a fundamental social institution. It is central to the nurture and raising of children. It is the "social glue" that reliably attaches fathers to children. It contributes to the physical, emotional, and economic health of men, women, and children, and thus to the nation as a whole. It is also one of the most highly prized of all human relationships and a central life goal of most Americans.
—David Popenoe, Barbara D. Whitehead, "The State of Our Unions:
The Social Health of Marriage in America 2002," research report,
©2002, Rutgers University, The National Marriage Project

~~~~~~~~~~~~~~~

Why do we get so scared to commit to another? What ends relationships? Why is love said to be painful? What separates people, whether friends, lovers, or family? One favorite explanation I often hear is "People change."

I don't believe people change, nor do they need to.[1] Lasting relationships are not built upon the expectation of change in your lover.

THE INEVITABLE DESIRE TO CHANGE HIM. In my twenty-three-year marriage, after our early years of setting aside time to Communicate[2] for hours (and hours) to get him to say things as I wanted to hear them, I finally concluded that the reason we fought was that one of us wanted the other to change, to talk and do things in the way that would make the other comfortable. In my case, the way I would do them. Or, even better, the way that the mythical Everyone Else's Husband does things.

Not going to happen. The more I wanted him to be who I wanted him to be, the less I got from the relationship I had. There had to be a better way.

~~~~~~~~~~~~~~~

*". . . Divorce?" he said. "Divorce is about the little things,
the apple core in the ashtray, the toilet paper put on backwards again."*
—Statement by a sorrowful, recently divorced man on why he
"finally had to get out" of his marriage

~~~~~~~~~~~~~~~

If two people get to the place where they can look past the little things, they'll get to the big things, the things that matter for each of them, deeply and forever.

---

1. The influence of our genetics increases as we age. We become more of ourselves, incorporating the wisdom of the lessons we've learned. We mature, we don't change. (Based on work by Rutter and Rutter, *Developing Minds* (Basic Books, 1993).
2. Of *course* we worked at communication; I had taught the subject for years.

Giving up trying to change, improve, or adapt to others is difficult for most of us who are in the middle of the Bell curve. People with genius or, conversely, disabilities, can't help but focus on their strengths. It's us, the "normal" ones, who have the biggest challenge: How can we sort through all our options, hopes, possibilities, and parents' expectations to choose the best path?

ONE CHALLENGE FOR LOVERS: STOP FOCUSING ON NON-STRENGTHS OF YOUR PARTNERS. She's reading a romance novel. The hero is sensitive (he focuses intensely on the heroine) but tough (he beats up the bad guys), charming, very sexy, highly ethical, and strong enough to protect her (he lifts weights and sweats a lot in a manly, yet intensely alluring, manner before punching the villain). The love scenes in the book, described in scintillating detail, leave the reader aroused, and, this time, annoyed. Her husband has no clue about how to make love like the hero. In fact, the list of comparisons is running off her mental page: his inattention (he changes the subject to his own problems when she tries to tell him about hers) and his indecisiveness—not to mention his absolute cluelessness about anything she considers romantic. She reaches the inevitable conclusion. The thrill is not only gone, there is a vacuum (cleaner) where it used to be. He couldn't possibly love her. Worse, she probably doesn't love him anymore. She (sigh) merely tolerates him.

Concentrating on what she doesn't have and can't see, she dismisses her husband's tenderness in their intimate moments, the depth of feeling he shows in those times when no one else would really understand. She is setting aside how he continually demonstrates his protectiveness by solving family problems with his time, analysis, and concentration, how he celebrates her wins, cares about what she cares about.

He goes to his thirtieth high school reunion after all these years. Surprise! His high school sweetheart is, amazingly, much better looking, more mature, more vibrant, more excited by him—the way she looks at him!—than she was thirty-some years ago. "Whoa. Not like the little wife at home," he thinks. Okay, his wife has been loyal and a good mom, but she always has problems to solve, reminders of obligations. His wife is *work*. This gal is pure fun. Also pure fantasy. He "feels like a man" when he talks to her at this party; suddenly he's 18 again in a 47-year-old body.

He is blanking out the intimate laughter he has had over the years about things he and his wife have shared together. He is erasing the thrill he gets when she takes his arm and shares the victories they have with the kids, the grief of loss borne together a day at a time, when she was stronger than he would have imagined. He is dismissing the incomparable beauty of her in her unguarded moments when he catches her just so, those looks they share that say worlds of knowing one another.

Each of these people is focusing on his or her own fleeting feelings, the loss they feel because they expect another to fix those feelings, only to become depressed by their comparisons. What a swamp.

Overlooking your own strengths or those of your partner to focus on your non-strengths is a double whammy. You focus on a fearful reality and overlook the love available right in front of you. By doing so, you'll bust up the friendship, stop speaking, divorce, and change the will. You'll feel alone in the midst of company, dissatisfied with your love life, depressed with how the kids turned out, and alienated from your parents and siblings.

NEXT CHALLENGE: LET GO OF YOUR OWN BARRIERS TO LOVE. When we see another as the cause of our problems, we give up our power, our wisdom, and our peace, not to mention the basis for love of any kind.

What about Dad and all those mean things he did and said? If we forgave him, would we have to give up hauling out the Guilt Card, enjoy him as he is and, what, have a good time? What fun would THAT be? What might we have to look at next? Our own problems? Our own gifts and limitations? *Oh no!* The best way to stay on top of things is to get mad. Keep that distance. Maintain control.

Deep within, you know there is a better way. That is why ultimately, right or wrong, we will feel guilt for attacking another. *Every time we get angry, we choose to trade in love for being right—blaming another to create distance.* Guilt then undermines our self-confidence and esteem. We cannot be at peace, the defining state of love.

There are three barriers within us that we use to keep from being loving.

1. **WE REALLY DON'T WANT TO BE PEACEFUL.** Let's face it, what would we do if we forgave Susie for ruining the evening and started to speak to her again? Wouldn't it be embarrassing to admit we made such a fuss in the first place? People at peace can't be President, get the best sales figures, or win the tennis tournament, can they? Peacefulness must mean doing nothing, being wimpy, a pushover. The real fear of being whole, at peace, is to surrender the identity your ego has such an investment in protecting: achiever, author, breadwinner, single guy who won't be tied down, one of the abused, whatever. To even want to be peaceful, we need to remember what it is—and choose it. It is the identity of our real self and the foundation for a true partnership.

2. **WE MAKE THE BODY THE SOURCE OF OUR REALITY.** The body and all its hardware is indeed a miraculous thing. The reality it processes, however, is a perception of what the senses gather and the brain interprets, a mere fraction of the data available outside of us. Neuroscientists have measured that we register about 1/100th per second of what is in our environment. Their conclusion: We create our own reality. We interpret it to be painful or pleasurable. Descartes' conclusion, "I think therefore I am" asserts that our sensory awareness proves we exist. We extrapolate this to mean that because we are aware of emotions, pain, and pleasure, this sensory process defines us; i.e., we are created by our environment and what it registers upon our hardware. This fundamental error in self-definition creates the basis for most of what we do to keep from being in love and at peace within. The body is not the source of our reality, it is merely the hardware that expresses our spirit, or soul, or essence (whatever term you like), to allow it to operate in this world of measures and time. We arrive having wisdom far greater than we could ever gain in a lifetime.

Just learning how to speak and read are computing feats that are nearly incomprehensible. Our bodies must be taught; but our wisdom is already there, waiting for us to access it. Attachment to the body is the false promise of the ego—whose job it is to survive, and in doing so offers the false hope of living well and happily by having beautiful skin, full leather interior, lots of sex, and money to keep us safe. Problem: The body dies. No matter what. All the gorgeousness of the body and its accessories is a dead end. Spirit, expressed in love and realized with inner peace, never ends. The two different realities are mutually exclusive and distinct. Learning to hear the messages of love from within, rather than the seductive whispers of our fears for survival in our society, is the most challenging job of our lives. In doing so, we can see a whole new reality filled with opportunity and gifted people who are lovable. We feel worth loving. It takes a constant willingness to shift your vision from the ego's definition of reality to one that looks for and honors the best, most loving reality. This takes far more courage, far more strength than it does to react with our emotions.

3. **THE FEAR OF LOVE.** The ultimate obstacle in life is a fear of living from love, free and at peace, with no reason to get mad or care what people think. To offer your very best as an expression of that love, rather than to win. You may be thinking, Whoa, just look what happens to people who do that! When we listen to this fear, we lose the lesson that spiritual leaders

like Jesus, Buddha, Mohammed, Gandhi, and Martin Luther King Jr. were teaching in such a dramatic way: The loving spirit within us transcends the body and its accomplishments. The emergency workers who raced into the World Trade Center and the Pentagon were, no doubt, fueled by love for others, overcoming fear for self. Each of us is capable of this kind of love; we demean it by calling those who exhibit it "heroes," setting them apart from the rest of us wimps. Not true. WE EACH have this capacity, all the time, everywhere. Those who realize it are as happy and as rich as anyone has ever been. Those who claim it are unafraid. They show us how to heal.

A FINAL CHALLENGE: FORGIVE AND RELEASE EXPECTATIONS. Whatever is your personal case, the issues in relationships—with yourself or someone else—are always the same: Expectations about the body's behavior or appearance lead to anger when they are founded on what cannot be delivered. Peace comes from acceptance of who and what is. Life, as we often have been told, is school. Learn and love or suffer. Ego-based, left-brained comparisons of yourself to others and how you measure up in this world bring suffering ("I'll never be as smart," "I'm so much smarter"); connections made by the right brain bring wholeness and completion ("No matter what, we have a common bond, we are one in spirit"); whole-brained loving puts our bond into words and actions.

In my experience, it only takes one committed partner to heal a relationship and return to the love between you. Think how hard it is to turn away from someone who honestly admires and appreciates the best in you. You can't resist what is really true. And your gifts, not your flaws, are what is true of you. Know this and change your life.

~~~~~~~~~~~~~~~~~

What you focus on becomes your reality.
—A principle of quantum mechanics

~~~~~~~~~~~~~~~~~

To start, you must be willing to take some chances. Surrendering to limitations opens the potential for a limitless spiritual bond that only long-lasting relationships can give. If you have a close, longtime friend, you already know how.

WHO YOU REALLY ARE

You are a loving, wise being,
the sum of your very best—and more.
Your spirit,
your ability to love and care,
is infinite,
perfect,
right now.
Aligning your spirit
with your gifts
while forgiving your limitations
allows you to express yourself
masterfully
every moment.

To improve yourself, be MORE yourself.

TRANSFORM PERCEPTIONS, TRANSFORM YOURSELF

~~~~~~~~~~~~~~

It is the chiefest point of happiness that a man is willing to be what he is.
—Erasmus

~~~~~~~~~~~~~~

R OLE MODELS. CELEBRITIES. A recent quiz circulated anonymously on the Internet makes very relevant points about whom we honor as celebrities and role models, and why our egos are in charge of the process.

Try these questions:

➤ Name the five wealthiest people in the world.
➤ Name the last five Heisman trophy winners.
➤ Name ten people who have won the Nobel or Pulitzer prizes.
➤ Name six of the last dozen Academy Award winners for either best actor or actress.

So, how did you do?

These are no second-rate achievers; they are the best in their fields. Celebrities! Stars!

Notice how the applause dies, the awards tarnish, and achievements are forgotten except by the very few?

Here's another quiz. See how you do on this one:
- ➤ List a few teachers who aided your journey through life.
- ➤ Name three friends who have taught you something you'll always remember.
- ➤ Think of several people who have made you feel appreciated and special.
- ➤ Think of five people you enjoy spending time with.

If you're in your twenties or thirties, you may want it all: influence, outstanding achievement, and fame. You might consider the moral the anonymous author of this quiz added, in case you hadn't gotten it already: *The people who make a difference in your life are not the ones with the most credentials, the most money, or the most awards. They are the ones who care.*

~~~~~~~~~~~~~~~

Everything has been said before, but since nobody listens,
we have to keep going back and beginning all over again.
—Andre Gide, 1869–1951, Nobel prize-winning author

~~~~~~~~~~~~~~~

THE MULTI-BILLION-DOLLAR INDUSTRY: GOSSIP. PUT-DOWNS.

What do we read? Buy? Watch? *The National Enquirer* or an uplifting book? Trashy novels or inspiring biographies? "Action" (violent) soap operas or instructive documentaries? In a *New York Times* story (4/29/01) called "By the Water Cooler in Cyberspace, the Talk Turns Ugly," it was reported that "online gossip takes character assassination to a new level" as "hurtful and hateful gossip is laid out for all to see." Our new technology now allows us to read what has only been spoken over the centuries: "On [e-mail and chat room] message boards . . . employees are anonymously expressing thoughts they would not dare say out loud. They are freely showing their prejudices or denouncing other employees by name, sometimes accusing them of incompetence or misconduct or recounting salacious rumors about their sex lives."

Who hasn't, in the privacy of a close relationship, fired off blasting resentments and let the labels fly? Why do we love melodramas, soap operas, tabloids, and gossip magazines? We're supposed to feel better when the venting is over, when the divorce is final, when the villain gets her just deserts. What we're actually doing for those few raucous moments is shifting the label onto another: the deeply held, nagging fear that we are not OK. "It's not me! You're the one with the problem! See, I'm the one who is right, smart, and suffering because no one else can see just how right and smart I am. I'm innocent." This blaming and washing of hands adds to the toxicity of the world; it prevents solutions that move us forward. It creates a "Dilbert" cartoon life, where cynicism rules, and meanness equals cleverness. But those inner messengers of fear and loathing sent out to prove us right merely retrieve more jealousy, begin a cycle of revenge, and ultimately, end in isolation and self-loathing for the sender.

~~~~~~~~~~~~~~~

I'm just sitting here editing and judging myself day after day . . .
it's so painful because there's no escape from it. And the only solution is
kindness. Acceptance. Acceptance is not a passive thing. The more
you accept, the more you energize your whole being.
—Peter Williams, *New York Times Magazine,* May 7, 2000

~~~~~~~~~~~~~~~

HOW EACH *BRAINSTYLE* IS SEEN BY OTHERS *or*
HOW EACH *BRAINSTYLE* WITH A STRONG SELF-IMAGE SEES HIM/HERSELF

When we are *comfortable* with other *brainstyles*, we *describe* them in this way:

KNOWER	CONCILIATOR	CONCEPTOR	DELIBERATOR
Direct	Warm	Challenging	Systematic
Straightforward	Enthusiastic	Visionary	Neutral
Decisive	Accepting	Optimistic	Objective
Aggressive	Supportive	Sees the Big Picture	Private
Shrewd	Imaginative	Experimental	Thoughtful
Focused	Spontaneous	Inspiring	Cautious
Clear	Empathetic	Strategic	Methodical
No-nonsense	Charismatic	Philosopher	Tactful
			Professional

When we are *uncomfortable* with another *brainstyle* (or ourselves), we *label* them (or ourselves) like this:

KNOWER	CONCILIATOR	CONCEPTOR	DELIBERATOR
Dictator	Self-Absorbed	Manipulative	Rigid
Cold	Defensive, Reactive	"Blue-Sky"	Aloof
Bully	Wishy-Washy	Unrealistic	Overextended
Arrogant	Pushy, Needy	All Show, No Go	Unfocused
Inflexible	Personalizes Everything	Big Talker	Waffler,
Insensitive or	Touchy, Hyper-Sensitive	Different	Indecisive
Uncaring	Out of Touch	Weird	A Perfectionist
Type "A"	Moody	Incomprehensible	A Loner
Self-Promoting		Impractical	A Follower
Controlling		Unpredictable	Too Sensitive/
			Insensitive

Perceptions

I.

She does not *listen* to me.
I could shake her by the shoulders
    until her teeth rattle.
She is *forever* going to lose weight.
She still hates her body, her life.
She sees her defeats, never her wins.
She is a victim. She is depressed
    NO MATTER WHAT I SAY.
That's what I really hate.
My encouragement, support, little presents,
    advice, good cheer are never celebrated,
      nor received with the enthusiasm of my offer.
Her gifts are to be loyal,
    steadfast,
    unmoved,
    dedicated.
She is always on time.
She makes promises and keeps them.
She is independent, supports herself. She perseveres.
She is consistent. She moves through life
    a step at a time, one foot in front of the other.
She is a slow-paced Deliberator.
And I am not.

II.

He is talking about himself.
So is she.
He changes the subject from my story
    back to his own interests, projects, ideas.
She is preoccupied with measuring her achievements
    with the impact she makes.
He is preoccupied with his customers in dollars and cents;
    he is preoccupied with the sales of his book.
I am a comma in their sentences,
    an icon unclicked.

Until—
Unless—
I ask a question,
Pose a problem,
Offer a means to an end they care about.
They are Knowers.
I am not.

III.

She speaks a foreign tongue
    in my own language.
She looks right through me,
    then doodles on her pad.
Asks a question that I can't understand and changes the subject.
Her thoughts skip like a stone over a pond.
She is weird at times, laughing at her own jokes,
    then terribly, terribly serious.
She likes thinking.
She likes talking about things several times around.
    I get bored sometimes and impatient.
She seems to want to be friends,
    but is distant, preoccupied.
Maybe I'm not smart enough to get along with her.
Maybe she's moody.
She's a Conceptor
And I am not.

IV.

Who am I?
What value do I, can I bring?
Scattered as I am
        in so many directions.
Sure now, sorry later.
Deliberators receive Awards of Merit,
        Certificates of Accomplishment.
They stay the course, master a craft.
Knowers focus and tally the rewards.

Conceptors invent, or are working on it anyway.
I am jack-of-all-trades, master of none.
I am a mystery even to myself.
I cannot see what they see in me.
They tell me "I couldn't have done it without you."
I go about my business of
      doing,
      smoothing,
      finding and offering,
      entertaining,
      helping,
      getting excited about their ideas,
      gathering people together,
      making things happen for them,
      feeling it all.
The applause that is supposed to make it all worthwhile
      fades so soon.
I am a Conciliator.
They are not.

Transform Your Perceptions. Review Criticisms. An Exercise in Defining Your Strengths.

Check all items below that you have consistently been criticized for:

____ acting cold, indifferent, unfeeling

____ getting too emotional: too attached to others or too self-involved

____ talking about ideas by overgeneralizing, leaping to conclusions

____ being picky, trying to get things just so

____ having no focus, doing too many things at once, being disorganized, messy

____ being inconsistent, fickle, starting and dropping things quickly

____ taking too long to make up your mind

____ telling too many stories, rambling, being disjointed in thought

____ being arrogant, always having the answer quickly

____ being too quick with your opinion

____ interrupting, going too fast

____ going too slow, not open to change

____ being stubborn, not being willing to be influenced

____ changing your mind as often as you change your clothes

____ being selfish, talking about yourself all the time

____ being outrageous, taking too many chances

____ being too big for your britches, having too many big ideas

____ alternating between tough and tender, critical and understanding

____ being a chameleon, changing according to the situation

____ taking things personally

____ procrastinating, especially about decisions

____ making up your mind and never changing it

____ keeping things from others, not sharing information

Write in Your Special Flaw Missing From the Above List:

_____

_____

Where Criticism and Labels Come From.

- You compare yourself with an idealized other, a role model, and judge yourself as inadequate.
- Given your *brainstyle*, you get uncomfortable with another *brainstyle's* expression and make him wrong or unacceptable and demand she do things as you would do them.

Of course you next demand self-improvement (change) to meet some imposed standard that may have nothing to do with what can naturally be delivered.

AN EXPLANATION OF "REFRAMING." Criticisms are a reliable predictor of your strengths. How? Things you do or ways you behave over time that stick out are your natural abilities, exhibiting the way you think in the most natural way for you. When these natural abilities flower into maturity, they serve the human community by adding your unique contribution. As we grow up and become socialized, we often decide to believe what we're taught: There is a right way to be. Some of us (often the more left-brained) believe clearly we know what that is and act from it.

Yes, some rules are necessary for social interaction, which require learning how to behave caringly in a group, i.e., the Ten Commandments, traffic lights, etiquette that respects others. Many of the social niceties, however, are based on institutionalized demands imposed by one group at the expense of any other (the Taliban movement in Afghanistan, the stereotypical Mother-in-Law-From-Hell who imposes her Ways to Behave, and Political Correctness leap to mind).

As we interact with others, we expect them to make us comfortable if they really care for us. (Can you hear the whine?) Take an example from the list above: "keeping things from others, not sharing information." If this is true for you, you may also legitimately be called a private person, an independent thinker. You may be labeled controlling, accused of withholding information from others, being secretive, a poor communicator, when you are actually protecting someone, being loyal, or respecting another's confidences. You also may not trust others who do not deal with information as you do. By reevaluating the labels you have accepted, put up with, or actually use against yourself (and others), new solutions can emerge that are natural, liberating, and focus on the strengths of all concerned. By beginning with respect for yourself, outcomes can be respectful with more successful outcomes.

What do you need in order to be more forthcoming without giving away your boundaries? What if you started by reframing the judgmental word into a more neutral term that describes strengths more clearly? This gives you a more solid platform on which to stand, one that does not need defending. Your communication automatically becomes more neutral, detached, and more open; you change a slanted battlefield into an even playing field.

Being able to relook at behavior for the gifts beneath is the most important step you can take to a successful and satisfying life. Criticisms are indicators of *brainstyle*. The previous list has been reorganized under the *brainstyle* category most likely to exhibit it.

Note: All *BrainStyles* exhibit

—interrupting, going too fast.........when they have.........high energy

—pausing, slowing down, going blank.........when they have.........lower energy

Using the lists below, find the critical statements you checked and their corresponding underlying strengths. Take time to rethink an event, reevaluate the gifts of the critic, and rewrite the criticism as the gift it truly is.

Don't be confused if your items correspond to several of the *brainstyle* categories. Criticism is always focused on behavior, or occasionally a group of behaviors grouped into an "attitude" (poor communicator, stuck-up, mean) that you have to untangle to get at the specific behavior the attacker has in mind. Criticisms are projections on you of the speaker's feelings of discomfort, based on his own *brainstyle* gifts that determine his standards for the Right Way to do things.

~~~~~~~~~~~~~~~

I must be honest. I must be true to myself. *These words are almost always a preamble to a speech of abandonment or betrayal.*
—Hugh Prather, *Spiritual Notes to Myself*, Conari Press, 1998, 40.

~~~~~~~~~~~~~~~

EXERCISE: REFRAME CRITICISMS INTO STRENGTHS
Review the list on pages 204 for the items you checked. They appear below with the *brainstyle* reason for the behavior.

THE KNOWER *BRAINSTYLE* IS CRITICIZED FOR	BECAUSE OF THESE UNDERLYING STRENGTHS
— acting cold, indifferent, unfeeling	— left-brained, unemotional analysis
— being stubborn, not being willing to be influenced	— ability to sort information quickly to reach a logical, practical, A or B conclusion
— being arrogant, always having the answer quickly	— rapid summary of facts
— making up your mind and never changing it	— creating a logic stream that leads inexorably to a measurable goal
— keeping things from others, not sharing information	— an ability to shut down and focus

REFRAMED STATEMENTS:

As a Knower, I have been criticized for _____.

My underlying strength(s) is (are) _____

_____.

My non-strengths are_____

_____.

THE CONCILIATOR *BrainStyle* IS **CRITICIZED** FOR	BECAUSE OF THESE UNDERLYING **STRENGTHS**
— getting too emotional: too attached to others or too self-involved	— rapid, right-brained processing of information, which adds emotion, empathy, images
— having no focus, doing too many things at once, being disorganized, messy	— *ideaphoria,* an ability to rapidly generate and associate thoughts and images
— being inconsistent, fickle, starting and dropping things quickly	— an ability to imagine possibilities, dream, focus on the future and generate alternatives (with delayed, left-brained analysis and logic)
— telling too many stories, rambling, being disjointed in thought	
— being too quick with your opinion	— associative (nonlinear) thinking, often visual, which is the underlying ability to learn language and tell stories, brainstorm, get "out of the box"
— changing your mind as often as you change your clothes	
— being selfish, talking about yourself all the time	— spontaneity, rapidly putting feelings into words
— alternating between tough and tender, critical and understanding; inconsistent	— delayed access to left-brained logic
— taking things personally	— an ability to introspect or learn from experience that must be thought through or verbalized to remember
	— rapid right-, delayed left-brain access
	— attaching experiential and nonverbal interpretations to incoming data

REFRAMED STATEMENTS:

As a Conciliator, I have been criticized for _____.

My underlying strength(s) is (are) _____

_____.

My non-strengths are_____

_____.

THE CONCEPTOR *BRAINSTYLE* IS **CRITICIZED** FOR	BECAUSE OF THESE UNDERLYING **STRENGTHS**
— talking about ideas by overgeneralizing, leaping to conclusions	— rapid synthesizing of visual and logical input, a mental ability to hold contradictory thoughts
— being outrageous	— an ability to formulate a new system, take risks
— taking too many chances	— seeing beyond limitations with foresight
— being too big for your britches, having too many big ideas	— right-brained imaging, coupled with left-brained analysis; storing whole ideas that build upon and then eliminate contradictions in the specifics
— being selfish, talking about yourself all the time	— a need to explore right-brained, non-verbal, image-based ideas out loud

REFRAMED STATEMENTS:

As a Conceptor, I have been criticized for _____.

My underlying strength(s) is (are) _____

_____.

My non-strengths are_____

_____.

~~~~~~~~~~~~~~

There is nothing either good or bad,
but thinking makes it so.
—William Shakespeare

~~~~~~~~~~~~~~

THE DELIBERATOR *BrainStyle* IS CRITICIZED FOR	BECAUSE OF THESE UNDERLYING STRENGTHS
— being picky, trying to get things just so	— sensitivity to specifics, awareness of details
— taking too long to make up your mind	— an ability to assess thoroughly and methodically; a planning ability
— going too slow, not open to change	— sequential thinking, collecting and synthesizing information to reach a single conclusion
— being a chameleon, changing according to the situation	— able to gather a large volume of information in the moment, observe and monitor self and the environment, synthesize the information, and put forward a response appropriate to, or a summary of, the current situation
— taking things personally, especially about your competence (right-sided Deliberator)	— synthesizing facts with personal experience; maintaining high standards by assessing what could be better, more efficient, more accurate
— procrastinating, especially about decisions	— a need for time to synthesize a wide range of experience, input, and information, and formulate it according to internal values or standards
— acting cold, indifferent, unfeeling (left-sided Deliberator)	— ability to think rationally

REFRAMED STATEMENTS:

As a Deliberator, I have been criticized for _____.

My underlying strength(s) is (are) _____

_____.

My non-strengths are_____

_____.

SOME ELEMENTS OF REFRAMING.

TRUST. Trusting others starts by trusting your own ability to manage challenges that arise. This means you don't have to retaliate when criticized, labeled, or defamed. Trust begins by knowing your own limitations. Trusting others also requires knowing their strengths and limitations. Your responses can be more understanding, more thoughtful, wiser, respectful, more mature. Just by using *BrainStyles* timing, you will be able to start reframing for strengths today—right now—and expand the circle you influence by many magnitudes.

BE KIND IN YOUR RESPONSE. "You can say anything you want to someone if you really care for them when you say it," says a seasoned executive and highly successful people manager. Honesty can come from the ego or from love. Ego-honesty is based on the intention to separate, put down, build up, or in some way isolate. This kind of honesty "is for your own good," or "meant to help," but does just the opposite. Ego-based listeners commit the same error of isolation: No matter what you say, you're trying to hurt them. A loving intention, however, conveys connection, care, ultimate respect, and speaks of a knowing about the person that is a grander view of who they really are. I'll bet you, too, have had the experience of someone saying, "That was really stupid," to you, and you felt absolutely cared for and respected—you knew she was on your side and knew you were better and bigger than you had just demonstrated.

For instance, to review an example above, the private person might keep in mind that other, more responsive *brainstyles* may want to know that silence isn't a personal rejection; or in another example, the person with all the details might need to know that you just can't track them as well as he can. You can tell each of them, kindly.

DESCRIBE WHAT YOUR *BRAINSTYLE* CAN BRING to the situation by using a more *neutral* (not self-justifying) vocabulary.

LIKE THIS: I know it seems like I get off the subject, but I use associative thinking to consider other aspects of a situation that just might expand our thinking.

NOT THIS: I can't think in straight lines! It's boring! Narrow-minded! *Loosen up.*

EXPLAIN YOUR TIMING. Describe how your timing compares to hers:

LIKE THIS: It helps me to get clear on the goal/end/target first. I need time to do that now.

NOT THIS: Look, I'm faster than you are in getting to the point. Try to keep up, okay?

LIKE THIS: I'll never be as fast at deciding as you are. What I can do is offer an accurate, thorough assessment. And you can take that to the bank.

NOT THIS: You're a hip-shooter. That's why we have so many screw-ups and spend so much time having to redo everything.

~~~~~~~~~~~~~~~~~

Faster? Slower? No apologies, just a desire to deliver your best will neutralize the subject. If you are shy (an introvert), get the focus off yourself by mentioning how your quiet and thoughtful listening intends to draw out someone else—and that you may need some time to do so. Actually, you may just need rehearsal in order to drop them dead in their tracks with your pertinent insight, considered opinion, or well-thought-out conclusion. Give up being insulted or demeaned by those who dismiss your considered comments as if they had just popped into your head—as theirs do. Explain that you have more to add, if you have, or that you need more time, if you do.

If your comments or information are designed to prove how right you are, remember:

You get to be right. Or *you get to be happy.*

Happiness comes from seeing the impact of your ideas in life, from participating fully. What natural abilities have you been told to fix, get over, or stop? What have you overlooked, downplayed, or tried to adapt to please someone else? Quietly or loudly, you have a contribution to discover.

You may begin noticing, as some have who have tried Reframing for a while, that your remarks to yourself are kinder. You stop the self-name-calling and labeling, the giving yourself a hard time, and instead you treat yourself more like the friends you're being gentle with. Sometimes the process is reversed and you're kinder outside and then start being more gentle with yourself. In either case, there is no phoniness or real effort involved. In both cases, you win.

~~~~~~~~~~~~~~~~~

Knowing others is intelligence;
Knowing yourself is true wisdom.
Mastering others is strength;
Mastering yourself is true power.
—Tao Te Ching

~~~~~~~~~~~~~~~~~

CHAPTER

CREATE A LIFESTYLE YOU CAN LIVE WITH

~~~~~~~~~~~~~~~

Getting married is very much like going to a restaurant with friends.
You order what you want, and then when you see what the other person has,
you wish you had ordered that.

—Anonymous comment from the Internet

~~~~~~~~~~~~~~~

RELATIONSHIP AGONY AND ECSTASY: You may have experienced both and more in your own home. Your lover, the one you really, really depend upon, the one whom it turns out you have the least control over, is the very one you may have entrusted with your very well-being.

An examination of relationships heated up with a book written in the '50s by sociologist David Riesman. In *The Lonely Crowd,* Riesman told us we were "inner-directed" (you have an inner sense of worth) or "outer-directed" (you look to others). Riesman observed that in America the nuclear family had been expected to supply all needs for the children, propelling and reinforcing an outer-directed society, where the expectations for Mom and Dad to make us feel worthwhile were huge, rarely fulfilled, and often led to blame and suffering. This set up a pattern of expectations for life with our lovers. What to do?

WHAT'S UP WITH FAMILIES TODAY? As you may have heard, the 2000 U.S. census revealed that a mere 25 percent of all families is the traditional nuclear mom, dad, and kids. More single parents of both sexes are raising the children, if children are even in the picture. Committed relationships in America, it would seem, are too scary or take too much time away from our real goals. Fewer of us come from an intact, financially stable, two-parent family which has a faith[1]. The commitment of marriage, these days, is just an option.

Childlessness is reflected in continually decreasing birth rates in the U.S., and staying together to take care of the children is only a very minor factor when considering divorce.[2] The purpose of marriage for most Americans, namely raising a family, is just not the trend these days.[3]

TWENTY-FIRST-CENTURY PARTNERSHIPS. David Riesman had it right: We are still challenged to live as inner-directed (spirit- or love-directed) responsible beings. Failing this, we are doomed to forever listen to our egos and look outside for someone or something else to make us whole. So life, as we often have been told, is school. Learn and grow, or suffer. As the Buddhists teach, attachments to an idea or a person ("Before I commit, I must find someone who meets my standards, like my parents/friend did.") derived from left-brained comparisons and right-brained idealizations bring suffering; connections made from inner wisdom bring wholeness and completion ("We have our differences, but we are one in spirit"). Couples who have successful and long-lasting partnerships have something larger than their own needs and feelings to reflect upon when all else seems hopeless. Having a common faith or set of spiritual principles for living to turn to is their bedrock to sustain one another.

Think about this:

Jesus' life didn't go well. He didn't reach his earning potential.
He didn't have the respect of his colleagues. His friends weren't loyal.
His life wasn't long. He didn't meet his soul mate. . . .
—Hugh Prather, *Spiritual Notes to Myself,* Conari Press, 1998

---

1. "Cohabitation, Marriage, Divorce, and Remarriage in the United States," Centers for Disease Control and Prevention (CDC), July, 2002, a report based on interviews with nearly 11,000 women 15–44 years of age. The report is available at *www.cdc.gov/nchs/releases*.
2. See "The Top Ten Myths of Divorce" by David Popenoe (on The Marriage Project Web site), that debunks many commonly held beliefs on the subject.
3. Then as now, cultures built on extended families offer choices of many adults to satisfy relational needs, along with stability and bonding with others. The pressure is less on the family, the sense of community greater, and the reliance on tradition and ritual builds in structure and markers on the road to maturity. The search for the inner self is less a self-conscious rite of passage and more a natural outgrowth of values and faith established in the home.

WHAT WE LOSE. Families provide the intimate setting to grow as a whole being, confront your limitations, and learn. Each relationship you commit to—whether a marriage, a life partner, a member of your family, an adoption, or a friend who becomes family—brings the potential to explore the inner vastness of joining minds, not bodies, to create a spiritual union that opens the soul. You just can't get this alone or on the job.

Here is the view of a woman cohabitor of nine years who, along with her Significant Other, had been married before. The man was terribly gun-shy about committing to marriage, still smarting from bitter divorces. Defying statistics, he recently popped the question. Here's what the bride-to-be has to say about cohabitation and the difference making a commitment brings:

> You asked why we think we'll beat the odds of couples getting married that have lived together. It's already worlds better—like the pressure has been lifted or a barrier removed to the relationship that should never have been there in the first place. NOT getting married kept us separate, guarded, angry (for me), hypocritical (we expect our children to do the right and moral thing; why are we exempt?), and looking out for ourselves more than each other. . . . [Now] we know each other will be there for one another through anything . . . and that is what security and love is all about. It's all about a commitment to the end together—the biggest unknown we face—and making the best of the time we have left.

She now views this time together as a foundation for the future with a larger goal:

> We've established some wonderful family traditions which serve to solidify and support our commitment to each other and our family, and we take great delight in helping those we love grow personally and experience the happiness life has to offer. What more could someone want?

~~~~~~~~~~~~~~~

If we can see the oneness with just one other person,
we become the light of the world.
—Hugh Prather, *ibid.*

~~~~~~~~~~~~~~~

HELP IS ON THE WAY. To make your journey with all your family more loving, authentic, and nourishing, here are three simple tools to start you on your way. These tools will also help you open to greater possibilities than you may be considering in those tough times when the other looks incorrigible, intractable, and not worth the effort.

1) **LOOK FOR UNDERLYING BRAINSTYLE GIFTS** in order to look beyond and forgive behavior and bring out the best in the other. This will allow you to be

neutral more of the time, peaceful instead of reactive, confrontational, or on the defensive.[4]

2) **REFRAME CRITICISMS** and personal affronts with your understanding of *brainstyle* gifts and timing. This allows a release of your expectations for others to think and express caring in the way that you do, and

3) **USE TIMING** to honor gifts—yours included.

~~~~~~~~~~~~~~~

CREATING A MARRIAGE DAY-TO-DAY. To the outsider they are an odd pair: he, the carpenter; she, the intellect. He, the quiet Man of Few Words; she, the public speaker and business consultant who Knows How Things Work. They have discussed their differences in the past and agreed that they love each other "fundamentally" but have a lot of trouble with the day-to-day. More commonly today, she is the main breadwinner. If truth be told, this was an undercurrent of difficulty between them in the early years of their marriage. It was a common enough version of the Golden Rule: The one who brings in the gold makes the rules. Having the financial high ground, she has learned that if she wants the marriage to work (just as breadwinners and bosses and leaders everywhere must learn), she must go for the win-win. It is not always easy.

She made a comment one night—something off the cuff, something neutral to her—something like "I can't be saving for *both* our retirements" to encourage him to put IRA money away annually. A sensible remark, a practical suggestion. Much later she was to figure out that it was this remark that was an axe to his pride that cut deep.

THE BOMB. He is a big man, burly, strong, and physically imposing. Younger, more introverted, and less educated than his wife, he is a Knower who has very few words even when he feels like talking, which isn't very often. He shows his commitment to her by doing and building things for her, making sure she's safe and protected. He shows his dedication to their family by endless hours of Little League coaching, home repair and expansion, continual dedication to his son's welfare, and problem-solving of family issues with the quick clarity and lightning focus that takes his wife's breath away at times, as she says. His face registers nothing as he issues the unexpected edict. In fact, he really doesn't look at her directly until after he launches his Words of War, using the momentum of the anger to carry him into meeting her horrified gaze.

---

4 Respect for another flows automatically and authentically from appreciating and honoring one's own strengths and limitations. Thus no effort is required to improve your communications or adapt to the other's way of relating by trying to change yourself—which you know doesn't work because you resent the effort and fakery and so give it up as too much of a sacrifice.

"Well, here it is then: One roof, two lives. We'll just live together until our son is gone, and then it's over." His main point seems to be that he is already so detached from the situation, he doesn't even use his own son's name.

It's a Knower heart-stopper. The Conciliator wife's heart obligingly stops. Eyes like glassy headlights, she registers the incoming missile. Duly noting the kill, he is gone. Scorched-earth policy. No prisoners taken.

She is a strong woman, physically able, a Conciliator business professional who works full time, and does the housekeeping, cooking, shopping, and carpool duty for her son when she's in town. She is also deeply and openly feeling, sensitive, articulate; when she has chosen to use them in the past, words and feelings have been her weapons of choice. Knowing this, he fires his round and spares himself her anguish by evacuating quickly.

There were no words for days. Ships passing in the night, as she recounted it, they each retreated into neutral corners of their dual careers and separate turf of the home to nurse wounds. That he had been wounded, she had no doubt. It took four days to find out what had hurt, given their workdays, and even then the symptom is never the illness. What we are angry about is rarely, if ever, the source of the upset, for the source of the anger is never outside you.

THE FOUNDATION:
- One thing she believed: It takes only one to heal a relationship.
- One thing she declared to herself: Love is a decision.
- One thing she committed to: her vision for their marriage where both could be "bigger" than their emotions to create a loving family for the long term.
- One thing she trusted: Her husband could get over his anger.
- Her premise: She could neither change him nor change herself.

COMMUNICATIONS THAT HAD NO REAL IMPACT:
- Expressed herself authentically. "This is hurting. I hate this."
- Tried to engage her partner with the goal. "Would you throw this [marriage] away?"
- Set limits. "I'm not willing to live together in some pretense, separately. Do you want to go now?"

These tactics, expressing her own feelings and concerns, did not seem to make a lot of difference in engaging her husband to resolve the issue between them.

WHAT SHE DID THAT WORKED.
- Applied her understanding of their *brainstyles* to their marriage.

She knew he was logical and decisive first, and later he'd show and express his feelings; she knew she would feel first, get objective later. She realized that she was so much more competent at managing a relationship and expressing her feelings that she overpowered him. This kept her from "chasing him down" and demanding an encounter where, she'd learned, "he always perceived himself the loser."

She used timing, waiting for her own objectivity to settle in and recall what she must have said or done to cause his hurt and anger, and more importantly, she waited for an opportunity to talk that would work for *him.*

- Acted as a partner.

After several days, he mentioned that he was going up to some property they owned together to take care of a sick animal. She insisted on going with him, enduring the silence of an hour-and-a-half car ride that was "terribly punishing" for her. "The trip to the ranch helped me just be on his page, his activity, his ground, and learning [from him], helping, and supporting him," she said. Active in the care of the animal, she enjoyed sharing in it and was openly helpful. There was a shared experience to talk about on the way home.

- Persisted.

"Do you want to work this out?" By the time she asked this question, she had demonstrated her willingness to be with him no matter what. She demonstrated her commitment to both him and their son by continuing her responsibilities in the home and on her job.

WHAT SHE DIDN'T DO.

- Take revenge nor "punish him" in return.
- Use her verbal and emotional prowess to hurl emotionally charged words as "weapons" to make the situation worse—no badgering or emotional blackmail, as Conciliators are equipped to do.
- Stop being herself.
- Stop listening.
- Give away her values for the marriage.
- Allow her victim feelings to rule the day.

She apologized for hurting his feelings. He responded with the most vulnerable of replies: "No, it was my own doubts and fears about things that was the problem." "Then," she says, "he expressed his huge and solid sense of the miracle of our marriage, family, our son, our blessings, which he very rarely expresses. Melting, I said, 'You are my rock.' Then he said something funny and it was over with a big hug."

And they just went on with their day.

~~~~~~~~~~~~~~~

Okay, you're saying, "She's a saint," especially if you're a female Conciliator or Deliberator. This comment means you are judging her husband in light of this situation and your own *brainstyle*. If you came to that conclusion, you are overlooking a few things. Namely, it takes two saints to create a partnership. The husband had to use his own introspection responsibly to get past his own hurt feelings, his own horrible hurdles at expressing them, and receive her overtures with care and then tenderness.

More than that, you are a saint every time you put larger commitments ahead of your own feelings, and instead use forgiveness and your strengths to support your lover, your family, or any other who has caused pain.

To create a lasting partnership, you must learn to choose love over fear. As the wife above demonstrates, this isn't always easy, but it is always possible. To do so, begin noticing your daily choices to be right, get mad, and feel in control rather than peaceful, your choice to listen to your body's emotions and pleasures rather than your greater wisdom. Ultimately you'll overcome your fear of peace, intimacy, and love to have the joys and depths of a lasting commitment.

What more could someone want?

~~~~~~~~~~~~~~~

If you want to learn to love better,
you should start with a friend who hates you.[5]
—Quoted from anonymous 4–8-year-olds when asked to define love

~~~~~~~~~~~~~~~

---

5. Or business partner, husband, sister, mom, father-in-law, grandma, cousin, snippy waiter— or take on an HMO receptionist if you're on a roll.

EACH *BRAINSTYLE* CAN HEAL A RELATIONSHIP WITH ITS STRENGTHS.
ALL EXPRESSIONS OF LOVE ARE MAXIMAL.

The Knower Can	The Conciliator Can	The Conceptor Can	The Deliberator Can
• Love deeply and show it by solving and preventing problems, protecting the family from harm and the lover from unproductive and stressful entanglements. • Define an outcome and spur others to achieve results they didn't know they could achieve. • Minimize fears with logic; demonstrate honor, loyalty, and confidence in the face of obstacles. • Show how to work smart, not hard, to reach confidence-building goals. • Define measurable targets to eliminate the stress of ambiguity. • Support others' goals by solving problems that bring order and efficiency and allow them to pursue their dreams. • Set boundaries for the family and lover so they feel safe. • Act as an ally without reservation.	• Love openly by illuminating the best and highest motives, gifts, and visions. • Touch, demonstrate affection, and openly nurture. • Enthusiastically support the lover and the family's strengths and goals. • Bring everyone together with a loving intent. • Respond to problems empathetically. • Bring personal meaning to tasks and people who touch the heart. • Forego credit, acknowledge others. • Solve problems intuitively in areas where people and ideas come together. • Be tolerant and celebrate differences. • Demonstrate forgiveness. • Directly influence the lover's and family's self-esteem with openly expressed, unconditional love.	• Love deeply by creating a larger purpose for the family and the partnership. • Support by declaring and uncovering the basic principles and assumptions of the partnership and reframing them to be loving. • Heal old wounds by seeing the overview and forgiving them. • Create new solutions to inspire others to overcome fears. • Give new, unseen reasons why people are lovable or smart. • Make people right by using their ideas in new ways. • Create a future that includes everyone, valuing them for how they think rather than what they do. • Clarify underlying principles and underlying assumptions that promote integrity and success for all. • Forgive mistakes by putting them in a larger context.	• Love deeply by attending to the cares and needs of the family and lover. • Show affection by doing things that matter to others. • Open new areas to the family and lover by learning and curiosity. • Take the sacred role of a follower who creates leadership in others. • Set an example of personal growth, steadfast gentleness, and adherence to principles/faith. • Honor the growth or learning of others by sharing their own and guiding with values. • Bring out the best of another by challenging with ideas or tasks, then discussing the lesson. • Be tender, attentive, and caring by listening and helping when needed. • Make things less risky, more realistic, and understandable, to calm fears. • Demonstrate honor, loyalty, and trust.

"Till death do us part? Hey, I thought this was just supposed to be a starter marriage!"

CHAPTER **12**

CREATE YOUR PARTNERSHIP

~~~~~~~~~~~~~~

Most people enter into relationships with an eye toward what they can get out of
them, rather than what they can put into them. . . .
There can only be one purpose for relationships—and for all of life:
to be and to decide Who You Really Are. . . .
Your personal relationships are the most important element in this process.
Your personal relationships are, therefore, holy ground. They have virtually
nothing to do with the other; yet, because they involve another, they
have everything to do with the other.
—*Conversations with God, Book I,* Neale Donald Walsch, 122, 128

~~~~~~~~~~~~~~

WHAT **ACTUALLY WORKS IN A MARRIAGE OR COMMITTED PARTNERSHIP?** Conventional wisdom prompts the questions, "Don't you have to have sexual chemistry? Don't you have to instantly like each other to stay together?" Clutching that insight, singles use dating and having sex to size up whether they have a future together.

Look just a bit deeper, as one couple, who have been happily married for nearly two decades, did recently. Neal and Susan readily agreed: It's more than being friends that makes a difference; it's a friendship based on respect. Actually, you like someone as more than an acquaintance over time because you respect his or her values, thinking, and decisions. Effort and communications skills be darned. Common interests? *Fuhgeddaboutem.* They change all the time. Chemistry? Brain studies track the slide from the initial whoopee pheromonal passion to the thrill-is-gone stage, which, when allowed to, deepens into serotonin physical closeness over time. As chemistry recedes, choices begin. It is respect that is the foundation, the glue, the key to lasting love, the real source of friendship, intimacy, and a lasting, loving commitment.

TECHNIQUES. The findings of behavioral researcher John Gottman at the University of Washington are often cited as statistics on marriage, as he has studied 130 couples over six years and he claims now to predict their marital success or divorce by observing how they fight. In a *Los Angeles Times* story in February 1999, the headline grabber is "Just Say Yes. Research finds that the happiest marriages are those in which husband gives in to wife,"[1] based on Gottman's research. Reading the article, we find that learned communication techniques "are just too hard for the average person. . . . Active listening, in which one partner paraphrases the other partner's concerns—'So what I hear you saying is . . .'—is unnatural and requires too much of people in the midst of emotional conflict."

RESPECT, RESPECT, RESPECT. Gottman's main finding? It is the underlying respect that is the key factor in a relationship—NOT the tricks you use to communicate, but the intent to recognize legitimacy in what the other is saying—that allows a partnership to thrive. Gottman's research found that the marriages that did work well all had one thing in common: The husband made his wife a partner. The research continues, "We found that only those newlywed men who are accepting of influence from their wives are ending up in happy, stable marriages." Getting down to the specifics, the researcher warned the women about whining or firing emotional missiles to get something changed: "Women who couched their complaints in a gentle, soothing, perhaps even humorous approach to the husband were more likely to have happy marriages than those women who were more belligerent."[2] Marriages that worked included "gentleness in the way conflict is managed." And why would you be gentle? Treat your mate as a partner? Settling into natural strengths allows these very things. Aren't you more open, trusting, and gentle with someone whom you respect as a person? If you see what he truly brings and stop comparing him to someone else, what remains?

---

1. Note: This finding was going to be included no matter what, *especially* this specific sentence.
2. Extroverts, whether male or female, Conciliators, Knowers—are you paying attention?

BEYOND SEX. "The only way to change marriage for the better is to improve the quality of friendship between a husband and wife and to help them deal with disagreements differently," Gottman says. Isn't this how you already treat your friends? Why change at home? Said another way, treat your mate with respect for who she is, just as she is, and watch miracles occur. Gottman's research addresses the male who doesn't listen, the wife who whines. Listening to many married couples where the woman is the left-brained one, and more and more often the higher income producer these days,[3] the dynamic is reversed. The man is the open and nurturing one who complains, the woman the impatient major decision-maker. Gender is trumped by *brainstyle*.[4]

B. Smaller

"I'm not saying that I don't have intimacy issues. I'm just saying that I prefer to work on them by myself."

---

3. It is estimated that some 30 percent of married women are the primary breadwinners in the United States.

4. Trickier still is when *brainstyle* and the task don't match. This is attributed to gender without looking for underlying gifts. A Wisconsin study of 2,682 people between 18 and 77 for ten years found that men who take over child care and house cleaning have an 82 percent (!) higher death rate than career men. Psychologists concluded that househusbands are required 1) to do more multi-tasking; 2) without social support. Both of these factors are expressions of *brainstyle* gifts. Executive women were found more likely to have heart attacks than their junior managers. Psychologists look at gender expectations; you can look at the pressure to deal with conflict and make faster, bigger decisions more often, and what *brainstyle* gifts apply, and then come up with your own answers to make the best choices.

NEWLYWEDS. A young couple (Mancy, twenty-five, Kevin, twenty-eight) has been married less than a year. He speaks of the long term, she of the immediate. He manages their investments and the big items, she the daily life. He is a Deliberator with a strong, open-ended, right-brained approach to many things; she a Conciliator. They are a wonderful team in the making.

I ask for factors that influenced making a commitment to a marriage after five years of dating. Their answers reveal their values, yet their conversation is about the smaller daily issues that obscure those values. The petty things, the ebbs and flows of emotions—when becoming the focus of attention—are the things that can devastate a relationship.

The window afforded in a new marriage, that heady time of finding your way, setting your boundaries in the midst of all those fast-diminishing pheromones, is an unsettling period at best. Patterns get established that, depending on the depth of emotional memory of each partner for this time, are difficult to change.

Let's start at the beginning. Why did you marry?

They each split 100% among the following factors:

HIS ANSWERS:		HER ANSWERS:	
Religious faith	60%	Religious faith	50%
Desire for a family	20%	Financial considerations	25%
Peer expectations	10%	Desire for something more formal	10%
Desire for something more formal	10%	Peer expectations	5%
		Desire for a family	5%
		Parental expectations	5%

Kevin and Mancy have the most important things covered: a common faith, similar values for a committed marriage, and a similar desire to have children in the future. Note her emphasis on his earning capacity and his ability to provide a stable home, which was how she explained "financial considerations." He did not consider finances a factor because he assumes his own success. Their common need for a certain standard of living with a home in a certain price range as a criteria for family is based on the values for stability they share.

> *BRAINSTYLE CLUE:* The brain values outside what it is structured for inside unless you tell it to make more choices.

Lifestyle can be a major challenge to a partnership, one that love and commitment can overcome, but not easily. Why? Amazingly enough, this preference

CREATE YOUR PARTNERSHIP / 227

for lifestyle can have a genetic base, according to the twins studies conducted at the University of Minnesota. "Conservatism" was found to have a genetic base among twins, governing values such as risk-taking and adherence to tradition. Even though they have different *brainstyles*, they each were predisposed to value tradition, which equaled lifestyle for them.[5]

IF MAMA AIN'T HAPPY, AIN'T NOBODY HAPPY. According to Barbara Graham, a Dallas psychotherapist with over twenty years' experience counseling couples, there are key elements required in long-term relationships.

- Men want to know that they are respected; however, they care as much or more that their wives are happy.
- Wives want to know that they are cherished, protected, and provided for by their mates.

Graham adds that the sexual relationship has its seasons, but the mutual respect and cherishing of mates are constants. Lose these elements and the relationship falters. Another author/psychotherapist, David Richo, PhD, underscores this point in a recent book[6], "A relationship based solely on sex, rather than on a fulfilling friendship that includes sex, can turn to ashes in the years to come. Such relationships can endure thirty years of marriage, but they will be stale, non-nurturant, and sorely regretted. *An adult makes the transition from attraction as* [physical] *charge to attraction as choice.* . . . As we become healthier and more adult, we no longer seek sex for joy but share sex because of joy."

THE BEGINNING OF THE PARTNERSHIP. Of course these newlyweds are in love, but more than this, each has a deep appreciation of the other. The latter has been put to the test. "I grew up with him," she says. Mancy was only twenty when they started dating. In her first committed relationship, she openly admits she had to learn how to take care of herself. She felt dominated by Kevin, not knowing how to ask for her own schedule, not knowing how to say No (non-strengths for the Conciliator). She stopped seeing him for three months because he was "totally taking her for granted," not being "romantic" (flowers, calling ahead), doing what *he* wanted to do; and she was going along with it, canceling her plans to meet his last-minute invitations. She had to date other people because she knew she had to learn how to "stand up" for herself. (A non-strength for Conciliators is setting limits.) "Even though I'd drive to another guy's house crying because I'd rather be with Kevin, I did it because I was miserable the way it had been. I

---

5. Her sister and his brother, raised in the same family environments, do not value a traditional lifestyle.

6. *How To Be an Adult in Relationships: The Five Keys to Mindful Loving,* David Richo (Shambala Press, 2002), 95.

thought I wanted a courtship." When she actually was "courted" by other guys she was appalled. Those she dated were, like herself, "romantic" in the full sense of her word: quick to express their feelings with poetry(!), songs, candy, and lots of phone calls. She found this "cheesy" and "weird." She couldn't take them seriously. "What I found out was that I wanted a courtship from *him*. When we got back together, he was romantic and brought the flowers I wanted and paid more attention to me. Everything changed. [But overall] I have realized that he isn't really a Romantic, and that's it."

What can she do with this conclusion?

CHOOSE YOUR PARTNER. Her little adventure clarified what she prizes in the man she wanted to marry.[7] Choosing your partner for real occurs many times in a marriage or long-term relationship: You choose him instead of the sexy guy at the party; you choose her when she's barfing in the toilet—when he's broke or mad at you, when she's stupid and bitchy. It's the day-to-day definition of "for worse" in the marriage vows.

She concludes it is the depth of the expression of this Deliberator that she values, well, loves. When he focuses on her, he means it because he's thought about it—no impulsive lyrics are tossed around by this guy.

CHANGE YOUR PARTNER. But then, of course, after the wedding she has immediately set out to change him, to train him to be more romantic, as she calls it, even though (she says) she knows better.

Don't be smug. You know you've done this, too. Our *brainstyles* demand comfort by expecting another to do things the way we do them ourselves.

What does he need to fix? He doesn't spend time thinking of what to buy her the way she does for him. He doesn't enjoy music as much, but since "he knows how important it is for me," she gets angry when he doesn't show up on time to listen to music with her as she has asked him to. In her perception his lateness equates to a lack of caring. She was "so mad I couldn't enjoy the music," fuming about his unwillingness to "spend an extra fifteen minutes just *once a week*" for her.

Is her expectation realistic? All she wants is an expression of caring in her own terms. But of course, it's an expression that is natural for her, unnatural for him. After all, hasn't she gone along with his (hobby, friends, movies, etc.)? (Fill in your

---

7. Statistically, we tend to do best with those who complement us. Her own *brainstyle* was *not* what she wanted as a mate. Anthropologists say that this comes from a primitive need to survive by covering all the bases for survival with different skills. Psychologists say we choose another to complete who we are.

own blank.) It's *quid pro quo* time. I did this for you. Now you owe me. I ask her if her demands are not the same things she left him for: being dominating, selfish, inconsiderate. Tears come when she realizes—and owns—what she is doing. She is seeing in him what she hasn't owned in herself. *Projection* is the term for this.

Sound familiar?

FOR BETTER, FOR WORSE. Their fights have been terrible, passionate, loud "word wars" where hurtful things have been said. They "set each other off" with huge, emotional reactions to small, "stupid" things as they explore one another's sensitivities and react to expressions of their differences.

After the initial conversation, the Conciliator wife realizes how she has equated love and its expression with presents and doing things her way. She is ecstatic to see the new possibilities for valuing her husband as he is. She feels less guilty.

She is open to, and getting a sense of, what it takes for a real partnership.

He wants to read about their *brainstyles* and grabs the book. He wants more information, as a Deliberator does.

She is creating an opening for her more introverted husband to feel appreciated for himself, without pressure. She says she is "learning so much" about him that she had just "overlooked." Couples who have been married for decades say the same thing.

TIME TOGETHER. TIME APART. She wants time together. He does too, but then he loves fishing. Alone. It's thinking time, relaxing time. She needs less of this than he does. "She likes routine more than I do," he confides, which is an interesting contradiction when you think of it.

> *BRAINSTYLE CLUE:* The Deliberator finds "play" in getting away from his natural ability to structure; the Conciliator needs structure that she can't naturally create, in order to play.

As we discussed this difference, I speculate that he is not so much learning about himself as how to apply his strengths in their marriage. I mentioned to him that he was a planning professional at work and wasn't bringing his gifts home. That was sloppy and inconsiderate, and he knew it.

As a single guy, Kevin liked to go out at a moment's notice. But now, as he grows into their partnership, he is planning ahead, letting her know about plans, parties, and trips, so she can plan too, she reports, respecting her need for structure to work within. This is treating her like a partner instead of a date.

As he demonstrates more of his best, rather than who he was as an adolescent, he is giving himself permission, in *BrainStyles* terms, to apply his gifts at home, not just the office. Maturing in his application of his gifts, the reward is being happy *together*.

TIMING: THE RHYTHM TOGETHER. In a sexual union, novices say that timing is everything. It's certainly true in ballroom dancing. In sex, timing can express many things: openness, consideration, kindness, fear, tenderness, respect, or the state of our health. Each partner must choose his own interpretation to ruin or create intimacy. Healthy relationships see sexuality as just one expression of their love.

~~~~~~~~~~~~~~~~~~

Sex is not a game. It gives rise to real enduring emotion and practical consequences. To ignore this is to debase yourself and to disregard the significance of human relationships...An active sex life within a framework of personal commitment augments the integrity of the people involved and is part of a flourishing liveliness.
—Epictetus, 50–138 AD, Stoic philosopher

~~~~~~~~~~~~~~~~~~

As we learn about one another's rhythm, we constantly choose how much time we spend together, how much time we can stand in closeness and physical separations, and the timing needed to interact lovingly. This is a way that the left brain measures reality, and it easily translates to something to fight over and be right about. She is the one in this couple to be martial about being on time. He's always late. She fears becoming a nagger—what she promised herself she would never become—to get them places on time, to follow through on appointments. They argue about this continually.

Being on time counts as a way to demonstrate consideration and respect for another, to dance with another. Is it more important than the partnership? In my marriage, our roles are reversed and I am often the late one. My husband has gotten furious, time and again, to make his point. When he began to simply remind me of the time we had to get ready, I took responsibility to get there on time. It is still a struggle for me, as I can get lost in my own world of Just One More Thing, so I must consciously choose to be on time to honor his values, which I respect. Going out for an evening, relaxed and in sync, is a much more pleasant way to start.

For Kevin and Mancy, she must set realistic timetables and give him reminders when it's important, as a demonstration of respect; he can be responsible by being on time. Beyond this, they can give up using time as a way to be right, use their natural rhythms, and take away the emotionality of the issue. Ultimately, our spirits don't know about time; our bodies do. Keeping spirits in alignment is the prize. Matching rhythm and being considerate, I must admit, is more important than just taking your own time.

~~~~~~~~~~~~~~

*I learned from BrainStyles that I was demanding everyone in my life
to do things according to MY time.*
—A Mexican professor in a *BrainStyles* seminar, Chihuahua, Mexico

~~~~~~~~~~~~~~

CHANGE YOUR PARTNER, PART DEUX. The premise that you cannot change another person is in the vocabulary of this couple, but the true depth of what that means takes practice. As with most of us, when the chips are down (a *Time Zero* event), she wants him to do things her way; i.e., match her rhythm, see issues, and act the way she would in a similar situation. On the other hand, he is appalled at her quick, off-the-cuff, irrational, or hurtful comments. Why can't she be thoughtful, reasonable (i.e., slower or match his pace better)? It's reflex to want another to speak your language and match your *brainstyle*, especially in emotional, high-stakes situations.

> *BRAINSTYLE CLUE:* The time required for making decisions creates your rhythm together or apart. Taking charge of that rhythm takes discipline and intention.

Kevin is not willing to just launch into an introspective discussion, but, of course, Mancy is eager to do so. Introspection and sharing about emotions are her gifts, after all. He wants time. Time to research and think it over. Time to consider his answers. She is on the phone talking, talking, to a friend and to her mother about all the new insights. She realizes when we talk again that by the time she tells her husband, she will have gotten over the initial blush of excitement of her discoveries, robbing him of her initial thrill. A Conciliator's right brain demands to be expressed and heard. Her choice to make is when will that sharing come? When she needs to share, or when he can hear her?

> *BRAINSTYLE CLUE:* Timing is the problem. Timing is the solution.

After time passes and there is some time for more experience with the *brainstyle* principles, the Conciliator wife reports elation on her part, romantic cards and flowers from her hubby. She has, she says, "with practice," caught herself critiquing her husband for not doing things as she would do them. "Instead of sniping [making indirect or sarcastic comments about his "failings"], I'm asking more directly for what I want, and we're talking more openly. I still have to work on saying No, but I'm getting better at having a nego-tiation instead of giving an ultimatum."

> BRAINSTYLE CLUE: Conciliators who learn to be on time, set limits, or make requests can be very defensive about any skill acquired in a non-strength.
> This holds true for all of the *brainstyles* in any acquired skill in non-strengths.

CREATING A PARTNERSHIP FOR REAL. Kevin is the one with the insight that she most remembers: "We each see negative qualities in one another that we hate in ourselves." *This is wisdom to last a lifetime;* it is a res-olution for *any* fight. If you know how to look for and define strengths and non-strengths, you skip the cause of most upsets. You own projections.[8] Acceptance and neutrality come quicker and easier. Fights disappear. Healing occurs.

What is the bedrock of this partnership? What will keep it together?

First, couples must have a bigger purpose for their partnership than simply being comfortable (having the same interests) together. Since the foundation for this couple is a common faith and a strong tradition for family, they are both motivated to learn from their interactions. The principle is universal: A successful business, church, team, or family requires the same. You must have a long-term mission and a reason for learning from others. If this is missing for you, this is the place to start building. Next, they are learning to respect one another for the strengths they each have. Doing so automatically releases expectations and demands for change based on one's own *brainstyle*.

MORE ON WHAT WORKS. Two studies get to the very heart of a rela-tionship and point the way to a spiritual partnership. In a section called "Intimacies," a magazine cleverly captioned an item that goes to the heart of part-nerships: "Is Your Marriage Everlasting . . . or Just Lasting Forever?" The item referred to a study done at Bowling Green State University in Ohio that showed that "couples who view their marriages as sacred—those who see the divine in each other—tend to be more satisfied, experience fewer conflicts, and settle their differ-

---

8. Reminder: A *projection* is a psychological term coined by Sigmund Freud to mean a defensive mechanism where we seek to disown our feelings. Doing this, we see in others the sins that we don't wish to acknowledge or take responsibility for in ourselves. To ensure that the projection stays outside us, we literally forget the projection, which allows us to feel hurt or justifiably angry over how others treat us unfairly.

ences more quickly than couples who lack that spark."[9] The article refers to a National Institute for Healthcare Research report by Dr. David Fenell of the University of Colorado, who identified and interviewed nearly 150 couples whose marriages had lasted at least two decades and whose unions were rated highly satisfying to both. These couples rated the ten most important traits in their marriages, many of which our newlyweds have already addressed:

➤ Lifetime commitment to marriage (the notion of a "starter marriage" is OUT)
➤ Loyalty to spouse (as in sticking up for the partner with others)
➤ Strong moral values in common
➤ Respect for spouse as best friend; i.e., someone you can forgive, confide in, and enjoy as a person
➤ Commitment to sexual fidelity
➤ Desire to be a good parent
➤ Faith in God and spiritual commitment
➤ Desire to please and support spouse
➤ Good companion to spouse (As a whole person, you can enjoy his or her enjoyment; love him or her for the interests which you may or may not share, and have fun when together)
➤ Willingness to forgive and be forgiven

As you can see, the values embedded in the above list are decisions made over time, which is another way to define *values*. As all of us know, sometimes living from those values is a decision to which we must recommit on a daily basis. This is how the commitment to a partnership builds character and becomes sacred. Living this way, we become wiser, more powerful, clearer, and more clearly who we were born to be.

> *BrainStyle Clue:* Values are decisions created over time.

Looking beyond the immediate behavior for another's gifts, refusing to generalize the upsetting situation into Always and Never, and keeping your eye on a loving, longer-term goal is what will allow you to do more than hang in there. It will allow you to realize your own magnificence as a human being as well as the magnificence of those you love.

Supporting the idea of a sacred, committed context where each partner becomes whole and brings his or her best self to their partnership is another

---

9. As reported in *Spirituality & Health*, Winter, 1999, 13.

remarkable study on the impact of marriage counseling. *Science News*[10] reported a study conducted with forty-six couples in marriage counseling over twenty years. The couples who participated in behavioral counseling for marital problems (they changed things they did and said to one another) had a significantly higher divorce rate (19 of 23) than couples participating in insight therapy. The latter helps individuals resolve past emotional issues (previous decisions) that block communication and has much longer-lasting effects, promoting autonomy for each person. (Only one of 23 couples divorced after this type of therapy.)

To change your routine, rather than one another, try the following exercise. It is the basis for a marriage contract that requires honoring—and then drawing from—your mate's or partner's strengths to create a real rhythm between you, to make your life together a dance . . . with timing to share the leading and following. And always, always, the band is playing the music of love and forgiveness.

It's the basis for a lifestyle known by successful partnerships all over the planet.

An EXERCISE. Each partner makes four lists:
- ➤ **How he or she will see my strengths**
- ➤ **How he or she will see my non-strengths**
- ➤ **The strengths of my partner as I see them**
- ➤ **The non-strengths of my partner as I see them**

~~~~~~~~~~~~~~~~~~

The sharing of your perceptions, supplemented by the research about *brainstyle* strengths and non-strengths, can serve as the start of a more loving assessment for your partnership. *The Strengths Contract* (chapter 15) is the method to apply this information to big projects, which require the application of your differences to make decisions—exactly the place where angry, deadly spiders live in webs that look a lot like a new boat purchase or room renovation.

~~~~~~~~~~~~~~~~~~

When my grandmother got arthritis, she couldn't bend over and paint her toenails anymore. So my grandfather does it for her all the time, even when his hands got arthritis too. That's love.

—Anonymous quote from a 4–8-year-old when asked to define love

~~~~~~~~~~~~~~~~~~

---

10. February 23, 1991, 118.

RETIREMENT. *TIME ZERO*. MARRIAGE CRISIS. We have the children raised. We have worked hard. We're ready for travel or play. Or we've hit it big in the lottery, sold several huge deals in a row, and now, at 45, are thinking of retiring. Whether 45 or 70, the issue is the same: We think we are what we do. I'm a mother, an athlete, a professional. Our egos identify with what we learn, what we achieve or don't achieve in our lives, to give us a sense of purpose and worth. It follows that a large change in lifestyle with new rules, new things to learn, and very different things to control and learn can promote personal crisis. When the kids leave home, "empty-nesters" grieve, cling, and, hopefully, regroup into a new and more full adulthood. Retirement can be even more disorienting with the many losses of structure, identity, control, and focus. To paraphrase General Norman Schwartzkopf, commander of the U.S. troops in the 1991 Gulf War, yesterday I had 500,000 troops at my command; today I can't even get a plumber to fix my toilet.

Recently,[11] the business journal on National Public Radio reported a study done with retired married couples. The worst situation (which put the most stress on the marriage) was one where the husband retired first, while the wife continued working. Why? The wife saw the husband's availability in the home as her long-awaited partner in chore completion and household repair. The husband viewed retirement as the long-awaited reward for his years of labor. Expectations were at loggerheads. Resolution came when the partner in the home rolled back the standards for household tidiness and the retiree pitched in on some on the chores. The transition takes, on average, about two years to move from separate careers, and therefore interests, to a merged career and melded interests.

My husband sold his company and retired in the last several months, so I can vouch for the *Time Zero* situation in which we now live: no structure, no nine to five, no business trips, no deadlines. Some days it's scary, sometimes liberating. Our lives are a *Strengths Contract*[12] every day. Using knowledge of *brainstyle* gifts bolsters self-worth; gifts transcend the activities they are applied to, otherwise we can confuse who we are with what we know.[13] As a pre-retiree at Pepsi said to me, "I used to be able to walk into a [bottling] plant and tell you what each piece of equipment was and what it could do. Now, I can't . . ." He clearly showed his depression and loss of pride as he added, "Now I don't know anything worth

---

11. July, 2002
12. Chapter 15.
13. I am discovering more of my own competency and confidence, as my social skills become more visible for us. I consider this a new personal beginning. David is taking time for friends and family that he never had time for during his career. He is "a new man," his children and brothers and sister say.

anything." As we discussed the lie he believed about himself and what the truth of his gifts allowed, his life began to open to new possibilities where he could use the same gifts that mastered manufacturing to master new explorations in travel, learning, and projects to build at home.

LIVING TOGETHER WELL PAST FIFTY. START NOW. But what kind of retirement will it be if you aren't healthy? To enjoy the life that you've worked so hard to create, you need to feel physically well. In "the longest and most comprehensive study of human development ever undertaken," Harvard Medical School gave psychological and medical tests to over 800 people over the course of six decades to find out what "attributes were vital to successful aging." Dr. George Vaillant, the study director, reports these findings as essential for a long and happy life:

- Orientation toward the future. The ability to anticipate, to plan, and to hope.
- Gratitude, forgiveness, and optimism; i.e., the ability to see the glass half-full.
- Empathy. The ability to imagine the world as it seems to the other person.
- The ability to reach out. "We should want to do things *with* people, not do things to people or ruminate that they do things to us," says Dr. Vaillant.[14]

Especially important was a feeling of acceptance. Vaillant concludes: "Worry less about cholesterol and more about gratitude and forgiveness."

If you want to live long enough to share your golden years with someone, start thinking healthily now. Use *brainstyle* information to understand clearly and simply the magnificence of everyone in your life. Give up your grudges by changing your expectations. Look for reasons to love the best in others. Have a good time.

~~~~~~~~~~~~~~~

No matter the problem, love is the answer.

~~~~~~~~~~~~~~~

"It's important to never give up," she said. "It took me years to forgive myself and forgive Doo [her husband]. I had to let go of guilt and blame. After he died, it was hard for me to think of anything really bad he'd ever done. That's because love overrules everything. When you look back, it's love that remains. And when you die and close your eyes, the thing you see is love, the face of God."
—Loretta Lynn, commenting on her "tempestuous marriage" to Oliver "Doo" Lynn, and why she made it last through 48 years of infidelities, physical abuse, major illnesses, and chronic drunkenness

~~~~~~~~~~~~~~~

---

14. The study is published in *Aging Well: Surprising Guideposts to a Happier Life from the Landmark Harvard Study of Adult Development,* 2002 (Little, Brown).

CHAPTER 13

PARTNERSHIP OR PARTING?
ROMANCE AND SPATS

CONVENTIONAL **F**EARS OF **S**INGLES. Jokes reveal our fears and beliefs. Here's a sample.

I didn't know what true happiness was until I got married. . . .
Then it was too late.
I married Miss Right. I just didn't know her first name was Always.
I take my wife everywhere, but she keeps finding her way back.
Statistically, 100% of all divorces started with marriage.
—Attributed to Rodney Dangerfield, comedian, quoted on the Internet

~~~~~~~~~~~~~~~

PICKING A **M**ATE. The short answer: Yes. Our chemistry supports our spiritual joining and our longing for oneness, our dreams of closeness, and our union of spirits.

CHEMISTRY AND **M**ORE. Finding a mate is known as "the dating industry," if marketers, talk shows, *The Bachelor,* and *Sex and The City*[1] have anything to do with it. Finding Mr. Right is sexy, fun to talk about, and if you've ever asked a

---

1. Currently popular U.S. television programs focus on the dating game, emphasizing one's appearance and the difficulties encountered in the win-lose contest to find the right match. Dating is a contest, an elimination competition, currently portrayed in the U.S. on *The Bachelor* and *The Bachelorette,* and even more sleazily on *Joe Millionaire.* The "plot" is to have 25 applicants for the affections of the star and then to have these be eliminated one by one for various subjective reasons. A "relationship" is supposed to develop, but since it's all for TV, the "winners" of each game haven't yet stayed together. The values portrayed are sex, physical looks, and material lifestyle. Illusions = "reality TV."

couple how they met, gets that glow going. Listening to the answers of couples who have been together for some time, there seem to be some factors in common: There is an inexplicable chemistry that attracts them to one another; the settings are random; and almost never do common interests make a lasting difference. As author and minister Hugh Prather points out, "Many couples feel a deep oneness with each other and still have 'very little in common.'" He cites the lack of common interests between parent and child where there exists the most open and deeply intimate bond as proof.

HOW OUR CHEMISTRY ACTUALLY INFLUENCES DATING.

"When two people find one another attractive, their bodies quiver with a gush of PEA (phenylethylamine), a molecule that speeds up the flow of information between nerve cells. An amphetamine-like chemical, PEA whips the brain into a frenzy of excitement, which is why lovers feel euphoric, rejuvenated, optimistic, and energized, happy to sit up talking all night or making love for hours . . ."

Addictive, isn't it? Now researchers at the New York State Psychiatric Institute have proven that "attraction junkies," as they call them, are those addicted to these brain chemicals, and so the Romeos and the heartbreakers who love 'em and leave 'em over and over are simply looking for a fix of PEA. Brain chemistry rules in the feel-good junkies, but it has no depth, no soul. But there *is* an answer for both the attraction junkies (as well as the socially anxious) in chemistry itself: Antidepressants allow the unstable, fickle ones to "choose partners more calmly and realistically."[2]

Our hardware and natural chemistry for love are factors supporting or hindering our commitment. The good news: We know how it works. Today we can choose to manage it with the values we decide upon, the life purpose we define, and the new medical and health choices we have available.

~~~~~~~~~~~~~~~

Debra:

I've known him for seven years. He's been my best friend. We went to this event together, as we've done so many times in the past. This time, though, we hadn't seen each other for six months. He told me back then that he couldn't see me as a patient anymore because his feelings had changed for me, and he didn't want to compromise our professional relationship, nor the relationship I had with another man at the time. I was really sad, missed him, but I just didn't feel "that way" toward him.

---

2. Diane Ackerman, *A Natural History of Love*, ©1990, 1994, Random House, Inc. 64.

This time, on the first evening, we were sitting across the room from one another and *BAM*. We just looked at each other, and it was instant. People started telling us how we were the perfect couple after only two days. We couldn't stand being apart.

Our first date was Friday night, and I met him at the door. We embraced. We actually just hugged for the next two hours. We couldn't let go of each other. It was the most incredible thing I've ever experienced.

He called last night, and. . . we talked for hours, and then, then we were just quiet and each of us could feel the other's energy all over our body. We had whole-body orgasms, and we weren't even in the same room. It's the most perfect thing I've ever known.

She is 40, he, 44; she was married once at 18 for a short time and promised herself to never make THAT mistake again. So she has dated for all these years, found her career, supported herself, and found that exercise and spiritual pursuits are enlightening and a great way to spend her free time. In fact, that's where she met Russ for the first time. Russ, who is now The One. Russ, who has somehow caused her world to tilt, her view of reality to alter dramatically, and her eyes to glaze when she talks or thinks of him, for that matter.

Perfect. It IS a lightning bolt. It IS instantaneous. You DO know in a heartbeat. You do feel it all over. Your brain chemistry does literally explode. What a terrific foundation: friendship first, attraction later.

~~~~~~~~~~~~~~~

"When . . . love relationships fail . . . they fail because they were entered into
for the wrong reason. . . . Most people enter into relationships with an eye toward
*what they can **get out of them, rather than what they can put into them.**"*
[emphasis added]
—Neale Donald Walsch, *Conversations with God*

~~~~~~~~~~~~~~~

Most of us, like Debra, rehearsed by dating other people in relationships that didn't work out, assessing what mattered and what didn't. In her last relationship with a younger man, who shared her interests but not her spirituality, she enjoyed a wonderfully physical relationship. She learned, however, that she must have spiritual values in common or she could not truly connect. In her case, as a physical therapist who enjoys sports and the outdoors, she explored her spiritual Self by going to more and more retreats that dealt with mind, spirit, health, and fitness. It was at one of these that she saw her love anew, right across the room.

One young man named the safety, ease, and spiritual connection with the woman he was to marry by saying, "She makes me laugh."

It is significant that Debra's "soul mate" was right in front of her all along. This is the definition of a miracle: To simply change your perception from one of fear (fear of the intimacy in an authentic, loving relationship) to one of love and acceptance. It is the greatest thing you can do at any time, this mere shift in perception; you see the person, the world, and all of reality anew. You perform a miracle. It is no more than and no less than that. If you can see the deeper love available within a dear friend, you can also shift your perception any other time, about your chosen partner, a colleague, an event, your entire family, even an illness—everything. You can realize a new life, a spiritual path of joining with others and healing as you go.

~~~~~~~~~~~~~~~~

Deep sexual attraction—love—prior to marriage isn't necessary to make a marriage work. . . . If a couple feels comfortable when they are together, they know they can trust each other, then the relationship has a BIG chance of surviving. I also believe that incompatibility (different likes and dislikes) can add depth to a marriage, so long as both parties respect each other's ways, likes, and dislikes.
—Dave Vorback, husband of 37 years, father of three, grandfather of two, New Zealand; a Deliberator

~~~~~~~~~~~~~~~~

CHOOSING A PARTNER. If you are reappraising your current relationship, entering or leaving one, what would it take for you to consider the following thoughts as a new approach to your love life, regardless of the statistics on marriage and divorce (see Appendix B)?

~~~~~~~~~~~~~~~~

There is simply no mistake to be made in picking a mate. . . . You will end up with someone who has far more flaws than you originally thought. And obviously it's true that people who have multiple relationships tend to carry the same problems into each one. . . . This is not because they are choosing the wrong person, but because they are not yet healed. Dynamics form over and over for the uncomplicated reason that we pick a partner with the characteristics that could most facilitate our growth, and then turn around and do battle with those characteristics.
—Hugh and Gayle Prather, *I Will Never Leave You* (Bantam, 1996), 62.

~~~~~~~~~~~~~~~~

Consider this: Parents and children have almost nothing in common, "and yet feel their oneness . . . deeply," write the authors/couples' counselors. The Prathers also divulge that they were "highly incompatible" in the beginning, yet by creating a broader context of learning from one another, came to see that "the differences in [their] strengths contain[ed] the potential for healing." They have used their lessons to practice a ministry and counseling practice for couples over several decades and have put their wisdom in their wonderful books. The Prathers summarize relationships simply and eloquently: ". . . the yearning for oneness is the source of the love instinct. The ego's resistance to oneness turns love into war."[3]

The ego's job is to keep us alive. In *BrainStyles* Land, this is the job of the left brain. Love is clearly not rational or measurable, and so the commitment, the feelings, and the inner wisdom that draw two people together can be said to come from the right brain, or our connection with the soul, the intuitive and immeasurable knowing we are all capable of. It is this part of us that can be trusted, will remain changeless, and is the true guide to life. We have but to listen past the conscious loud worrying and questioning of our left-brained comparisons. The Prathers suggest overriding the left-brained analysis of, say, marital testing with that inner knowing that may be aware of the unseen potential in a relationship. "A test can't tell you what you will have if you walk beside this person for a lifetime, but the peace of your heart can inform you whether to begin."[4]

So if the question is, "Should I marry or partner with my opposite?" then the answer has to be in terms of your goal. If learning is your goal, then there are no mistakes or accidents. If getting the right answer[5] is your goal, only you know who the perfect mate is for you, and your fearful process of generating criteria and matching candidates to them (as one left-brained Deliberator who didn't marry until 40 will attest) can take a long, long time.

A spiritual relationship is one where minds join. All relationships are spiritual, because bodies cannot truly join; a partnership is one where those involved choose consciously to join for a larger purpose. When bodies are the reason for joining, separation is the result, for bodies can only experience the illusions of emotions and physical attraction which soon dissipate.

---

3. Hugh and Gayle Prather, *I Will Never Leave You* (Bantam, 1996) 62 (used with permission).
4. Ibid., 65.
5. Answer A: Avoiding the Mistakes Your Parents Made, or Answer B: Having a Marriage/Partnership as Good as Your Parents'.

~~~~~~~~~~~~~~~~

*We do not listen to and do not follow this voice within our own souls,
and so we become a house divided against itself.
We are pulled this way and that, and we are never certain of anything.*
—Ralph W. Trine

~~~~~~~~~~~~~~~~

AFTER THE CHEMISTRY WEARS OFF. OK, it was a bad day. We were having an argument. "You're not supposed to argue on a vacation," I thought. He was doing the shouting for both of us, so that left me to be calm. Odd how that happens sometimes, when you choose in that nanosecond before you speak to not react from your emotions. In any case, he was telling me just how angry he was by using low and inside, hardball four-letter words. It was painful. If I hadn't had the preparation of three weeks of his illness, pain, and frustration while we were supposed to be having so much fun, I would have been a lot worse off.

TIMING. As it was, I went for a walk and recalled how he had just confronted a huge, emotionally-laden financial situation in a marathon telephone call on my behalf, using the expertise and *brainstyle* brilliance I didn't have, and stressing himself terribly. So, I reevaluated in the little time-out I had given myself. I concluded (for the first time in living memory) that his anger came from sensitivity to me. Whoa! Isn't he the Man from Mars with Will of Steel and I the Vulnerable from Venus who was supposed to have all the feelings in the family? But wait. It must be that his feelings were hurt or he wouldn't be shouting like that. *Duh.* I used the time to sort out my immediate reactions to his tantrum from the facts of the situation. When I finally remembered what it was that I'd actually said, I was embarrassed. Sorry. I realized that my standard response to his answer, "How could you say that to me?" was off the mark. Nor was it appropriate to ask him, "What's really wrong, dear?" I already knew. No, nothing was appropriate except to affirm and act on the best from each of us. Forget the fight. He was a loving man, not an angry one, who was currently in pain. I was a loving wife, not the selfish and thoughtless wench I felt myself to be at the moment.

There were no apologies needed. No discussions. It was over. We would do whatever he needed to feel better, and that was to go right home from our dream vacation five days early. My disappointment disappeared as I settled into doing the right thing.

"Why am I talking this loud? Because I'm wrong."

© *The New Yorker* collection from cartoonbank.com—reprinted by permission

PARTNERSHIPS WHERE NO ONE CHANGES. Conventional wisdom points out differences. Our left-brained analyses serve up lists of obstacles to relationships: gender, finances, race, affiliations, religion. Where would Hollywood be without these lists? Where would the drama of our lives be without the conflicts? We say we want inner peace; we act to realize its opposite. Think about it. When are you aware of differences? Is it when you want something or someone to make you feel whole (sex, money, property, status, clothes) and another appears to have what you want? When you notice these differences, are you able to be authentic? Kind? Have an intimate and natural relationship? Do you not have to get past your envy and comparisons first? This is the turf of the ego, the part of us that measures our worth and believes we are incomplete and isolated—and need another person or achievement to make us whole and complete.

LET THE FIGHTS BEGIN. Every time you fight, you are upset with what exists. You want things or the person to be different than they are. Ecstasy, it has been said, is the opposite condition: experiencing the perfection of things just as they are, right now. Your *brainstyle* establishes the way you perceive reality, and when you're irritated, annoyed, and exploding with anger and impatience, you can bet that you want things done and said the way YOU would do and say them given your *brainstyle*. That's why families are the place where we get so upset. Of ALL the people we should be able to count on, of ALL the people in the whole world who should understand and say it the way it needs to be said, THEY SHOULD . . . and then they don't. They say it their way.

~~~~~~~~~~~~~~~~

The battle of the sexes . . . is mostly a draw these days.
—Maria Russo[6]

~~~~~~~~~~~~~~~~

Fights are driven by *brainstyle*, not gender. You can count on each *brainstyle* fighting according to its strengths. Understanding how each *brainstyle* contributes and with what timing is critical to release unrealistic expectations and therefore prevent conflicts.

Actually, fights are a concern for only two of the *brainstyles*: the Deliberators and the Conciliators. Knowers and left-sided Conceptors approach disagreements or fights with much more confidence, knowing they can resolve, squash, or out-maneuver the person and problem and get over it quickly. It is the emotionality that is tiresome and wearing for all of us. In (most of) western culture, we all agree with the left brain's distaste for unruly, irrational emotions.[7] The reframing of this right-brained expression as passion is how we are finally taking advantage of this gift. Emotional intelligence, as defined by Daniel Goleman, PhD, requires right-brained emotions informed by left-brained rationality.

> BRAINSTYLE CLUE: **Timing is the problem. Timing is the solution.**

Knowing about your own *Time Zero* reactions, you can manage your own fight buttons more confidently no matter your *brainstyle*; using timing, you can realize many more workable solutions with others when they get unmanageable.

---

6. *New York Times* book review, 5/26/2002, 7.
7. A distaste supported by brain functioning. Daniel Goleman's research into emotional intelligence as well as other studies on grieving show that emotionality is debilitating for brain chemistry, draining needed neurotransmitters and requiring a long recovery time. Those who move on to other subjects tend to get to similar conclusions and healing with less stress. These findings belie the maxim of the therapy of the last several decades to "get into your anger and express it." *Emotional Intelligence: Why It Can Matter More Than IQ* (Bantam Books, 1995).

BrainStyles Clues:

KNOWERS FIGHT EARLY over who is going to win. The situation is distilled into black-or-white options, often with an ultimatum or blame attached. This is "telling it like it is" to the left-brained ones. If seen as a statement of logic containing feelings, it can be problem-solved. Direct questions or statements are the most useful to clarify actions and statements. Avoid asking about feelings.

CONCILIATORS FIGHT LATER over personal issues of fairness (when they feel "wronged" and you can't see your own "mistake"). Initial explosions are emotional reactions that pass. Offer rational ideas or goals to get Conciliators to their left-brain analysis and a more reasonable discussion.

CONCEPTORS FIGHT EARLY over the big picture, the philosophy, values, and future impact. Look for the value in the idea presented and watch the emotion drain away. As soon as possible, move to discussing the future and see how to take advantage of what the Conceptor is presenting and become a partner instead of an adversary.

DELIBERATORS FIGHT BY ARGUING and DISCUSSING what is right, based on value and precedent. Use a step-by-step process that avoids pressuring for a decision, includes their ideas, and uses the situation as a learning experience.

HOW EACH *BRAINSTYLE* FIGHTS. The first purpose of a fight is to create emotional distance. You know, get a little time on your own. The second purpose, which explains the first, is to allow time for *brainstyle* processing. Check your intentions. You can get the same result by just asking for the time that you need to think.

The third purpose of an argument is to briefly project guilt, regret, or discomfort onto another by making them wrong and yourself right.

Choosing happiness and forgiveness, you can turn any argument into an opportunity to learn about yourself and deepen the partnership.

~~~~~~~~~~~~~~~~

I call you what I am until I can see it in myself.
—Byron Katie, *Loving What Is*[8]

~~~~~~~~~~~~~~~~

BrainStyle Clue: The more left-brained *brainstyles* and their opposites, the right-brained ones, are alternately tough, then tender. The strong access to one side of the brain creates wide swings.

8 Harmony Books, 2002

Conciliators and right-sided Deliberators, be aware that you are at your best and most confident being supportive and openly caring; at your most defensive when setting a boundary or confronting another. Prepare ahead.

Knowers, be aware that you are most comfortable and in control setting limits and reaching quick conclusions; least able to express and respond caringly to an emotional situation in the moment. You tend to give in or lay down the law. Give yourself some time to think before you unload on your partner.

KNOWERS take no prisoners. The rapid left-brain access means quick pronouncements, conclusions, and judgments. Usually heavy artillery is the first, not the last, option. Knowers do not recognize this as "conflict" but as simply setting things on course. "Conflict?" a Knower teacher asked. "There is no conflict. I am right." Declaring what is right or wrong, go or no go, A or B, and the consequences that will result from your choice of the wrong option come straight from their strengths. Edicts. Crystal-clear direction, boundary setting, well, orders, are to be expected given their gifts. The strengths prevent "conflict" because the treatment of everyone is much more "even-handed," as this teacher's colleagues attested. "She applies the rules to everyone." Other *brainstyles*, spending much more time on what things mean and the impact and significance of the details, end up having little time to sort out the issues that are so very clear to the Knower. Thus others have favorites and spend more time discussing or patching things up as they include and personalize. Knowers have no time for these activities. Although both the Conceptor and Knower can be combative, their tactics are distinct: The Conceptor can be more willing to negotiate early, the Knower will not. A direct confrontation ("No, that is not our policy") or a time delay ("I'll get back to you") can stop the Knower's logic and open discussion.

For example, a Knower wife announced to her new Deliberator husband at a social dinner that if he ever criticized her publicly again she would get up and leave, and he would be eating alone with his guests. (She drew the line quickly and surgically in a way he wouldn't forget. He thought about it, acknowledged he was being critical in a "socially safe situation," saw her logic, and from then on said what he didn't like privately.)

If you remember that the Knower's access to the right brain is delayed, you can anticipate that his or her first onslaught will reflect the Knower's problem, not yours. Being direct in your response with a request to consider your timing, plus offering a solution of your own, can impact the logic of the Knower to shift to new ground. Here is a punchline response to a confrontation by a Knower vice president ("Get to the bottom line, dammit! I don't have all day!" with a fist to the table for emphasis), given by a Deliberator manager. He was outgunned and outranked, and yet he looked his Knower vice president in the eye and told him, "I'll never make a decision as fast as you will. But I do have an answer that I have thoroughly analyzed, and you can take it to the bank. There are too many hip shooters around here. I'm going to give you something you can count on." When the Deliberator delivered what he promised, that Knower vice president became his biggest supporter and saw that he was promoted three times in the next three years.

DELIBERATORS hate conflict, avoid it at all costs, and thus can slide in zingers in protected social situations (like the husband above), where they feel safe in social conventions ("She can't fight in front of company. . . ."), rather than be directly confrontational. Best at assessments, a Deliberator's little criticisms/pointers/helpful hints can mount up and erode the relationship. Almost always these comments are neither kind nor loving. "But I was only trying to be helpful," or "I was just joking, dear," are lies. Will what is offered pass the Caring Test? You know when it won't and when it will.

In any confrontation, the Deliberator wants to slow down the conversation to use his or her substantial gifts for analysis and rationality; thus this *brainstyle* doesn't have arguments, it has discussions in which the topic is broken down, explained, understood, and assessed against standards of right and wrong. Key point: Discussions are NOT emotional. This is not to say that Deliberators cannot get emotional. No, they just do not want anyone else to get emotional in return. Losing control is somewhat shameful—and always unsettling—so many Deliberators brag about the times they put another in his place, had the last word, or sorted someone out. You can almost hear the door slam with the delivery of the long-formulated, righteous conclusion. Since confrontation is such a non-strength of this *brainstyle*, anytime a Deliberator carries off a confrontation (even if it is a one-sided affair), she is quite proud of her ego's victory. She has forgotten the rule about the tradeoff between being right or happy.

Because of the Deliberator's gifts, he can calm down the emotional maelstrom until it gets manageable. This ability to settle storms is what he brings to a conflict when emotions are involved. To move forward, allow time for thinking and sorting information with short discussions that allow for timing of all parties.

BRAINSTYLE CLUE: People don't dislike you or fight with you simply because you're different.

They dislike conflict with you for two reasons:

1) You don't like them.

2) You don't yet realize your differences are your gifts.

CONCILIATORS hate conflict also. Since their *Time Zero* response is from the right brain, which can carry the full force of their emotions, they have two basic responses: Sweetness and Light "Oh! I'm sorry!" or Going Ballistic (I don't think we need a description of what this sounds like here). The first response (without *BrainStyles* information) can set up volcanic revenge-taking for later. Other *brainstyles* may feel "manipulated" by a Conciliator's use of emotions to get his or her way, implying, "If you don't do what I want, I'll throw a fit," or by the indirect way of saying what they want, "What do you want to do? I don't really care" (when it turns out the Conciliator really does care but just doesn't want to create disharmony or make you unhappy).

The Conciliator needs time to slow down the speed of the logic and language to allow for all the right-brained associations he makes with incoming stimuli, and then to access the logic of the left brain, which is delayed by this process. Asking for time to think is often the most profoundly simple thing a Conciliator can do to maintain his own peace and the relationships he cares about so deeply.

Conciliators' timing in a conflict is the key to whether they are trusted and can maintain a relationship for the long term. So many Conciliators see a fight as an ending and leave a relationship—without understanding that it is the situation where their non-strengths are called upon (to make quick, logical decisions) that they seek to flee. Overwhelmed with feelings initially, Conciliators can make pronouncements that are defensive, vicious, and are later regretted.

CONCEPTORS, especially the more extroverted of the crew, want to take over quickly in order to simplify the issues, establish the overview, and stop the overwhelming number of facts and details that they cannot process in the moment. When a Conceptor is more introverted, they will avoid the conflict until it must be dealt with, and steer a discussion (not an argument) with these gifts. The strengths the Conceptor can bring to a complex argument help to sort detail into priorities, surface underlying assumptions, broaden the topic, and take it to new places. Conceptors who see the broader issues look at negotiations and confrontations as challenging, stimulating, and a real opportunity to win in the broadest of possible senses. Conceptors who go for the short-term win see it as a game, an opportunity to out-strategize their opponent. They have also forgotten a rule: You get to win now and lose later, or you get to win in the long term. Managing relationships is the criteria for getting ideas implemented.

Conceptors go for the win by defining the game itself: "These are the issues. Don't bog me down with the details." When angry, what better way for the Conceptor to take charge than by attacking the big issue, the broken rules, the future cost, the hot buttons of the other? Other *brainstyles* point out exceptions ("I did not say that . . . exactly"), or bring up what the Conceptor missed. Interrupting or other forms of resistance, and either smart-aleck or well-intentioned input, that interferes with the Conceptor's timing, that requires a left-right-left-brain exchange, can set off a full-frontal launch of the weapons in the Conceptor's arsenal: name-calling (stereotypes are merely generalizations that are not politically correct), ultimatums and threats (left-brained boundary setting), or personal attacks. Other *brainstyles* can be totally alienated. Conceptors who learn about others' strengths and timing avoid all these landmines that detonate their brilliance with off-target delivery.

~~~~~~~~~~~~~~~

The loss of an emotional or spiritual integrity may be at the source of our suffering. In a very paradoxical way, pain may point the way toward a greater wholeness and become a potent force in the healing of this suffering.
—Rachel Naomi Remen, *Kitchen Table Wisdom*, 75

~~~~~~~~~~~~~~~

FIGHT-STARTERS: COMPARISONS. ASKING FOR NON-STRENGTHS.

- **CONCEPTOR TO CONCILIATOR:** "Why can't you support me like (a Knower) does? She's not shy. She speaks up on an issue. You just disappear."

- **CONCILIATOR TO CONCEPTOR:** "You certainly embarrassed me out there, yelling like that. Why can't you be more polite like (a Deliberator)."

- **KNOWER TO DELIBERATOR:** "Well, you sure disappeared when things got tough. At least (the Conceptor) stood up for getting our money back. If it was up to you, we'd be out all our money and nothing would change."

- **DELIBERATOR TO KNOWER:** "Do you have to make such a scene? Can't you act more like (a Deliberator?)"

FIGHT-PREVENTERS AND PARTNERSHIP-BUILDERS: FOCUS ON STRENGTHS.

- **CONCEPTOR TO CONCILIATOR:** "I like it when you stay back and let me do my thing, then get people together afterwards, like in the lunchroom where you congratulated everyone."

- **CONCILIATOR TO CONCEPTOR:** "You certainly took over in an area I couldn't handle well at all. I appreciate how you got our money back."

- **KNOWER TO DELIBERATOR:** "You are so good at smoothing things over. The man almost looked pleased to give us our money back after you talked to him. Nice touch."

- **DELIBERATOR TO KNOWER:** "You were great, taking it to the mat like that. You're our fighter. You saved us a lot of money."

CONFLICT AND THE BRAINSTYLES SYSTEM®

Conflict is a way to create distance between you and another.

In order to transform a conflict into a new direction for the relationship, you must clarify your intention about the outcome: Do you want to be right? Or do you want to be closer?

TIMING IS THE PROBLEM.

DELIBERATORS

INITIALLY:
Want to be right according to personal values, knowledge, and other experts.

Will give lengthy explanations or background.

Demand to be heard.

Will look for exceptions.

May say Yes or No, but won't decide now.

KNOWERS

INITIALLY:
Want to win and/or end with a quick solution.

Will offer black-or-white options.

Will simplify issues quickly. Ends can justify means.

Will dismiss emotions.

Will decide now, feel later about the issues.

TIMING IS THE SOLUTION.

CONCEPTORS

INITIALLY:
Want to uncover the basic assumptions, then win by establishing new ground.

Love to negotiate, outthink, and strategize.

Can detach from the relationship and stay aloof.

May demand a new direction for the future or changes from you.

CONCILIATORS

INITIALLY:
Want to be loved and want to be right.

Want to be treated "fairly" according to a personal definition.

Want to maintain the relationship, even to the point of changing or fudging the facts.

May make an emotional "decision" now, then revise.

TO BRING OUT THEIR BEST, ALLOW TIME FOR THEIR STRENGTHS.

DELIBERATORS

Don't ask for a quick decision in a new area.

Offer goals, alternatives early for them to consider over time.

Respect their thinking and analysis. Build on what they offer.

Notice how they organize the idea or break it down into doable pieces. Listen to their questions and see what's missing. Watch how they anticipate risks to keep you safe.

KNOWERS

Realize the first decision will come fast. Confront it directly or ask for time.

Offer your goals early and ask to merge them.

Don't argue methods or history—they'll win.

Look for their gifts of clarity and focus to define what is unclear. See how they bring structure and limits to problems to make things work. Acknowledge this.

CONCEPTORS

Allow time for their generalities. Work on defining a mutual goal.

Allow time for specifics to be heard and understood by them.

Set up trial periods to allow emotions to fade.

Elicit their thinking rather than arguing facts or history.

Notice how they added depth or breadth to take you somewhere new.

CONCILIATORS

Refuse a quick decision. Reinforce their value to you and others.

Allow the left brain time to add logic and consider facts.

Expect changes.

Be openly supportive.

Look for their integration of differences, their personal touch, the enthusiasm and warmth. Appreciate this and they will offer more.

CHAPTER 14

BrainStyles Pairs
and Possibilities

~~~~~~~~~~~~~~

The happiest lovers are not the most realistic but the most positive.
They idealize their partners and expect their relationships to survive hard times.
—Martin P. Seligman, *Authentic Happiness,* ©2002, Free Press

~~~~~~~~~~~~~~

COMMON QUESTIONS ABOUT FINDING YOUR SOUL MATE. How do you tell Ms. Right from Ms. Right Now? Which *brainstyles* create the best partnerships? Should you choose the same *brainstyle* or your opposite? How can you increase your odds of staying happily together?

The following chapter describes the issues each *brainstyle* pair can encounter. There is no one best *brainstyle* combination, although some *brainstyle* couples will have more challenges than others. To stay in love, look for gifts. The pace of your intimacy—revealing your dreams and fears to one another and the trust you allow as you face life together—is up to you.

BRAINSTYLES PAIRS AND LOVING POSSIBILITIES. If you begin—or restart—your relationship by consciously offering your strengths to reach common goals, your admiration for one another can build, and trust grow. Your reliance on one another's integrity can increase. The product of your growing partnership will be interactions, including communications, where each partner will come away with respect for the gifts and wisdom of the other. Each partner will grow in self-respect and offer more to his or her lover. Joy becomes a natural part of your lives. With this foundation, you can consider possibilities together that expand your lives spiritually as well as financially. You will then give and receive the greatest blessing of all: you will expand the lives you lovingly touch as a couple.

To seek this outcome, to *intend* this outcome, to *insist* on this outcome, will create a spiritual partnership, richer than your grandest dreams.

~~~~~~~~~~~~~~~~

THE KNOWER-CONCILIATOR PAIR. (The original Mars and Venus pairing; and we all know which planet is supposed to be male.)

This is a marriage of opposites in which all the bases are covered in solving problems. The attraction for completing oneself by choosing a partner to fill in what is missing in oneself is just one of the many challenges for each partner. The line between appreciating differences and competing with them can disappear in a heartbeat. For instance, Knowers love to be told that they are good with people. In their own way they are, though never by establishing the closeness and bonding that their counterpart can. If they take over for the social lead of the couple, *uh oh.*

Conciliators like to be prized for their fast decisions, only to change their minds very quickly. There is a large potential for competition by the Conciliator to be as quick with left-brain logic and ideas. Conciliators love to be told they are logical. In their own way they are. If they try to outwit the Knower in logical areas, oh dear, *oh dear.*

Another trap for the Conciliator partner is to adapt to the clear demands and pace of her left-brained partner and lose the invisible value she brings to make the life of the Knower exciting, meaningful, and full of caring relationships. Conciliators may take the role of resentful followers, sacrificing their own lives and expressions to go along with the more rapid, practical direction of the partner (see chapter 4). The Knower, when male, is wonderful as the protector and boundary-setter; when female, as the problem-solving leader, often the breadwinner, or the independent contributor to the relationship who gets things started, going, and completed.

The relationship must be managed continually. The solution of one married couple which has these *brainstyles* is not to partner in the traditionally Conciliator-defined sense of that word. The Conciliator wife calls this partnership strategy "divide and conquer," meaning: split the turf into separate project arenas. This means the Conciliator had to give up her image of the mythical Perfect Partner Hubby, the one who would spend hours alongside her, listening, sharing, acknowledging her for her brilliant ideas, disclosing his intimate thoughts and insights, and reveling in the bond they would openly acknowledge. Nope. Won't happen. Accept this, and whole new worlds of collaboration open up, as shown by pre-breakfast hot tub times or special events where the Conciliator shares in the Knower's activity.

When upset, Conciliator tactics can be indirect sarcasm, covert revenge, and emotional storms; Knowers can be brutally judgmental or withdrawn. Fights can be messy with differences in *brainstyle* blamed as the cause for problems ("You never listen! You're always right! You are hysterical! You're so black-and-white!") when actually the *brainstyle* strengths are being resisted and denied. Refocusing on the benefits of differing strengths will erase the conflict.

The first thing this partnership must do is to discuss what it means to be a "partner." The two *brainstyles* define this term from opposite places in the brain. For the Conciliator a partner is a buddy, a close compatriot, someone to talk things over and decide with. For the Knower, a partner is someone to ally with in getting things done. A mate is something entirely different. A mate is someone you privately treasure and feel for, brag about to others perhaps, but show your partnership with tenderness rather than collaboration.

➤ Time and reviews help when new issues are raised. The Knower must allow time for the Conciliator to mentally experience and try out the new ideas and see how they feel.

➤ Conciliators must accept that they will best manage, first, their own personal growth and maturation and bring it to create the warmth of the partnership. The Knower takes charge of directing the tasks—except for the fun and "silliness" of parties and birthdays and holiday festivities. Sure, Knowers can plan them and figure out all the logistics, but not the nuances of seating charts and games to play (you get the idea). Knowers are, however, excellent at discerning what presents are best for whom. Conciliators often give what they want for themselves, or their latest good idea, to the dismay of the recipient of the weird new vase.

➤ Knowers can, however, plan a most romantic event, getaway, honeymoon, or vacation. Watch out for those rose petals. There just needs to be a target set, a date, or an event to catch their attention.

➤ Loving Knowers are tolerant of the Conciliator's ups and downs, learn to steady their partners' thinking, help provide focus, and include their partners' needs and ideas in the new projects. They are caring advisors, not unconditional listeners.

➤ Recognition for their right-brained gifts will be a source of personal concern for Conciliators without some inner work. Heaven for a Conciliator might include a great deal of fanfare, greeting cards, trophies, small, tasteful plaques marking meaningful events, or as one with this *brainstyle* said, all she wanted was worship. Focusing on your own gifts, Conciliator, with caring self-acknowledgement is the most important thing for you. Meditate. Pray. Go out in nature. A faith or philosophy that can help you differentiate between the pride of the ego and the neutrality of self-acceptance in doing these things is critical.

➤ Conciliators need to supplement the Knower with relationships with other supportive friends, and expect delays in personal understanding from their partners.

➤ If either partner has the intention to build and heal the relationship, it can be an extraordinary partnership to raise a family and build a business.

> BRAINSTYLE CLUE: Partnerships begin with common goals. Partnerships are defined differently by each *brainstyle*.

CREATING A SUCCESS WITH YOUR OPPOSITE BRAINSTYLE.[1]

Linda, the lifelong high-achieving Conciliator you have met previously, has learned to live with, and after twelve years used several personality tests to understand, her differences with her husband. They had reached a détente: "We loved each other in general; it was the day-to-day that was difficult." Then there came the discoveries.

Since learning about *BrainStyles*, I now say my husband is a Knower. When new information presents itself to him in our family dealings, he comes to a seemingly quick, clear, fist-pounding exactness that is a "this or that," "yes or no," "can or cannot" conclusion. I used to say, especially when we'd argue, that he was a black-or-white rigid thinker and that he was impossible to deal with. I would avoid talking about difficult subjects, because I knew that it would be so hard to change his mind.

I know that he is more an introvert than I (his personal energy is directed inwardly), so his analysis is not out on the table for me, our son, or his employees to observe, understand, or follow. Instead, his decision, which to us seems so abrupt and final, is delivered almost as a pronouncement.

---

1. This example supplied by Linda Bush, now master teacher of *The BrainStyles System®*, was written in the first few months after her training as a *BrainStyles®* Instructor/Coach.

You might think he's a snob or a control freak. That's what I used to think when I'd get mad at him. Yet when you meet him you'll see he's a gentleman, almost timid with folks. Then, as I discovered, you'll realize he's also very loving. I just couldn't see it very well before, blinded as I was by my own way of seeing things through my *brainstyle*, and by all that I had learned about human behavior. I had no idea how it blinded me to seeing who he really is.

He says he doesn't speak much around others, because he doesn't trust their reaction to his comments. He fears that his "pronouncements" will hurt feelings or offend in ways he doesn't comprehend. He listens to others' banter and shakes his head at their seeming indecisiveness and lack of clarity. He may even tune out their speech if it's flowery or lengthy. What I began to notice was that if they offer succinct, factual, declaratory statements, he listens and nods.

One evening I asked my husband to stay at the dinner table a few minutes to talk. (Usually, he clears the table as soon as he's finished, even if others are not, and leaves to unwind alone.) I explained how powerfully moved I'd been earlier in the day by the revelation *BrainStyles* had provided about our differences in seeing the world and making decisions. I told him I thought he was a Knower and explained to him the Knower's strengths of quickly analyzing and sorting facts to diagnose cause and provide clarity in murky, emotional settings. He had been telling me since we met that he has two speeds: fast and stop. And I've been telling him for years in a not-so-complimentary tone that he only sees things in a binary fashion, black or white, good or bad, yes or no. I told him I used to think he was narrow-minded, incapable of seeing relationships and contingencies. Now, I explained, I saw that characteristic as his strength, one that I valued and needed, as it's my non-strength. It's hard to convey what an insight this was for me, and what an admission this was to tell him.

For me, a Conciliator, new events and information are usually wonderfully intriguing and full of guesswork. I can't sort information quickly; it all stays present and messy for a seemingly long time. I react emotionally, sometimes to such a degree that I freeze and cannot find words to explain my quandary, let alone facilitate others' decision-making. Hours later, I decipher and clarify what transpired and can then think of things I should have said.

With my new perspective, I offered my husband the fact that I need him to keep the fog clear for me and to offer a simple, efficient solution to problems. I suggested that he could count on me to help him see aspects of an issue that he might have overlooked, such as people's reactions or emotions, or what the guidelines are, or how things fit into the big picture.

This was the first time in twelve years of knowing Gary that I have had his undivided attention for thirty minutes. His face softened, his gorgeous blue eyes remained riveted on mine. The relationship tension we had felt for so long by looking at our differences as a problem, a gulf between us, evaporated before my eyes. He said, to my amazement, he never knew I could need him. Then his eyes filled with tears. He gently reached for me and held me, as we wept together in joy, in relief, to release the past and reach a whole new definition of who we are together.

~~~~~~~~~~~~~~~

THE KNOWER-DELIBERATOR PAIR. This is a marriage of complements in which the common bond is a gift for analysis and rational decisions without emotional turmoil. The home or business is, most likely, thoroughly organized and structured with rules, values, and tradition. They can also give great parties. The more extroverted of the couple will take the lead socially.

➤ Even though courting can be intensely romantic, lovey-dovey romance will be more private, and settle down sooner than for the right-brained unless the Deliberator is the more right-sided variety. This couple is an unemotional pairing, tending to do things for one another rather than being demonstrably affectionate, especially in public.

➤ Parental expressions of love by this pair are especially important for Conciliator, right-sided Deliberator or Conceptor children to understand in *brainstyle* terms. It is terribly easy for the right-brained, immature child to interpret the left-brained expressions of love (protecting, advising, doing things, giving money) as uncaring and the critical comparisons the parents may make as "abusive," the favorite disempowering term of the '90s.

➤ Mutual interests for this pair are not critical, as each partner tends to be comfortable enjoying his or her own hobbies or careers. However, mutual values are critical. Respect for one another rests, especially for the Deliberator partner, on shared values.[2]

---

2. The famous marriage of President Lyndon Baines Johnson (a Knower) and his Deliberator wife Lady Bird survived his years of infidelities and depression because he relied on his wife for steady, unemotional support, and she completely believed in him and his values as a politician.

➤ The Knowers' patience with the more thoughtful decision-making of their partners is continually tested, thus the need to split up the turf each is in charge of managing. One couple, when buying a car, let the Deliberator husband do the research in *Consumer Reports,* and then they would decide together, often with the Knower negotiating the deal. Either can be an excellent negotiator, and together they are a formidable team.

➤ The Deliberator can easily take charge of the social, travel, and intellectual life, bringing in interesting new books, people, ideas, interests, and taking them new places. Knowers can be homebodies and work until it's time to play, then it's party time. This is not universally true, but in general, Deliberators are better networkers and so mix in more activities and interests, while the Knower maintains more focus with fewer friends and more associates.

➤ Fights have a potential to stay win-lose with each of the partners defending his or her own right answer. *BrainStyle* timing is therefore critical in disagreements. When emotions surface for either party, they are slow to build and slow to end. Grudges and silence are likely. Using a problem-solving strategy that lists all the disagreements in a logical fashion with the intention to resolve them is needed as soon as possible. The Deliberator needs time to assess, the Knower to consider another side.

➤ The Deliberator's ability to sort out the issues, look for compromises, and pose alternatives is most useful here. The other strength of this couple is the ability to stay fairly unemotional (well, compared to the right-brained). The need to be right and win is the biggest obstacle to peace between them.

~~~~~~~~~~~~~~~~

If you really want to be happy, nobody can stop you.
—Sister Mary Tricky

~~~~~~~~~~~~~~~~

A MARRIAGE OF STRENGTHS AS SEEN BY A KNOWER WIFE OF 30 YEARS. The husband is a Deliberator, the wife, a Knower. They are a good team, as each is quite independent, literal, and unemotional in general. They have raised two high-achieving sons, one Deliberator, one Conciliator. She writes this piece after learning about their *brainstyles* to clarify how they have lived together on a daily basis with respect in order to love each other today. Note the things the husband does that have been attributed to "women" by those who still promote gender wars.

PERSONAL STYLE:	**HUSBAND (DELIBERATOR):** Collects closets full of newspapers, magazines, clippings, resource material, stacks of files, and so much clutter he can't find anything when he needs it. **WIFE (KNOWER):** Impatient with inefficiency in herself and others; hates clutter; throws everything out; if she needs something later, she'll find it by phone or wing it.
MEALS:	**HUSBAND:** Prefers seven courses, served individually and in proper sequence. Unlimited embellishments. Different plate, fork, glass for each item. Needs two hours minimum to finish. **WIFE:** Throw it together, put on table, eat, clean up, gone.
DIRECTIONS:	**HUSBAND:** Draws elaborate detailed maps, lengthy explanations. **WIFE:** Turn right here, left there, 1901 Main St.
SHOPPING:	**HUSBAND:** Spends days/weeks pursuing item, massaging the salesman, reeling him in, buys for astonishingly low price. Salesman loves and adores him; friends for life. He loves to shop. **WIFE:** This is what I'll pay, take it or leave it; get good deal; salesman resents me; I don't care. Hate to shop. It wastes too much time.
RELATING EVENTS:	**HUSBAND:** Long explanations, unnecessary side trips, careful weaving together of facts, climax seems anticlimactic. **WIFE:** We went, we saw, we did. Loved/hated it.
CHRISTMAS CARDS:	**HUSBAND:** Matches persons to cards, envelopes show Mr., Mrs., Jr., III, all children. Sends to people he hasn't seen in 40 years. **WIFE:** Rather not. Envelope says "Smith Family." Takes everyone off list haven't seen in five years.
PROJECTS:	**HUSBAND:** Wife says he is sometimes unrealistic. **WIFE:** Husband says she is negative, always announcing pitfalls.

WHY DOES THIS MARRIAGE WORK? The Knower wife sums up the advantages of living with her Deliberator husband as follows:

[I] trust and respect his ultimate decision and actions because I know they are backed up with reams of supporting data and no stone has been unturned in thorough research. If I want names, phone numbers, maps, or schedules for any city, structure, or event in the world, they are amazingly retrieved from the archives of information he deems necessary. I respect his knowledge of cuisine, music, arts, history, politics, etc.

He is very reliable because he shows moderation in all things. He makes unemotional decisions and takes personal charge of the details that I have no patience for.

And what does he see as the advantages of his Knower wife?

He can trust her common-sense approach to running the household. He respects her judgment and "ability to think on her feet." She handles emergencies with cool efficiency. She never calls him at the office with household questions. He knows she is loyal, steady, and reliable.

So, in conclusion, she looks at how *BrainStyles* has helped their marriage:

Traits I used to find annoying I now attribute to *brainstyle* differences. This has helped me be more patient with those differences. I now realize how much I respect and rely on his strengths. It has also made me more confident in my own attitudes, to recognize when I need to back off and let his strengths prevail.

Observation: It is very difficult for a Knower wife to accept traditional domination by a spouse. I firmly believe that some failed marriages are due to mismatched *brainstyles*, when the partners do not or cannot learn to respect the natural strengths of a spouse. There has to be respect before there can ever be love.[3]

BRAINSTYLE CLUE #1: Don't choose a Knower partner or mate lightly; they don't.

---

3. This statement is supported by clinical research reported in the section on marriage. Respect for another *brainstyle's* gifts is the basic requirement for a marriage.

THE KNOWER-CONCEPTOR PAIR. This is an unlikely partnership, just because there are so few of each of these *brainstyles*; the odds of either being male is much greater, and neither have social skills as a strength. Most likely this partnership will exist in business, a combination which works very well.

➤ The Knower brings practicality and structure; the Conceptor the new and the possible. Exciting possibilities will be invented when Conceptors are free to get results in their own way or when they are in charge. The mature Knower who knows his limitations can explain how ill-equipped he is to entertain the blue-sky thinking of the Conceptor, and so will leave the Conceptor to flesh out direction and needed changes. The Conceptor often needs a supportive partner to brainstorm ideas into fruition at the beginning. Conciliators and supportive Deliberators are the best choices here. However, a Knower partner supports the Conceptor in being practical and efficient, and is an excellent partner for defining the future.

➤ Conceptors may need more intimacy and openness than the Knower is comfortable sharing. Knowers tend to keep information close to the vest, and the Conceptor is very dependent on good input. Neither is terrific at collecting information in depth, so both may vie for leadership in directing the future. (Business solution: Bring in a third *brainstyle*.)

➤ Depending upon the left-brained access of the Conceptor, the relationship can deal well with the future, but not as well with social or people issues, detailed analysis, or follow-through on projects. The Knower is best at nurturing by problem-solving and focusing the couple by getting projects done; The Conceptor is best at initiating change and bringing a more balanced perspective to family issues.

➤ These friendships with the other two *brainstyles* will complement the lives of this pair socially.

➤ If this pair parents the other *brainstyles,* open expressions of love by touch and words will be vital to bond the family.

THE KNOWER-KNOWER PAIR. Forget it. Allies maybe, but a real partnership? For those of you familiar with sports, the example of Jerry Jones, Knower owner of the NFL's Dallas Cowboys, who insists on controlling every aspect of the team, and his former Knower coach, Jimmy Johnson, who took the football team to two Super Bowls, come to mind. After an increasingly contentious relationship over five years, where Johnson had to continually fend off the attempts of owner Jones to control the coaching job, the pair exploded when Jones said publicly that anyone could have coached the Cowboys football team to a win. Johnson quit. Jones hired a Conciliator who would follow direction. Even though the team (with no real leadership) did manage itself to a Super Bowl win one more time, it fell to the bottom of the league for seven years thereafter without the intensity and focus of its previous Knower coach. The competition created a lot of losers.

➤ Two Knowers need a common cause and separate turf to manage. Maintaining the separate turf is a constant battle, given that each has the same non-strengths of compromise, social skills, sharing information, and inclusiveness.

~~~~~~~~~~~~~~~~

THE CONCILIATOR-CONCEPTOR PAIR. This is a union of exciting potential: both are visual, imaginative, and love the world of ideas, philosophy, self-development, or spirituality, to name a few possibilities.

➤ The couple can get in trouble when they each make an issue dramatic, personally meaningful, and the resolution a Significant Event. Emotional fights can get ugly and unruly, and fear-based anger can drive words that are regretted for a long time.

➤ Fights can occur simply to create breathing space between the two—most often things get too close, timing too urgent, and issues too personal.

➤ Neither is naturally good at following through. Bills and obligations can fall through the cracks unless someone takes on the job—usually the Conciliator.

➤ Both resist control—a problem when deciding who will lead. The Conceptor is best equipped to do so when starting projects new to the couple. The Conciliator is also an excellent project manager, leader, and initiator when balancing his or her opinions with others.

➤ If the pair agrees to support new ideas without worrying about who gets the credit or takes the lead, breakthroughs in new territory can occur. The Conceptor is most often the idea leader, the Conciliator the supportive, imaginative, and action-oriented implementer.

➤ The Conciliator is best equipped to manage the relationship, the Conceptor to raise and resolve major issues and promote decisions to bring constructive changes into their lives.

A CONCILIATOR-CONCEPTOR PAIR HANDLE LOADED TOPIC$ WITH TIMING. Sunday morning, with the papers spread all over the kitchen table, the Conceptor husband of a woman I'll call Emily changed the subject abruptly to confront a major issue he'd already broached on several occasions. They were stalled, which is what she really wanted. She didn't know how to handle the sophisticated finances involved, which were her non-strengths.

"OK, I'm going to try to talk about this once more," Mike* said at the breakfast table, "and get this over with." He got a pad of blank paper and wrote a number on it. "This is what I've saved to give Jesse [their son] as a graduation present. This is," he drew a line under the number, "a given. Done. This," he wrote a second number, "is what I've got put away to give them for a down payment for the house. And this," he wrote a third number, "is the price of the house I want them to get."

The next few sentences went quickly, the words were simple, and their voices kept rising.

"Why?" she asked.

"What?"

"Why do you want them to buy a house for that much?" Conciliator Emily looked at the sheet of numbers still facing husband Mike.

"I've talked to Jesse already. I've figured it all out. What I'm not sure of is what size payment they can afford." His impatience with his wife's non-strengths belied his own non-strengths: empathy and a step-by-step approach. He underlined the number for the home. "If Joanie gets pregnant and can't work, this is the size payment that's reasonable." He studied the pad, reviewing the future he had all mapped out.

TAKING IT PERSONALLY. THE GAMES BEGIN. Typical of a Conciliator, Emily first thought only that she had been left out, and since

---

* Not his name, nor the real names of others in this anecdote.

inclusion was one of her strengths, one that she expected from him *"if he really loved and respected me."* She was hurt. Her questions carried the tone. "Have you already talked to Jesse about all of this? When are you thinking of giving him this money? How did you get to that figure for the home? What if they don't want to do this? What if they want to spend more? It sounds like you're controlling the whole thing," she concluded, indignant now.

A CONCILIATOR AT *TIME ZERO* IN NON-STRENGTHS. Because of how she felt, the Conciliator ignored the inability of their son Jesse to deal with finances. She also ignored the clarity her husband's gifts had lent to an impossible situation for their son and daughter-in-law, who had never bought a house or dealt with any of these complex issues. Emily's brain was awash in the processing of her own emotions.

"I asked Jesse how much each of them makes and what size house payment he thought they could afford. I don't think they can make it if they start a family and Joanie can't work." The Conceptor had thought it all through, the finances, the legal issues associated with the financing, and the potential future problems. Thus he was impatient with the review he had to go over *again* with his Conciliator wife. Mike said, "Why do you always have to be so defensive?" sounding very defensive.

"I have questions," Emily defended. Her eyes were getting liquid.

"You're completely off the subject, irrelevant. Why can't I just make my point? Why do you have to bring up all this other crap that has nothing WHATSO-EVER to do with the point?"

> *BRAINSTYLE CLUE:* When one partner must decide using his non-strengths, impatience and lack of explanations increase the stress and make things worse.
> It is critical for the partner dealing from strength to respect the timing of the other by being more patient and respectful, pointing out what they each bring to the situation.

LOADED TOPICS = NON-STRENGTHS = CONFLICT. "You're only telling me punchlines, and I want to understand how you got to them." Emily's voice betrayed her distress even though her questions may have sounded assertive some other time.

"You just bring up everything you can to block this and make it difficult," Mike charged. "You argue with everything." The Conceptor read between the lines, and referred to her habitual and fearful approach to finances when it came to the kids. She either wanted to give them everything or teach them responsibility by giving them nothing. Her inconsistency and slower pace, he realized, was what annoyed him.

CONCEPTOR EMOTIONAL EXPRESSION—A NON-STRENGTH. "I have only asked questions. Maybe in the past I wasn't in favor, but I'm just trying to understand now. That was a past conversation. This is NOW." He wasn't listening. He was talking. "I can't talk about this with you; you can't talk about anything on this subject." He stood up. "So I'm not going to talk about it again." He stalked across the room. Emily not only wasn't valuing his ability to address the overview and make decisions, Mike thought, she was too emotional to be reasonable. He just wasn't going to spend the time to talk it all through this time.

She shot back, "You're just blaming me, so you don't have to explain it to me." Pause. Insight. Emily began to be aware of her resistance based on feelings about her past that was creating a *Time Zero* decision for her now. She offered, "This is outside my experience," thinking again of how her father had never given them anything but a loan. They had had to pay back every penny by years of budgeting to be able to afford their first house together. She was stuck in the past, in fear, in resentment of the impending generosity that she felt cheated of. Loving words were unavailable to her.

He doesn't really want to tell me anything, she thought. She was overlooking the fact that Mike had had a much poorer childhood than she, and yet had been an unresentful partner in paying back the loan to her father. He was in the process of creating a different future for the kids—one she hadn't imagined yet. She was outside her strengths at *Time Zero* and was reacting badly, she realized.

Mike was silent. It was a standoff.

BRAINSTYLES INSIGHTS: IT ONLY TAKES ONE. She knew enough about *BrainStyles* to wait. About thirty minutes later, after allowing for the insights to settle and logic to take hold, she realized that her timing was poor for Mike. Moreover, she hadn't been respectful. What to do? Return to a commitment to learn and make her relationship with her husband a loving one. Then, drawing from her ability to introspect, she realized that it was a loaded topic because it required her non-strengths. Worse, her active experiential memory vividly reminded her of the negative experiences she had had with her own parents. She acted from those feelings to bring a poor attitude to every discussion on the kids and money. She stopped. She was aware of her emotions and past resentments, and saw a new opportunity. "I must sound whiny," she thought.[4] She needed to get into the present moment by focusing again on her strengths.

---

4. Note the Conciliator's strengths at work: Insight. Empathy. Generating options. Drawing from right-brain experience. She needed time to balance her thinking with logic so she could be more neutral and less overwhelmed.

She realized she had reacted spontaneously and emotionally, putting her own feelings before Mike's gifts, not to mention his feelings on the subject. No wonder he was angry and charged her with lack of consideration for him. Doing so had effectively stopped the problem-solving on the entire issue. "I'm jealous," she thought. She was mortified.

When her husband talked about the kids and money, her choice to focus on the past blotted out her ability to think objectively, to draw from her newer experience and logic and use her gifts lovingly in the present. So she lost her cool. She reacted to HOW he said things, not the issue itself. She confided that all she was focused on was a laundry list of Mike's faults.[5] Her ego was then firmly in charge, seeing her own faults within him.

> BRAINSTYLE CLUE #1: When someone attacks you personally to get off the subject, it's a red flag signaling they are in their non-strengths and need time and understanding.
>
> BRAINSTYLE CLUE #2: When you start focusing on the behavior that annoys you, it's your ego talking. Love is gone, and fear is the basis for all your logic, all your answers.

TIMING AND MIRACLES. Later, after thinking about it, she could see wisdom in what he said. Trying to deal well in her non-strengths led to self-doubt. And jealousy? She tunneled deeper into self-loathing. What was left but her darkest fear? To hide her dumb questions and just go along, become an obsequious, yes-saying bimbo without a mind of her own?

When her husband walked away, he created the time she needed to reassess.

From her study of *BrainStyles*, she knew the place to start was timing: Allow her husband to present the topic in his own way, at his own pace, and allow some of his logic to penetrate, then ask questions based on what he'd said.

Her shift from fear, doubt, and anger to love began when she moved into her natural strength, empathy. Thinking from his point of view, she knew that Mike too had a lot of feelings on the subject that she just hadn't recognized, expressed as they were with his bottom line on a pad of paper.

She apologized. Told him what she had realized about herself. Blame was gone, support reestablished. Next steps? The same ones, over and over. Forgive herself and her husband by seeing there was nothing there to blame in the first place.

---

5. Note the focus on behavior of the other when going for your own needs, your own goals. All you see is what's in the way of getting what you want. Love sees what is inside, and looks for the best in each of you and for the outcome and beyond. Love begets love.

She replaced her own guilt and self-criticism with a list of her non-strengths and looked at how to handle them more responsibly in the future. She forgave her husband by replacing her judgment of him as a tyrannical clod to name how his gifts took on the tough family issues that no one else could tackle. Resentment disappeared. Partners again.

Later, when they met with the kids, it went very smoothly. She listened and was careful not to interrupt her husband's initial presentation; then she presented some gentle questions, openly gave her support, and helped to get the kids to talk. She included and involved herself and saw clearly how her gifts brought the personal side to the conversation that her husband could not.

~~~~~~~~~~~~~~~~

THE CONCILIATOR-DELIBERATOR PAIR. This is a union of strengths that complement one another well. The Conciliator brings the pizzazz and adventure to the Deliberator's steadiness, analysis, and realism. The Deliberator can offer the rationality and reality checks that make the Conciliator's dreams come true. This is a commonly successful union, as Kevin and Mancy demonstrated earlier. Here is a case that didn't work out as well, and why it didn't.

➤ Problems can arise when conflict is avoided for too long. The Conciliator can be seen as "too volatile" or the Deliberator "too cold and stone-faced." Timing can transform the fight into a discussion rather than a blowup.

➤ Fights can occur over small things and get complicated early. Personalizations abound. Semantics and name-calling are torture tools used to wound. Both demand lots of airtime.

➤ When the Conciliator wants to impress the Deliberator by meeting his mate's high standards for performance in business, managing the home, or raising the kids, he can make promises that, at the time, he really means and really feels strongly about. As you've read, logic and analysis (follow-through) come after the initial right-brained surge of emotional promises. Unless the pair can collaborate on delivering the promises, each can end up over-promising (lying) and under-delivering. All show, no go.

A CONCILIATOR-DELIBERATOR PAIR. UPS AND DOWNS. He is a ballistic Conciliator, so high-energy that the only thing that stopped his momentum was falling down a ski slope and breaking his shoulder. He put off surgery until the pain was so intense his arm wouldn't move. Ah, the driven Conciliator, often putting passion into a calling and a lifestyle, which along with high energy and impulsiveness can take him right to the edge . . . and over.

He is a charmer. A chef. A highly talented boss of a high-performing sales team with the best numbers of any district. He is a nursemaid, father-confessor, prodder, buffer, and superstar. He is also a demanding, high-maintenance, passionate husband. He expects a lot from everyone, plunging into life with red meat, lobster, high-octane fuel, and the best of everything he can afford and then some. To his credit, he takes nothing for granted. He has always worked hard. Studied diligently. Smart enough, he has performed with the best and kept up.

His first marriage was made too young, he says, and he was too full of himself. He had a gal in every port. He was the poster boy for Macho Man. Now he has found the woman he adores. She is a right-sided Deliberator, sensitive, intuitive yet grounded, realistic, and capable. He saw immediately that she was independent, professional, and aloof when they met. The first words out of his mouth when he first saw her were, "Will you marry me?" "Yes," she said. "When?" "How about Friday?" he replied.

Oooo, is that romantic, or what?

Their first date on Friday was dancing until 4 AM on the back of her boat. It was sexy beyond belief. She, the Deliberator, was swept off her feet in spite of herself.

I ask, "So when did you get married?" (Drum roll.)

"Four years later." *Badabing.*

No rushing on her part, that was for sure.

It is now fifteen years after that wedding (which she delayed to be sure of herself and the preservation of her "independence"). They had their troubles. In a nutshell their discomfort produces these descriptions:

➤ The Conciliator at his worst is demanding, impatient, unconcerned about any feelings other than his own, and insensitive to her timing, her schedule, dreams, and goals.

➤ The Deliberator at her worst is resistant, too slow, too methodical, overcommitted to her work and friends, always asking for time alone, and not spending enough time with him.

➤ The Conciliator husband feels betrayed—she doesn't care enough about him to put her own schedule (unprofitable as it is compared to his work; nourishing as it is for her) aside.

➤ The Deliberator wife can't come up with an answer for fear of hurting his feelings.

➤ They each tend to avoid conflict and so allow resentments to build and go unresolved.

➤ His schedule means a great deal of travel; the compromise is for her to travel with him, which is quite uncomfortable for her, unstable as it is.

➤ They each love boating, however, and share what time alone they have on the water.

They are additionally challenged by having no common faith or philosophy to support them, put in *BrainStyle* terms, that both subscribe to, different support groups for friends (his time is spent with co-workers and customers, hers with a women's support group he doesn't respect), and schedules that do not allow for the kind of closeness that the husband, especially, wants.

Their conversation about a recent conference he needed to attend goes like this:

Conciliator Husband: "You've got to come with me." (He wants the emotional closeness.)

Deliberator Wife: "I can't do this. I need a break." (She needs time to think and be alone.)

A compromise is reached: She goes along on the trip with her husband only to stay in the hotel working the entire time. He is unhappy and so is she. They return home to talk it out. After many hours (each has so many examples to explain), the bottom line is reached for her:

Deliberator Wife: "If this is what is required to have a relationship with you, I don't think I can do it." (The Deliberator, who sets the limits, says no, remains more detached.)

Conciliator Husband: "If it's that important to you, I was unaware of it. You matter more to me than our schedules. How can we make it work?" (The Conciliator, the peacemaker, the relationship-maker, the lover.)

Each partner felt pressured with time demands that were robbing them of thinking time, relaxation, and health. Each of the partners was willing to look for a loving solution, given the time to do so.

The Deliberator wife, using her knowledge of *BrainStyles*, used the elements of a *Strengths Contract* (see the next chapter) to offer a way that the partnership could work for both of them.

First, they each agreed on the goal of their relationship: to enjoy being with and loving one another.

1. He agreed to allow her time to plan, write, and just be by herself when she asked, honoring her timing.

2. She agreed to ask for the time for herself in the future, honoring his need for more direct and open communications.

3. In the conversation that created this agreement, each reaffirmed how much they cared for the other. Each emphasized how much they valued time together that was unhurried and relaxed.

It was a beginning. They did not follow through. Their promises were based on delivering in their non-strengths.

Without that broader context, they set no time aside to create a foundation together. They are now divorced.

~~~~~~~~~~~~~~~~

THE CONCILIATOR-CONCILIATOR PAIR. This pair is likely to A) be best friends; B) be over-the-top romantics who have thrillingly instant, heart-pounding connections *(My soul mate!)* that fade with the chemistry when the reality of the same *brainstyle* gifts appear on a daily basis; or C) have stormy make-up-and-break-up peaks and valleys when feelings get hurt. Successful long-term relationships are rare for this pair, as both are quick with emotional reactions that drive conclusions which compare the upsets ("How could he say that?" "She never loved me!") to the initial bliss. Each has delayed logic that might steady and clear the air.

This partnership can be great spiritual partners and playmates. Too bad if one of the pair is more serious or matures more quickly. Looking at the same *brainstyle* every day, you see your strengths and your foibles, and if you are not at peace with them, uh oh. If there is such a thing as getting "too close," it could happen here. Meanwhile, neither is minding the store. Left-brain jobs can go undone with fights about who is responsible.

▶ To avoid competing or adapting too much to the other takes frequent and honest discussions. Two Conciliators with the same interest, say, photography, can be tempted to not compete with one another, and so one may give up the field or subordinate his or her talent to make the other feel comfortable. This can often happen when the pair is a parent/child and the "child" chooses to show her love by trying not to outshine her "parent."

▶ One same-*brainstyle* couple made three lists at the beginning of their relationship: Things I Like To Do, Things I Hate To Do, Things I Can't Do. They worked out a schedule to take turns on the first two, and hired experts (CPA, office manager) for the third.

➤ Maturity is required for this pair to openly negotiate and avoid personalizing too much. Often time apart can allow objectivity to set in.

~~~~~~~~~~~~~~~

THE CONCEPTOR-DELIBERATOR PAIR. This is a partnership of opposites, in which all the bases are covered. When both have a similar energy level, things can go more smoothly because the thoughtful Deliberator will not slow down the Dream Machine of the Conceptor too long before the new home is built or the future of the family is conceived. Then the Deliberator can step in and create a step-by-step plan, moving at the same pace as her partner.

➤ The Deliberator needs to appreciate the changes the Conceptor loves to promote and bring into their partnership, gently eliminating or focusing the ongoing onslaught of proposals. Tolerance and respect are requirements.

➤ The Conceptor must value the steadiness and organization the Deliberator brings to ensure things get done, and not expect a passionate or enthusiastic audience.

➤ The Conceptor needs to manage his or her ideaphoria; that is, the gift of coming up with new ideas, which can overwhelm her partner with too much change, too much to do, and too much to consider—especially one's partner who is especially mindful of things like budget, time, and other limitations that can serve to make a project doable. The immature Conceptor can label Deliberator assessment as obstacles and negativity. Conceptors *can* include, reframe, and take advantage of the Deliberator's concerns. The Deliberator can pose concerns as a way to make their goal better. (See chapter 6 for the examples of this pair as lovers.)

> *BRAINSTYLE CLUE:* In a union of opposites, neither feels openly appreciated in the short term. Appreciations need to be openly and consciously expressed from time to time. Looking for *brainstyle* gifts creates new depth in the relationship.

➤ Fights can get ugly with Conceptor attacks and Deliberator withdrawals, but overall are necessary to air the unsaid. "Difficult" discussions can take the pair to new levels of intimacy if handled with timing and an intention to learn from one another. The Conceptor will get first to the larger issues, the tough decision to be made, and the ramifications; the Deliberator needs time to discuss the fine points, the downsides, the specifics. They can discover they live in different countries, but also what the countries contain, and where the boundaries are. Taking time to hear the concerns of the other promotes realignment. Both must take time to acknowledge the other.

If a major decision is to be made, one option is to make a place in the home where the issues can be written and left visible (like a big sheet of paper or a small whiteboard on a wall) so that each may look at them over a period of time. New perspectives can emerge. The complementary gifts of these *brainstyles* can create new, complete, and well formulated solutions. They are a formidable team.

➤ To work smoothly, opposites need breathing room. Stressful situations for the pair occur before, during, and after big decisions like moves or new jobs or the first child, where each needs a great deal of personal nurturance and the partner is ill-equipped to provide it in the language of the other. Each needs his or her own outlets or supportive friends.

~~~~~~~~~~~~~~~

THE CONCEPTOR-CONCEPTOR PAIR. This pair, as described by one Conceptor, "thought so much like one another we could finish each other's sentences. It was spooky." They were very close friends, but did not marry. The couple could pair out of a need to have someone they can really talk to. In the long run, same-*brainstyle* pairs (except for the Deliberators) have the issues of too much similarity, need for control in the same areas to express their strengths, and loss of the differences that intrigue and excite.

Another problem with the same-*brainstyle* relationships is that similar strengths tend to compete with each other; non-strengths are crucial to survival; and one or both may feel they are sacrificing too much for the relationship. If both Conceptors are coming up with new ways to do things, who pays the bills and makes sure the cleaning gets picked up? If any can, only committed and mature couples can survive in the more erratic and emotional lifestyles of the right-brained. If two Conceptors are lovers, who follows up the plans and who leads? One of the pair can easily feel he or she has sacrificed too much to make the relationship work, has been unsupported in doing so, and is unappreciated. Not a good formula.

The mature pair could bond with their strengths: a conceptual and spiritual approach to life and the universe, with endlessly stimulating discussions and inspiration for one another.

~~~~~~~~~~~~~~~~~

> BRAINSTYLE CLUE: Deliberators who have spent time in personal or couples counseling learning about relationships agree that the most important thing for them is to *communicate* everything with one another to maintain the partnership.

THE DELIBERATOR-DELIBERATOR PAIR. The Deliberator *brainstyle* is the universal donor of partners, the one most apt to get along with all other *brainstyles*. Think of the gifts and see why: the ability to take in and entertain a great deal of information translates to patience and listening, the curiosity and desire to explore new topics means either bringing in new ideas or being interested in others' lives.

Deliberators can attune to the stability and lack of conflict of their own *brainstyle* best, most often choosing a partner who is in their own *brainstyle* but who is just different enough to be interesting. Key: the partner must have similar values. Communication for the Deliberator partner is the air she breathes. This is a way to exchange caring, by attending to the other's life. Perhaps more important, each partner must encourage the other to express resentments or appreciations. Deliberators whose marriages failed went their separate ways, leaving conflicts unexpressed rather than confronting tough issues. (See chapter 7.)

Deliberators can also love the logic and no-nonsense approach of the Knower, the ideas and exciting insights of the Conceptor (although this can be trying), and the spontaneity and warmth of the Conciliator (adding excitement with the emotionality while patiently listening). Most, however, choose their own *brainstyle*.*

➤ This is the union that tends to stabilize early over common values and last the longest with the least conflict.

---

* Often two Deliberators compare themselves to one another, focus on differences and assess their gifts as a Knower-Deliberator or -Conciliator pair, which means they miss the similar *brainstyle* foundation they share and can build upon.

➤ Partners tend to have discussions rather than arguments.

➤ Plans, budgets, and projects can stretch out endlessly, unless another *brainstyle* is brought in to move things along, provided either will take an outsider's advice. However, since each has similar timing in decision-making, this works well most of the time. Patience is the gift here.

➤ At least one partner needs to offer a goal, set limits, and stick to them. Unpleasant in the short run, this can be done when it supports the family's agreed-upon values. Reevaluation periodically can bring new commitment when rules are explained and love included.

➤ Serious conflicts can consume endless discussion in business or, in personal relationships, create irreconcilable rifts. Since neither party deals well with conflict, often just airing the issue can help with time to decide delayed.

➤ Also, individual counseling or learned techniques (such as the *Strengths Contract*), can provide useful structures Deliberators prize because they create boundaries for more open conversations. As Deliberators underscore, talking openly and resolving resentments or concerns is crucial to keep the love alive. Covert grudges and eroding respect can destroy the partnership, all for the sake of avoiding the temporary discomfort of disagreement.

➤ The intention of each partner must be to deepen the partnership rather than be right.

~~~~~~~~~~~~~~~~~

Happily loving, long-term Deliberator partners continually mention the heart of their partnership as a common faith or set of values that puts a larger vision above daily concerns.[6]

---

6. See chapter 7 for extensive examples of Deliberator partners who built and maintained their partnerships and those who did not.

SUGGESTIONS ON HOW TO BE A MORE EFFECTIVE PARTNER WHENEVER YOU WANT TO TAKE THE TIME:

1. Write your current list of priorities. Ask your partner to write his or hers. Share them. Are they similar enough to support your relationship? What will it take to make this happen?
2. Get absolutely clear on your own strengths, timing, and limitations, especially in decision-making.
3. Honestly appraise your ability to honor your own strengths. Re-evaluate arguments you are having. Look for areas where you are competing with your partner, or where you feel challenged instead of confident, and refocus on your strengths. After practicing this assessment, notice what happens to your expectations for your partner.
4. Notice how your gifts complement your partner's gifts and vice versa. Write them down or talk them out. Ask your partner to create or share his or her own list as the topic of conversation on a date or during some private time together.
5. Acknowledge your partner for specific ways his or her strengths have created value for your home, for you, and for your family. Do this regularly and watch what happens.
6. List two or three areas of conflict between you. Ask your partner to do the same. Discuss how each of your strengths and timing needs can address the conflicts differently.
7. Discuss with your partner ways each of you can bring out the strengths of troublesome family members—children, siblings, parents, and friends.

~~~~~~~~~~~~~~~~

EVALUATE. If you try some or all of the above items, notice how your home changes. Is it more peaceful? More open to others? Is your self-talk kinder? Are you happier with one another?

APPLYING *BRAINSTYLES* TIMING TO SOME COMMON PARTNERSHIPS: SOME TIPS.

THE KNOWER-CONCILIATOR PAIR	THE DELIBERATOR-KNOWER PAIR	THE CONCEPTOR-DELIBERATOR PAIR	THE DELIBERATOR-CONCILIATOR PAIR
Will work when:	**Will work when:**	**Will work when:**	**Will work when:**
The Knower quickly determines the solutions, sets goals, and outlines how to approach the tasks in the matter; the Conciliator visualizes how to get people excited, involved, and motivated. The Conciliator presents limited information, asks for advice on a problem, or suggests preferred options for the Knower to consider. The Knower listens and offers summaries that help focus the Conciliator. Subjects are reviewed more than once, and the Conciliator has the time to think things over.	The Knower sets the direction and goals, which the Deliberator can challenge before ensuring they get done efficiently and accurately. The Deliberator presents clear choices for action so the Knower can stay in control; the Knower respects the values of the Deliberator's choices. The Knower breaks projects into small, clearly defined pieces; the Deliberator sets and keeps dates. The Knower brings focus; the Deliberator ensures inclusion of the right people and the elements that add the beauty and art.	The Conceptor defines direction; the Deliberator thinks through the plan to make it happen. The Conceptor depends on the factual assessment of the Deliberator to maintain credibility and follow-through. The Deliberator can keep improving how things get done while keeping things calm. The Conceptor does not create confrontations but uses timing to present ideas. The Conceptor works on multiple projects at the same time, but is careful not to overload the Deliberator with too many To-Do's.	The Conciliator brings the sizzle, and the Deliberator makes sure there's a steak. Each will listen to the other. Both think through plans out loud and need a good sounding board. Time needs to be set aside for reaching agreements. There is clear turf and shorter-range goals each can discuss and contribute to, OR each is clear about how his or her strengths contribute. Each helps the other not to take things personally; the Deliberator needs explanations, the Conciliator needs empathy.

All Charts ©1997, 2003 *BrainStyles*, Inc. No reproduction without permission. *www.brainstyles.com*

THE KNOWER-CONCILIATOR PAIR	THE DELIBERATOR-KNOWER PAIR	THE CONCEPTOR-DELIBERATOR PAIR	THE DELIBERATOR-CONCILIATOR PAIR
Will NOT work when:	**Will NOT work when:**	**Will NOT work when:**	**Will NOT work when:**
The Knower shows impatience with feelings, new ideas, and the Conciliator's quick reactions. The Conciliator uses feelings to get his or her way. The Conciliator competes for control of the project rather than for the part of the project which needs his or her gifts. The same goes for the Knower.	The Knower wants control of how things get done and won't allow time for the Deliberator to do it. Either insists on one right answer and his or her own timetable to reach it. They have not agreed on the goals and ethical ground rules.	The Conceptor cannot take enough time to explain what he or she means, or institutes too many changes. The Deliberator critiques too early and insists on a logical explanation for concepts. The Conceptor's values are out of bounds for the Deliberator or vice versa.	Their values disagree. There is a need for many new decisions in the situation: the Deliberator can procrastinate, and the Conciliator can change his or her mind too often. They do not set deadlines, or get help from a third *brainstyle*, to help clarify goals and a realistic timeframe.

CHAPTER 15

CREATE PARTNERSHIPS THAT CHANGE YOUR LIFE *WITHOUT* CHANGING WHO YOU ARE[SM]

~~~~~~~~~~~~~

When we fall in love, we fall in love with another's uniqueness—his or her differences.
When we love for a lifetime, we use our differences to nourish one another.

~~~~~~~~~~~~~

CREATING A SPIRITUAL PARTNERSHIP. The following step-by-step process, the *Strengths Contract,* came into being as my husband and I learned how to live without the conflict we'd assumed was just part of married life. Over the six years following our first meeting to write *BrainStyles* in 1988, our arguments evaporated. We used timing instead of communications techniques, bargaining, and formulas. Our respect deepened, as did our intimacy. The examples that follow are true, lived by people who have applied the principles we learned over the years. They are couples just like you, willing to pause for just that second and look again, choose something besides their own right answer, their anger, or a need to remain distant by focusing on the externals. They have found a new way to relate to their lovers by giving up the idea that they could change them.

> BRAINSTYLE CLUE: Natural gifts are most acutely experienced in new—thus stressful—situations, where you must think to make a decision. It is at these times that you are uniquely yourself, different from your partner. It is at these times that you most fervently want your partner to respond to you in the language most comfortable for you: your own.

STRESS SITUATIONS. Under the gun, when money is on the line, or when big decisions must be made, it is most natural for us to use our *brainstyle* gifts to try to convince another to agree to our Right Answer. We've all been there: This is serious. Do it *my way.*

Typically the *brainstyles* will use their strengths to win with the following approaches:

THE DELIBERATOR will use the force of the information and facts she has collected to overwhelm another *brainstyle* with references, precedent, explanations, the reasons for her view of reality, and the inevitability of her argument.

THE KNOWER will use the force of his logic and rapid sorting of facts into two categories, Right and Stupid, to eliminate all other answers but his own. Discussion over.

THE CONCEPTOR will outmaneuver and confront with the contradictions in the other's thinking, making her own answer inevitable. She will draw from emotion, analysis, and/or logic to point out horrible consequences and glorious opportunities.[1]

THE CONCILIATOR will offer testimonials, stories, and examples that prove his point: It feels right, the right people are doing it, and not going his way will create a huge loss of opportunity, not to mention his own personal devastation. When all else fails, he'll sulk or get emotional and attack the person and/or the idea he disagrees with.

When the partner resists, bargaining and compromise begin, so that everyone has to give up something.

A question: How much satisfaction have these approaches given you so far?

So what can you do if you want to live and love and get something important accomplished together?

---

1. Extraordinary and inventive salespeople, Conceptors use foresight to predict and strategize around them using these same abilities.

A BRAINSTYLES TOOL: THE STRENGTHS CONTRACT™

The *Strengths Contract* conversation aims to overcome difficulties by establishing how each party can contribute from his or her strengths to the larger goal or outcome. It can take 30 seconds or 30 months. In order to be successful in reaching an agreement with another, you must intend to have it work between you. Using your knowledge of his or her strengths and non-strengths, you start with the premise that no one needs to change. Instead, you trust your partner for what he can actually deliver, ask for him to use his strengths, and give up hoping that if he really loved you enough, he would automatically know what you need and do it. No one is a mind reader, even though some seem like they are when they finish your sentences.

When you begin a project or need to make an agreement with your partner, you need to use your skills in reframing criticisms of underlying strengths and non-strengths. To do so, you need to remember the core strength and non-strengths of each *brainstyle* (the strengths of the other *brainstyles*). You need to enter with an outcome in mind *and* a willingness to let your idea go and explore what will work even better for the two of you. You also prepare by remembering what you love and respect your partner for and be ready to remind her of her strengths at any time in the conversation. *Hint:* It's the same way you treat your friends.

Additionally, you might also:

- Forgive yourself for your part in any past conversations that failed to reach an agreement. Acknowledge to yourself what you may have done to prevent a workable agreement and this time be aware of how you can give up trying to be smart in your non-strengths, be right, or trying to get your way.
- Enter the conversation ready to identify and honor the strengths of each of you.
- Examine your previous expectations for the other to say or do things to make you comfortable or for you to win in some way. Use your knowledge of *brainstyle* strengths and non-strengths to reestablish your expectations for this conversation.
- Intend to reach a win-win outcome. Don't give up. Don't give in. Use timing.

THE VERY FIRST STRENGTHS CONTRACT. The move from The Way We've Learned to Behave to an application of a *Strengths Contract* takes a bit of time and practice. This is what we went through in our beginning. You'll read about how, as the Principles and tools became clearer, others incorporated the same ideas into their own marriages, some with stunning transformations as they have applied the *BrainStyles* Principles evolved over the years.

THE ISSUE: WE HAD DECIDED TO RENOVATE THE LIVING/DINING ROOM.
TRADITIONAL APPROACH: All I could think of was my résumé. My professional credentials were far more important to me than my strengths—the gifts I was just learning to define. I thought of the fact that my husband had had experience renovating two previous homes. I had none. I feared that I wouldn't be taken seriously because of my newness to the game, so I tried to compensate by brainstorming lots of ideas (my strength) in the initial *Time Zero* meeting, competing with others to be heard, trying to be smart, interrupting my husband and the contractor.

> *BrainStyle CLUE:* Strengths used in fear never produce the results you can produce with those same strengths when calm and caring.

A NEW APPROACH: DEFINE STRENGTHS AND NON-STRENGTHS OF BOTH PARTNERS. I was aware of our new success collaborating on the first book together (described in chapter 1) when I saw the full power of David's gifts at work and the win-win that resulted. I remembered this happened when I respected his Conceptor strengths and stopped competing to have the best idea with my quick Conciliator reactions.

A NEW APPROACH: A TIME-OUT TO ESTABLISH TIMING AND BRAINSTYLES STRENGTHS. The meeting with the contractor was directionless; we were all talking at once. David asked for a time-out. He pointed out that I was trying to contribute ideas in an area of his strengths (establishing the project overview). I instantly recognized this was true and did not defend or try to explain myself, as in the past. He needed to start the project by defining the shape and structure of the new room; I needed to contribute after this overview was established.

Given his *brainstyle*, his experience with a previous home, and his knowledge of my *brainstyle*, I asked where he thought I could make the biggest contribution. He suggested that I could coordinate the whole project between the contractor and the decorator (with his vote on major choices). I would be consulted on major structural choices (my concern). I was not only relieved, I was pleased. He set the boundaries, provided direction, and outlined the future; I was free to do what I knew I could do well, résumé or no: generate aesthetic alternatives for furnishings and decor, form relationships, and facilitate communications to keep the project on track.

THE WIN-WIN SOLUTION: We worked together for the next eight months with more collaboration than we'd ever experienced. NO arguments. We were onto something. We began to compliment one another on decisions made. He relied on my gifts to maintain open and friendly communications with the decorator, while he set limits with spending and structure with the contractor. He was patient and interested as we tried out color choices. Moreover, when a serious financial issue arose with the decorator, I consulted David and his gifts to work out how to confront her (my non-strength). Our marriage had become more of a partnership, something I thought impossible with the pressures of each of our careers.

APPROACHES WE AVOIDED:

ASKING THE OTHER TO SPEAK MY LANGUAGE:

We each knew the other's strengths. Neither expected the other to "say it my way."

COMPROMISING, GIVING IN, BARGAINING: (LOSE-WIN)

We stopped the typical negotiating we had used before that had always ended in a stalemate ("We agree we can't agree") or unhappy settlement; i.e., "I'll do it your way this time. You do it my way next time."

DEMANDING MY WAY: (WIN-LOSE)

Neither of us tried to railroad the other into decisions. There were some guesses made in the project where neither knew the right answer. We reviewed the project as we went along and used one another's ideas and opinions to see what might work better.

Our competition of the past was simply unnecessary. I didn't just go along to get along; I asked for time to think when I wasn't sure. David did the same. Demands were unnecessary. Stalemates were unstalemated; we trusted each other, and if we didn't like the result, we did so forgivingly; we knew we'd do better next time. Communications skills were forgotten; we simply communicated. The partnership was finally more important than the petty things like who had the best idea, or whose taste prevailed.

I learned for real how compromising and all its cousins lead inevitably to resentment because of their basis in a system of *quid pro quo,* or trading favors— the way Congress runs. Tracking and measuring love by counting how many times he does things your way, for instance, precludes love or respect in any form. Some couples who designate one partner to handle the entire project for the home may realize splendid outcomes and gain efficiency, but also may miss some of the shared intimacies of working through the agonies and ecstasies together. On the other hand, the delegation may keep their relationship together.

> STRENGTHS CONTRACT CLUE: Trying to win is the ego's play at home or at work. Win today, lose tomorrow.

THE WAY THEY WERE. A couple married for 34 years was having an argument they had had many times before. It was more intense this time, it seemed, because for the first time in their lengthy married lives, they both had an office at home. Together. All day. Every day. This was not a fun *Time Zero* for the couple.

THE ISSUE. She, a popular and therefore busy Conciliator caterer, had clients clamoring for her fabulously creative and beautiful gourmet presentations. But she had screwed up her bookkeeping—again. The balance sheet erroneously showed that she had lost money on a huge order.

"It's so *simple,* I've shown you a dozen times already. I don't know why you keep screwing this up," her Deliberator husband said irritably as he pointed at the computer spreadsheet that was blinking at her.

> BRAINSTYLE CLUE: Fights focus on non-strengths.

"I'm wrong, wrong again," she thought. "This is infuriating. He's infuriating. I'm so stupid. Oh, I'll never get this. *Why* do I have to do these bloody figures? I *hate.* . . ." Her mental harpies went on in the steady stream of invective she'd heard so many other times when all the numbers muddled, and it felt as though all her work, all that slogging and lifting and organizing and preparing had gone for NOTHING. . . . And he was just standing there criticizing.

> BRAINSTYLE CLUE: Remember, your gifts end where different *brainstyle* gifts begin. As you honor your partner for his gifts, the natural response is to reciprocate.

It sounds so glib to say you have limitations and you need to call on others' strengths. To do so is to make the single most gut-wrenching admission of your life. To be vulnerable enough to go into a relationship whole, as totally you, unlike another, with the fullness of all your strengths, is to risk it all. This *BrainStyles* business is not for sissies. To admit to what you lack and what another can supply is true vulnerability. It contradicts the momentum of the drive for personal responsibility for one's own problems, of self-reliance. In reality, to be able to truly have a relationship with another takes buckets of courage and gallons of self-acceptance.

When under stress, we expect—demand—others to see the world the way we see it, to think the same way about things, to understand things from our point of view. The faster we go, the more we assume our view is The Truth. The only way we have a ghost of a chance to open our minds and points of view to another's reality is to slow down and think about it.

Oh, but you're thinking, "Not when there is an emergency. Not when there is a need for a decision. Not when there's a deadline." Those are times when people get on our nerves, don't understand us, act stupid, and—we think—need desperately for us to tell them what to do. And how to do it.

In these times, fear can define us. We can get ugly. Issue ultimatums. Threaten. Get emotional. Stomp out. Stonewall. We are not using our problem-solving, serotonin-based cognition; we are being driven by primal urges from the limbic fight-or-flight hit-'em-where-it-hurts part of our survival systems. According to one California writer and lecturer, Ashley Waugh, we have a mere two seconds of choice before we are lost to the "animal brain" and revert to survival on automatic pilot—fear over love.

Timing can save us. Staying consciously present in the moment, we can choose to be aware of our *brainstyle* and respect the strengths involved right now, instead of the other's discomfiting behavior. We can choose to respond from our strengths. This is nothing more, and nothing less, than a holy instant, a choice of love over fear. You create a loving miracle that will transform your relationship into a spiritual partnership.

~~~~~~~~~~~~~~~~~

Men are disturbed not by things, but by the views they take of them.
—Epictetus, 50–138 AD, Stoic philosopher

~~~~~~~~~~~~~~~~~

Here are some situations that you may encounter.

CONFLICT: WHAT YOU RESIST PERSISTS. In an emotionally loaded (i.e., family) situation there is bound to be friction, if not angry disagreements. Given the *brainstyles* involved, especially the Deliberators and Conciliators who hate conflict and will avoid direct disagreement at all costs, the following *brainstyle* positions can eventually explode or erode relationships at some point, if not defused. Resisting will keep them coming at you, have you noticed? Your stubbornness fuels the fires of competition and gets the adrenaline going to prove you, the obstacle, are wrong and can be won over or squashed with his or her need to win. Here are some pointers, mere suggestions to give you ideas on how to respond rather than defend.

WHERE SOME LANDMINES LIE, OR HOW EACH *BrainStyle* DIGS IN:

- The **Deliberator's** ability to process and recall a great deal of information can be used to control information, its interpretation, and application to the answer she has rationally put together. This becomes a rock-solid position: She's right, you're wrong.

POSSIBLE RESPONSES BY OTHER *BRAINSTYLES* TO MOVE TOWARD A STRENGTHS CONTRACT:

➤ "You've put a lot of thought and preparation into that answer. I'm not as good as you at collecting and assembling the facts, but I can offer the emotional impact this may have on others. I'd like you to hear me out and consider seriously what I'm saying."

➤ "I'll never be as thorough as you are at this analysis, but still, I cannot go along with your answer. Here is an option for you to think about."

➤ "I can't grasp the level of detail that you can, but I can look at the overall goals. Here is where I see problems in the future that haven't been addressed . . ."

- The **Conciliator's** and **right-sided Deliberator's** doubts of their personal value or emotionally based or abstract positions can be defended stubbornly with emotion or stonewalling. This is their way of gaining time. ("You always say that! You just don't get it.") The right-brain's associative ability can attach emotional meaning to facts, plans, or figures, and so make things destructively, fearfully personal.

POSSIBLE RESPONSES BY OTHER *BRAINSTYLES* TO MOVE TOWARD A STRENGTHS CONTRACT:

➤ "This is a loaded topic, and I hear you feel strongly. Would you postpone making a decision now and think about it for a day or two? We don't have to go forward until (deadline) and you need to be comfortable. Let's discuss this again tomorrow. I want to answer all your questions and work out where we disagree."

➤ "This sounds personal. What does this mean to you?"

➤ "If you could do what you wanted to do, what would it be? Do you think we can afford that? What would be something you know we could afford?" (Use his associative abilities to come up with new ideas and his need to be in charge of the direction to get him to assess and set his own realistic limits.)

➤ "What's scary about this idea?" (Note: To access left-brained logic, the right-brainer needs time [airtime, usually] and language. Putting things into words is a left-brained function. Writing or speaking allows the personal reasoning to be assessed, calling upon the left brain. So do time-outs. These strategies allow the issue to move from the personal association to a more objective view. These same approaches can work with other *brainstyles,* which are emotional about a topic.)

➤ Meet several times on the same issue. Each time you meet will be less emotional and more rational.

• The **Conceptor's** ability to see the overview without the ability to recall and debate with detailed evidence can come across as broad accusations or baseless generalities to other *brainstyles.*

POSSIBLE RESPONSES BY OTHER BRAINSTYLES TO MOVE TOWARD A STRENGTHS CONTRACT:

➤ "This idea is exciting. I want to help, but I can't think in such broad terms. What do you mean by _____ ?" (Assist the Conceptor to add the specifics.)

➤ "I like the direction you're suggesting. I can't see how it'll work yet."

➤ "I need time to think about this. I want to pose some concerns now and get back to you with answers." (Note: The Conceptor is best prepared to answer and create options in the moment, continuing her persuasive argument. It is the other *brainstyles* that need time to think it through. To have the best reception to your concerns, the best first response is a positive one, with the knowledge that the Conceptor is most able to use your concerns and logic to expand the idea or change his or her mind later.)

• The **Conceptor's** ability to see the forest for the trees allows for disengagement from a situation, rather than creating what he can see is a potential blowup. Conciliators can feel unsupported and abandoned; Deliberators can conclude the Conceptor is deceptive; Knowers can decide the Conceptor doesn't know what he is talking about.

POSSIBLE RESPONSES BY OTHER BRAINSTYLES TO MOVE TOWARD A STRENGTHS CONTRACT:

➤ "Can we talk about this again so I have time to think it over and add some ways to make it work?"

288 / B R A I N S T Y L E S   F O R   L O V E R S

➤ Build on the idea with examples before bringing up obstacles or downsides.

➤ "What do you need from me to make this a reality?"

➤ "I can't think in such broad terms, but I can offer some examples to test."

• **The Knower's** ability to state things without emotion can come across as Take It or Leave It, an ultimatum or threat. (Note: Actually, Knowers can be the most detached when making these kinds of statements. The ultimatums of other *brainstyles* are much harder to unwind, given the associated emotions.)

POSSIBLE RESPONSES BY OTHER *BRAINSTYLES* TO MOVE TOWARD A STRENGTHS CONTRACT:

➤ "You're faster than I am in getting to an answer, but I can add things you might have overlooked."

➤ "You've made the choices for this entire issue really clear. I want to start . . . ." (Note: Knowers want direct, clear rebuttals, preferably unemotional statements, then with the speed of the left brain can change their minds when presented with a clear and logical contradictory argument. If you are emotional about their conclusion, merely ask for time.)

➤ "I don't know how to deliver what you want. I need to think and give you a better answer."

➤ And the best: "You're right. I can work with that goal."

If any *brainstyle* issues an ultimatum or threat, allow time. If at all possible, speak to the thinking/feeling behind the ultimatum and not the ultimatum itself.

STRENGTHS CONTRACT CLUE: To create a partnership, you must start with a simple willingness to have a more respectful relationship. This intent is what makes a *Strengths Contract* work. Next, you need to respect your own strengths and non-strengths. Finally, the way you expand a partnership is by learning from your limitations and mistakes to openly admit that you need another to get to the best answer.

Preparing your own caring, respectful position will automatically generate the right words, tone, and approach that will be authentic and natural with your partner.

Same Song, Second Verse: A *BrainStyles* Strengths Contract in Practice. There they were again, in the home office, locked in mortal combat about her inability to do the books. Her husband, the financial guy; she, the insulted chef. Suddenly a new thought came. A small piece of insight she'd read in her *BrainStyles* book.

Recognizing Strengths. Hands on hips, the Conciliator faced her Deliberator husband and said, "You are so good at this, it rolls off your tongue." She pointed at the four-color *Quicken*™ display on the computer. "And I, I am just as good at what I do. I refuse to take any more abuse for not being as good as you are at what *you do best.*" He looked at her pose and registered the logic of her words.

"I didn't mean to just criticize," he said in a much lower, more patient tone. "Here, here's what you can do to make it easier," he said, sitting at the keyboard and punching in things that magically made other things stop blinking. "I know, I know. You're the chef. I'm the insurance guy."

"I'm sorry for sounding shrewish," she said. "But I've always felt so stupid for not being good at this stuff, and you know how tangled up I get with numbers and balance sheets."

She stopped being defensive. He stopped being offensive. The fight ended in a hug. They were partners again. The partnership was instantly recreated when she realized she didn't have to put herself down because she wasn't good in something besides her own gifts. She relaxed. She asked more gently for help.

She learned, magically, to prevent her husband's criticism by giving up her own statements of "I'll never get this! I'm such an idiot with this simple stuff!" Her defensiveness waned as she quit critiquing and railing at her *own* non-strengths. She was nicer to herself in these situations. Her husband's tone changed to a kinder, more patient one. A week later when the same problem occurred again, it was resolved quickly and simply. She asked, he advised, she fixed it. Boom.

> *Strengths Contract Clue:* The way you act as a partner is to speak to the strengths within—both your own and your partner's—the best thinking you are each capable of, not the emotions or language used in the heat of the moment.

A 30-Second Strengths Contract. Anytime you offer to apply the strengths of both of you, you create a *Strengths Contract.* Here are some quick examples:

- Conciliator woman applying for a bank loan to the Deliberator loan officer: "You're so good at this. If I can say it back to you in *my* way, then I know I've got it."

- Deliberator husband to his Conciliator wife: "If you'll just give me time to consider your ideas for the new barn, I'll give you a better answer." Her response: "How about if we go out for coffee on Saturday and talk it all through again?"

EXERCISE 1: Prepare some of your own responses for better results with those in your life. Think of a situation with your partner. Write a couple of sentences that describe what your *brainstyle* brings to that situation; NOT what you know or have experienced, but how you can approach the issue with your strengths.

ME	State your strengths in this situation. (Strengths = how you approach decisions; NOT your solutions, opinions, history.)

_____

_____

EXERCISE 2: Now do the same for your partner.

YOU	Point out his strengths, how he thinks and what he does well. Acknowledge what her *brainstyle* brings to decision-making. Emphasize what she can contribute by using her natural abilities (her *brainstyle*).

_____

_____

BrainStyles Principles of Influence.

➤ You are most influential when you allow others to influence you in return.

➤ You are most influential when you honor the other's *brainstyle* with respect for what he brings, not simply as an obstacle to overcome.

➤ You create win-win outcomes when you truly appreciate your own strengths and offer them to serve your partner.

WAYS TO INFLUENCE EACH *BrainStyle*

THE KNOWER	THE CONCILIATOR	THE CONCEPTOR	THE DELIBERATOR
• Make clear that you are not trying to take advantage of or outmaneuver them. • Go to them for the practical, simplest, or most efficient answer. • Challenge the pronouncement or decision directly. • Honor their strengths; you attack, you lose. • Ask advice; allow them to help you with their gifts. • Propose another solution of your own choosing. Back it up. • Focus your ideas or thinking before the conversation. • State openly that you want it to work for both of you and stick to this. • Do not personalize the Knower's comments.	• Be supportive; most times that's all that's required. Most often personal support is needed before he will consider your solution or idea. • Use stories or examples of previous successes. • Start with a punch line. • Look for ways she can gain in credibility or learn new things that are meaningful. • Make it safe to talk—he hates conflict. • Ask for her reactions; help her create her own reason for doing things. • Spend time on your personal relationship. • Offer personal or expert references and endorsements, i.e., drop names.	• Ask the Conceptor to see the pattern; give insights of your illustrations or examples. • Don't pile on facts; use examples, show trends. • Honor his thinking by asking him to tell more. • Influence her after initial thinking or an event, when she can take more information. • Ask for interim decisions by discussing the issue. Take your time. • Ask questions rather than listing facts or history. • Confront his ideas directly and overall; he will dismiss exceptions. • Stay neutral; she'll get there.	• Remove time pressure when you need a decision. • Offer an alternative early for him to assess. Help focus it. • Give a deadline to help him with boundaries. • Discuss a loaded topic a bit at a time. • Offer more information to study that fits within a timetable. • Appreciate his expertise. • Be prepared and, if possible, try to present facts neutrally, i.e., without emotion. • Offer corrections by first noting his progress. • Remember: a Deliberator doesn't get mad, he gets even.

A $TRENGTH$ CONTRACT FOR REAL MONEY. Linda Bush is the master facilitator for *The BrainStyles System*.® She tells the story of what she learned about living with and loving her Knower husband by applying each of their strengths in a new way.[2] Note in the following example that she isn't "compromising" or "negotiating" a way that each of them is going to act to make one another comfortable. That was the old way. This time she was going to reclaim her best self, trust her husband to apply his strengths, and enter into a real-life, rubber-meets-the-road decision involving the toughest, most dangerous subject of all: money.

"Last winter,[3] I learned about the depth of our individual strengths and how to apply them with the *BrainStyles Strength Contract* process as I attended the Instructor Training. Since we are asked to live the *BrainStyles* Principles in order to teach them, I decided to take this process home."

BrainStyle Clue: To initiate a *Strengths Contract,* you begin with respect for your partner's strengths and trust his ability to apply them. This requires a willingness to release your ego's need to control and an embrace of a new partnership between you.

THE WAY WE WERE.

"I'm accustomed to high stakes negotiating, including several house purchases, corporate contracts while at IBM, and ongoing vendor/supplier deals in my consulting business. Thus I've acquired the role for our family as the leader in major acquisitions. To be honest, I was self-appointed, in spite of my distaste for such tasks as negotiating price or comparing details and facts. And I received praise from friends and family members for 'handling it all.' However, things were different now: I had a new tool. Using the *Strengths Contract,* I chose a different role when Gary and I made our next major purchase of a new boat."

---

2. At this writing, she and her husband are building a long-time dream home/ranch/lodge with NO CONFLICT. This project has taken *two years* longer than the original estimate and required living in temporary, terribly cramped housing without indoor plumbing, to house both their offices and their 12-year-old son, along with all the changes of a new city, school, and full-time jobs.
3. February, 1998.

The ISSUE	Open by stating the problem you're having and your intention to resolve the problem by collaborating.

"We wanted to buy a new boat for waterskiing, a major purchase for us."

ME	State your strengths in this situation. (Strengths = how you approach decisions; NOT your solutions, opinions, history.)

YOU	Point out his strengths, how he thinks and what he does well. Acknowledge what his *brainstyle* brings to decision-making. Emphasize what he can contribute by using his natural abilities (his *brainstyle*).

NEW FAMILY TEAMWORK.

"Because I now understood just what it means that he is a Knower and I am a Conciliator, I tried a new approach. 'You're best at sorting the facts, sorting information, and focusing on the finances. I'm best at relationship-building and imagining the possibilities. Let's approach this purchase in a new way.'"

GOALS	What goals can you both agree to?

"We wanted to purchase a new boat that was within our budget and met Gary's criteria for value and mine for doing so with a good relationship with the sellers." (Note how both of their goals are included.)

PLAN	The plan must be based on 1) the gifts of each *brainstyle*, and 2) the timing most natural to each *brainstyle;* also, it may need to include other *brainstyles* as resources.

"We both pored over the ads. Gary called the sellers and asked the initial pertinent questions and narrowed the list of candidates to visit. We made the visits together, and when we saw a boat we really liked, I facilitated a get-to-know-you-and-trust-you conversation with the sellers, while Gary asked blunt [translation: direct, factual] and focused questions as he crawled in, around, under, and through the boat.

"Here are some of Gary's left-brained questions:
- Has the prop ever been replaced?
- Are those the true hours on the engine?
- Have you done mostly fishing or waterskiing with those hours?
- How many offers have you already had?
- What were they? Why didn't you take them?
- Have you done the maintenance yourself or had it done at a dealership?
- Where does the moisture in the storage compartment come from?

"Here are some of my own right-brained questions:
- How long have you been boaters?
- How many children do you have? How old are they? Any grandchildren? Do they go along?
- When did you start teaching the kids to water ski?
- What do your kids think about your selling the boat?
- How have you managed to keep the seats in such nice condition?
- What will you do without a boat? New interests? Buying another one?

"It's obvious just how differently we approached this new decision."

> BRAINSTYLE CLUE: Once you start looking for your partner's gifts instead of your differences and lacks, loving miracles will occur for each of you.

What is not so obvious is how much Linda appreciated Gary's gifts, although they had already had an initial intimate session when she told him what she'd discovered about his strengths. It was then that he discovered that this high-powered, self-reliant consultant needed him and his gifts, deeply and truly, which created a very special new bond between them. This situation, however, put her money where her mouth was, the Real Deal for both of them. It was transforming—and more—for the relationship.
- Note how they each still have doubts and judgments as they proceed—and follow through anyway. You, too, may be experimenting with a new way of loving the first time. The difference between trying this accepting approach and "faking it" is the loving intention and the goal you seek. You already know how to love, so effort lessens; you have to work harder each time you pretend.
- Note how strengths are trusted more as they proceed, how they start relying more on one another, and how they are the team that Linda always dreamed

they would be—once she was willing to risk a new way to be a partner. Clearly she had to let go of her ego's demand for her former control. Her husband also stepped up with his own willingness to be a responsible partner in this new way. He did not bring up "the way it used to be," or "Why didn't you think of this before?" He was just there, in the moment, using his gifts.

ME	State your strengths in this situation. (Strengths = how you approach decisions; NOT your solutions, opinions, history.)

YOU	Point out his strengths, how he thinks and what he does well. Acknowledge what his *brainstyle* brings to decision-making. Emphasize what he can contribute by using his natural abilities (his *brainstyle*).

STRENGTHS CONTRACT: PART DEUX.

"At first I thought some of Gary's questions were too blunt and probing and sounded untrusting. I wondered if I should soften his interaction. Gary later confessed he thought my questions were too personal and sometimes irrelevant and wondered if he should distract me. Happily, we both let each other interact in our own way."

> *BRAINSTYLE CLUE:* Trust the process. Trust yourself. Trust your partner. Forgive mistakes. Grow together.

"From our research, the seller's price was reasonable. I felt good about the couple who was selling the boat and wanted to just give them their asking price right then. Gary was prepared to walk away if they didn't take his offer that was $1,000 below their asking price. When he offered, they declined. We left in the rain. No boat, no deal. In the car, I expressed my disappointment. Gary said, 'Honey, there are lots of boats.' All I could think was how perfect the color of this one matched my new Expedition and his truck."

• Note again how their strengths impact the outcome of the situation: the Knower is unattached and therefore the perfect negotiator. He uses his detachment to reassure and help his partner move on. Her emotionally based approach, common to Conciliators, means less focus on their goals and criteria and many more personal connections.

THE WIN-WIN.

"Two days later, the sellers called us, expressed how much they liked us, and said they would meet our offer and throw in competition water skis, a kneeboard, six life jackets, two tow ropes, and a canvas boat cover. Gary asked how soon they could meet us at the bank to transfer funds for title. They arranged to meet us in a couple of hours.

"I released control of the negotiation, and we got the boat we wanted, at the price Gary wanted, with $1,000 worth of barely used equipment. I marveled at the incredible way we each used our gifts in a new way. We were respectful of one another, we worked seamlessly as a team, and I saw the impact of our strengths in ways I had never even noticed before. There was now a whole new level of trust in our marriage."

You can't see the light in Linda's eyes as she tells this story, but I can vouch for it and for the continual deepening of their loving partnership. They fell in love again that day. There have been many more days like this since for Linda and Gary.

There can be similar days for you.

> BRAINSTYLE CLUE: Applying your knowledge of strengths is a bold move which will propel you into a spiritual partnership that deals with the grandest, most eternal of things.

Here's an exercise to prepare you for the Big Decisions. The daily interchanges with your lover will start transforming automatically as you settle into the new definitions of your strengths and non-strengths.

RECALL YOUR SUCCESSES.

1. Think of a situation in the past where you successfully reached a mutually agreeable solution with another.

2. Recall the situation. Did you want things to work differently? What was your intent? It is not necessary to accurately recall what was said nor to focus too much on the topic resolved.

3. Write the Problem Situation as you saw it in the beginning.

_____

_____

4. Write the Mutual Goal it became for you to resolve. If all you can think of are fights and unresolved issues, return to the chapter that describes your *brainstyle* and review your strengths. _____

_____

_____

_____

5. Which of your strengths did you employ to reach a resolution?

_____

_____

6. Think of another success where you handled a tricky situation well. How did you feel? Why do you think you handled it well? What did the other person say that led you to believe that he or she was pleased as well? If he or she wasn't pleased initially, was it still a win for both of you?

_____

_____

7. You're on a roll now. Think of any other times where you stood in your strengths and, without apology, asked for help from another who had strengths you didn't have. How did you take responsibility for the outcome? What worked?

_____

_____

> *BRAINSTYLE CLUE:* The foundation for your personal integrity and leadership is clarity about your strengths and non-strengths.

CHALLENGES. One of the most difficult times—and most vital—to create a *Strengths Contract* is when the issue demands your non-strengths. For instance, a legal and financial issue for the right-brained can be a nightmare of details and technical specifics that are outside their strengths. A tangled, emotional family situation can be a living hell for a left-brained, literal, structured thinker. Having participated in a situation like this, I offer the following hard-won lessons, including some suggestions for actual statements you might try.

I have also observed divorces and firings that were irreconcilable at the time and no *Strengths Contract* was possible. At least one of the partners had no idea of his true gifts, demonstrated by his (often unwitting and well-intentioned) reliance on non-strengths and consequent lack of personal integrity. Worse, he blamed others for his unhappiness or failure. This is such a simple diagnosis, yet so profound. Some of us need a lifetime to accept and come to peace with who we are and what we truly have to offer.

HOW TO HANDLE SITUATIONS THAT REQUIRE NON-STRENGTHS. You'll know you're in your non-strengths by some simple clues: You're (pick any from the following list): tense, dreading the event, nervous, anxious, defensive, reacting strongly, irritable, picky, feeling picked on, isolated, or misunderstood.

When you are using your strengths, you're confident and willing.

1. **FOCUS ON YOUR STRENGTHS.** The most critical thing you must do when you're in over your head, outgunned, and overwhelmed is to focus on your strengths. How? Any way you can. Every way you can. Ask your partner to tell you what gifts he appreciates you for. Make a list to tell yourself. Read your *brainstyle* chapter again. Tell those you're involved with how they can use your strengths. Here are some corny, clunky ways to offer your gifts so you'll get the idea. The words you use must be your own, offered in as neutral and kind a tone as possible:

   a) The right-brained person in a left-brained situation: I am slower with the technical/legal/medical terms and requirements than you are, so I'll need to ask questions or rephrase your words or take some time to think things over. Some things you can count on me for are . . . (e.g., generating possibilities, helping us work together, looking for the emotional impact of our project/plan, etc.).

   b) The left-brained person in a right-brained situation: I tend to get uncomfortable in these kinds of events and don't like to spend much time around all the socializing and discussion. I'm not good at it. I'll help though, from behind the scenes. I can . . . (e.g., clarify direction, check the financial goals, and assess your plans by giving you a reality check). If necessary, I am better one-on-one.

2. **BE CANDID ABOUT YOUR NON-STRENGTHS** and gain respect for your honesty; you'll set the tone for everyone. Start by admitting them to yourself. Nothing is worse than dealing with the Wanna Be, the pretender who is going to hype her way through a situation when she doesn't know what she's talking about—or worse, is stuck on her position, confusing the truth with her opinion. When in such a situation, **you must get a partner** who has the required gifts to help you deal with the situation. He can be your interpreter. He can put the issues into terms you can understand or take notes to think about.

3. **APPLY THE GUIDELINES FOR BRAINSTYLES TIMING.** This is a must, especially in your non-strengths. When you're working outside your gifts, things are processed more slowly. This does NOT mean you are stupid; it means you understand the situation differently. You can contribute in areas others cannot.

4. **AVOID GETTING ATTACHED TO YOUR SOLUTION** or taking a position that cannot be modified. For me, this is a real challenge. I'm a fighter, and once convinced, especially in a family argument, I dig in and go for the win. This has not served me well. Once anyone in any family gets locked into a

position, timing is the cure I have seen: sometimes it takes years, in some cases decades, to appreciate Dad or Mom's strengths and the contribution they have made. If you take the point of view that it only takes one to heal a relationship, that one can be you. Returning to your strengths, your true values, you are grander than the argument, even when it involves money or lifestyle. You have access to a gentle, loving, inner wisdom that can support you in letting go of your right answers. As has been said so many times, let go and let God take over the ultimate solution. In so many cases, including mine, I have heard of deadlocks being broken after a particularly intense prayer or meditation time where there is a heartfelt desire for the best, most expansive answer. There has been a release of one's own "right" answer. Miracles in partnerships have occurred shortly thereafter.

THE STRENGTHS CONTRACT. As you have already read, entering any conversation to reach an agreement starts with an intention to honor the strengths of each of you. For those whom you dislike, distrust, or disrespect, it may be difficult for you to think of them with anything approaching respect. What you can do is to remain true to your own intention to be as kind and honorable as you know how to be—no matter what. You'll know you succeeded if you respect the person you see in the mirror at the end of the day.

INTENTIONS MATTER. What counts is the intention behind the words, and the intended goal for the conversation, which can be conscious and acknowledged or unconscious and a tangled waste of time. A kind or loving intention in communication is often the simplest, and has the greatest impact—at home or at work—not how you say it or even what you say.

BRAINSTYLE CLUE: It is not the words you say or the work you do that is your real contribution; it is the spirit-driven intention that illuminates what you offer and makes it stick.

To have a relationship where a loving intention drives communications, you must start by honoring yourself for who you are, and then you will honor your partner similarly with no extra work or techniques. The extent to which your partnership works is the extent to which you are able to be yourself, with responsible self-regard, and in turn offer respect. Communications are then authentic and effortless.

There is no more sacred ground than where former enemies now stand as friends. As you forgive another, you forgive yourself. Your ability to act as a whole person, caring, influential, forgiving, expands; your ability to act as a lover, a spiritual partner who touches others with love, becomes unlimited.

YOUR OWN STRENGTHS CONTRACT.

> **EXERCISE:** Write out how you can approach an actual situation that you want to resolve.

The ISSUE	Open by stating the problem you're having and your intention to resolve the problem by collaborating.

ME	State your strengths in this situation. (Strengths = how you approach decisions; NOT your solutions, opinions, history.)

YOU	Point out her strengths, how she thinks and what she does well. Acknowledge what her *brainstyle* brings to decision-making. Emphasize what she can contribute by using her natural abilities (her *brainstyle*).

GOALS	What goals can you both agree to?

PLAN	The plan must be based on 1) the gifts of each *brainstyle*, and 2) the timing most natural to each *brainstyle;* also, it may need to include other *brainstyles* as resources.

CHAPTER **16**

THE LONG TERM

~~~~~~~~~~~~~~~

*This is the true joy in life . . . being used for a purpose recognized by yourself as a
mighty one . . . being a force of nature instead of a feverish, selfish little clod of ailments
and grievances complaining that the world will not devote itself to making you happy.
I am of the opinion that my life belongs to the community, and as long as I live it is my
privilege to do for it whatever I can. I want to be thoroughly used up when I die, for
the harder I work, the more I live. I rejoice in life for its own sake.
Life is no brief candle to me. It's a sort of splendid torch which I've got to hold up for
the moment, and I want to make it burn as brightly as possible before handing it on to
future generations.*
—George Bernard Shaw, 1856–1950, Nobel prize-winning author, playwright

~~~~~~~~~~~~~~~

A **MAP OF WHERE YOU CAN GO.** Over the years of living and teaching
BrainStyles, I have found there are five stages leading to Personal Mastery; that
is living from your best, in the zone, experiencing joy and fulfillment, and making
contributions that define you as a master and that allow you to create a spiritual
partnership with those you have chosen to live with and love. These stages do not
occur in sequence necessarily, but emerge and recede as you direct your attention
past labels and open to more respect, more love, and your own wisdom.

The Stages to Personal Mastery:

Stage One: You begin to focus on your strengths.

Stage Two: You see others anew.

Stage Three: You achieve detachment and neutrality with others.

Stage Four: You forgive enemies.

Stage Five: You act from a peaceful, centered place within, wherever you are.

Learning and Living Using *BrainStyles* Starts You on Your Own Path to Personal Mastery.

Stage One: You begin to focus on your strengths. Attend to your strengths by reviewing your *brainstyle* description. As you begin to understand what your hardware provides, you start forgiving yourself for not being perfect. Then, by reviewing what you always considered your "weaknesses," your real strengths—always available, just overlooked—can emerge as your authentic self.

Look at all the criticism people have given you and that you now use to nag yourself. These criticisms target your gifts, the tip of the iceberg of your natural abilities you have not honored, and so not taken full advantage of to further your relationships or your life. You can easily spot those folks who use this form of self-derision; they cannot take correction easily or well. They take suggestions as personal affronts. They overinflate and idealize their abilities. They mull. They worry. They try to please. They boast outrageously. They miss the mark. When fearful, they become the critics pouring out the sarcasm, downloading correct answers with venom fueled by assumptions of their own inadequacy. Cloaked in self-righteousness, their aim is to deflect correction and protect their own right answers.

To recapture your authentic self and move smartly forward on the path of real success, you can start by reevaluating what you've been told. Your personal transformation starts when you stop making the Two Basic Errors of attending to your "weaknesses" and overlooking your strengths. This does NOT mean you simply disregard others' sensitivities and needs by replying, "That's just the way I am, take it or leave it." Oh, no. That's just hiding and being right. The choice is always between being right and alone, or joining with another to love and grow by putting your gifts at his or her service.

People who know who they are (and are not), have self-esteem, lead from confidence, are less aggressive, have higher serotonin levels (which promotes a further sense of well-being), and tend to negotiate situations rather than fight or impatiently demand their own way. How can you be a lover unless you start with a real sense of what you bring—and do not bring—to a relationship? You can start now to focus on what you do well, give up reacting defensively to criticism and instead respond with an intent to learn.

STAGE TWO: YOU SEE OTHERS ANEW. As you begin a new inner dialogue based on your strengths, you will automatically and effortlessly have new openings in relationships with others because you affirm and are more accepting of yourself. You will just naturally look for others' strengths. You will not have to work at "communicating better," you will just do it. You'll be authentic and respectful, too. Self-esteem works that way.

Need I say that criticism and righteousness are the elements of any partnership that is dysfunctional? That it takes two to tango? That at any moment, either party could stop and choose closeness over separation? Forgiveness over righteousness? When you are blinded by emotion or stuck in your own thinking, it is often terribly unclear what a loving response might be. Begin by entertaining the principle that *it only takes one to heal a relationship.* All that's required is a little willingness for you to be that one.

STAGE THREE: YOU ACHIEVE DETACHMENT AND NEUTRALITY WITH OTHERS for longer periods of time. To see who people really are, to see their highest and best selves, to create an interaction where you each are looking at one another with a new acceptance, you simply learn to look beyond their behavior and appearance. By doing so, you are less reactive and more attractive, and freer to choose between two universal responses: love or fear. Looking for gifts, you shift into your personal power where you are neutral: fine with the outcome, fine with the way they're doing it, fine with their mistakes, and confident you know how to use your strengths to guide, resolve, or heal the situation in the time required.

STAGE FOUR: YOU FORGIVE ENEMIES. "Enemies" are simply those you do not yet see as teachers. With time and a willingness to forgive yourself for mistakes, you will have fewer enemies for shorter periods of time and more teachers for the rest of your life. You will become a natural teacher yourself. You will have the real wisdom of your experience to stand upon and teach from.

STAGE FIVE: YOU ACT FROM A PEACEFUL, CENTERED PLACE WITHIN, WHEREVER YOU ARE. Have you ever noticed that when you want something really bad, you can't seem to get it? Then, when you give up trying and pushing and demanding, it just seems to happen? This has been true for me all my life. My conclusion: You surrender to the Spirit within you, allow your hardware to work in concert with that Spirit, join your partner in a loving purpose, and all becomes possible.

Finding your path means first choosing what you want to contribute, then daring to use all you've got to make the biggest difference you can to deliver it—right up to the end. It requires taking risks, getting hurt, hurting, losing—you know, all of that. A desire to employ your gifts to serve others and the world demands maturity. Those who have stuck with it are remarkable people whom you and I respect and are inspired by. Be one of those people. All it takes to start is to honor who you already are. Have the courage to live from your gifts so your opinions are useful, not just contentious; your talents serve others; and what you produce with them has impact that expands people and ideas.

~~~~~~~~~~~~~~~

Our trail through life can be seen only in retrospect. It does all add up, but not in advance of the steps taken. If each small step is guided by the present instead of by a hodgepodge of fears about the future, we can discern a lovely wake flowing from the actions we have taken, including even our mistakes. There is a beauty, a just-rightness, within the course of every life, but so often the individual is blinded to it by constant worry and second-guessing.[1]
—Hugh Prather

~~~~~~~~~~~~~~~

Wherever you are in your life process, consider the wisdom offered by Hugh Prather to own your life as you would a priceless painting, and enjoy, marvel, at the way you are creating it to teach yourself the most priceless lessons. Give yourself permission to be on the right path, doing exactly the things you need to be doing to learn what you must learn. Centered in your gifts, your only questions can be "How much fun can I have today?" or "How much love can I offer today?" Mastery comes from joy.

Here is the wisdom of someone who used the onset of debilitation and disease to reach her own personal mastery.

A WOMAN AT PERSONAL MASTERY. Beverly is in her mid-forties now. She has Parkinson's disease. Noticeable muscle tremors take charge continually, even though her gaze is steady. She discovered the onset of the brain dysfunction several years ago when, as a single parent supporting her household, she was working full time and getting a PhD in behavioral medicine. Since she had had five traffic accidents in recent years, the diagnosis was complicated. Her lifestyle was stressful, fast, controlled. When Parkinson's disease was discovered, everything came to a stop. Flat on her back, she "let go of control, of the map, of MY path."

---

1. Notes on *How to Live In the World . . . and Still Be Happy*, 1986 (Doubleday & Co.), 119 (used with permission).

Beverly replaced her career urgency with faith, the ultimate form of trust in life. She chose to learn from the illness.

"What has Parkinson's given you?" I asked. "It's given me *living*. I was in such a hurry before, controlling things, pushing things, I was not living. That's why I had the five 'accidents,'" she said, saying the word with the irony it deserves now. Her insights carry personal depth and perspective. No academic answers this time. This is real life: life as she is creating it, as she stares down a long and constricting tunnel of physical challenges. She does so with an extraordinarily bright spirit. She is happy, upbeat, thrilled to be alive. She is unburdened by the excess of choices that those with health and physical wellness have. She has stopped taking life and small things for granted. "How did this come about?" I ask. The answer in an e-mail loses the power of her affected speech delivered with the serenity of her eyes. "I completely and totally surrendered to God," she says. "It was then that I began the accelerated journey of joy with God's spirit being my strength rather than trying to do it under my own [power]."

What she is telling me is given added heft by the results she has experienced, for example, in her personal/professional life. She coaches others in writing and has ghost-written books and articles. Since taking on this new approach to life, she has had the financial wherewithal to support herself, her son—and, last year, her sister and brother-in-law with emergency medical problems. In the process, she has listened to new Guidance. Her boundaries have gotten clearer. In what some would view as a desperate situation, she is no longer desperate. She has turned down a writing project with a nationally known psychologist. ("It wasn't the right thing to do.") She cancelled a huge project with a multinational corporation, only to find out later that it fell apart when in progress. She is being sought out by others to start new projects that are bigger and broader, and draw from who she is. No longer does she try to adapt to fit the client's need and language, force-fitting her life and work into another's specifications. She IS her work. She is at peace. When she works, it is with her whole self.

Here are some of her conclusions for daily living:

1. Set very simple goals which allow God's abundant answers.

This is not like planning and imagining an outcome or setting a goal. That, she discovered, can limit the answers you receive. This is a more open, more expansive process. The goal might be immediate yet juxtaposed with infinite possibility. Outcomes occur without your control, only your acceptance. For instance, when I recently learned to ski, I only wanted to be able to exercise, to stay balanced and safe, and to have the experience of muscles supporting my direction. Doing so in incremental, even tiny, steps allowed very rapid physical progress without my control. In fact, getting to the top of the mountain that day filled me with wonder and joy far beyond the simple goal I had set in the beginning.

2. Step aside, mentally.
3. Don't ask why. Let go of the need to know why.
4. Take action only to teach or heal oneself.

"I believe we seek healing for ourself, but it is God who does the healing." Offer your example and lessons to others to take from them what they will for, as Beverly said, "What blesses one, blesses all." In this process, the possibility of discovering your own unique voice or contribution to others emerges.

5. Turn inward and "listen upward" (as she put it) for Wisdom and direction. Follow what you hear. Stop second-guessing.
6. Celebrate the outcome as though it has already happened.
7. Know with certainty that you already have the talent, information, insight, and abilities to express something of value, without effort.

In her words, "You have access to words beyond what you hear; others will hear beyond what you say."

8. Take one step at a time.

One project at a time. Stay in the moment, aware, listening, whether silent or active. "See God in everything," she says.

9. Begin.

Beverly says she begins everything with this notion: "I can hardly wait to see what happens," as opposed to the old days of "I can hardly wait to get this done, off the list, completed." She is a master who has found the power of her limitless spirit by accepting the limitation of her hardware.

~~~~~~~~~~~~~~

Learn to get in touch with silence within yourself and know
that everything in this life has a purpose. There are no mistakes, no coincidences,
all events are blessings given to us to learn from.
—Elisabeth Kübler-Ross

~~~~~~~~~~~~~~

MASTERY FOR YOU. Heal your mind, heal your body. Accept your physical hardware, your mental abilities, along with your thighs, your weight, your face, your hair loss, without blame or shame or guilt, just as a lover does, and accept a universe that comes flowing from the inside out to show you a loving world, job, family, boss, mother-in-law, and traffic jam, for which you are grateful moment by moment.

~~~~~~~~~~~~~~~

The world you see is merely a reflection of your perceptions,
the inner reality you have created and seek to prove true.

~~~~~~~~~~~~~~~

You must have had times when you surrendered. When you stopped trying. You must also have experienced your fullness in those moments of peace, a knowing how everything works and fits together. Most of the time this awareness comes in short bursts: an insight here, a focused, intense time on a project there, and then back to the old soup. Those are mere rehearsals for your full expression, which does not have to stop.

Recall a time when you sailed through the day, and nothing bothered you— even people around you with their upsets and fears. What did you do to give yourself permission to feel that way? Were you in love with a new job or really happy to be on vacation or snug in your home? Were you in love with someone? You were in Love, no doubt about it, and the world and everyone in it looked different. Full of wonder. Perfect. Because that's how *you* felt.

Have you ever felt deeply grateful and happy? Glad to be alive? If you aren't feeling that way right now, you can. It starts with appreciating just how grand you are. You allow possibilities to unfold. You marvel at being alive. You don't push. You set limits easily and clearly. "No, I won't do that. I'll never be as good as you are or as fast as you are. But what I can do is give you the very best of me in this situation."

Then there's the energy you create around you, the pleasure you have and express when being with those you love. When acting from this place, everything makes sense. Everything. You are part of a grand Plan. You are miraculous. You are.

APPENDIX

THE *BRAINSTYLES*™ INVENTORY DATABASE

SUMMARY OF *BRAINSTYLES* DISTRIBUTION.

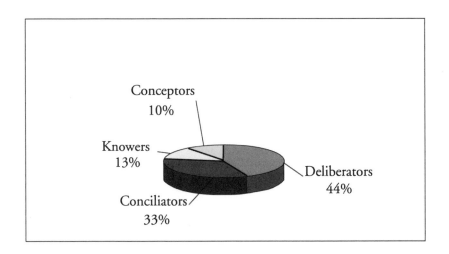

THE BRAINSTYLE INVENTORY DATABASE:
INFORMATION BY GENDER.

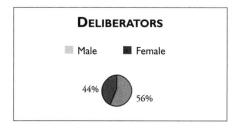

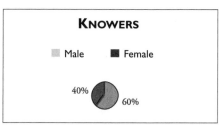

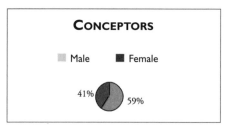

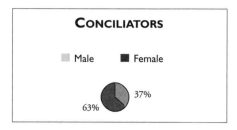

Total Male Sample = 1067
51% of the total sample was male

Total Female Sample = 1045
49% of the total sample was female

Deliberators: 521   56% of all Deliberators

Deliberators: 403   44% of all Deliberators

Knowers: 159   60% of all Knowers

Knowers: 105   40% of all Knowers

Conceptors: 129   59% of all Conceptors

Conceptors: 90   41% of all Conceptors

Conciliators: 258   37% of all Conciliators

Conciliators: 447   63% of all Conciliators

This sample has been drawn from representatives from 18–65 years of age in occupations as diverse as manufacturing/distribution, marketing/sales, finance, business administration, general management, human resource/education, law, engineering, media/advertising, health care, information technology, research/technical development, customer service, interior design/building and physical education/sports/athletics.

For correlation of representative occupations to the *BrainStyles* database, go online to www.brainstyles.com.

APPENDIX **B**

SELECTED RESEARCH AND BIBLIOGRAPHY

A CURRENT REVIEW OF RELATIONSHIPS IN AMERICA:

- There are more single people today than ever in history: 82 million in the United States, or 40 percent of the adult population, versus 37.5 million, or 28 percent, in 1970.
- Over 25 percent of households are single-occupant households, versus 17 percent in 1970.
- The marriage rate is decreasing and is at its lowest in 30 years.
- The divorce rate has remained stable since 1988.
- While the exact divorce rate is a matter of debate, experts agree that somewhere between 40 and 60 percent of all marriages will end in divorce, and that *for every marriage there is about one divorce* [emphasis added].
- Cohabitation has increased dramatically since the 1970s. It is the most common preference of people aged 27–35 to prepare for marriage, yet it ends in separation 150 percent more often than a first marriage in the first five years: (49 percent versus 20 percent); after 10 years, the rate of breakups of cohabitations is nearly double, versus marriages (62 percent versus 33 percent). Cohabiting couples have much more violence, with fewer benefits in health, wealth, and emotional well-being for the cohabiting couple than for a married couple.
- The percentage of young adults who say that having a good marriage is extremely important to them is increasing (94 percent in one study).
- The majority of first-born children are now conceived by, or born to, unmarried parents.

- Half of all children will spend some time in a single-parent family.
- Forty-three percent of first marriages will end within fifteen years.
- Thirty-nine percent of remarriages end within ten years.
- More than 85 percent of all adults marry at least once. That rate has declined, and singlehood is increasing.

The above findings are part of a summary of a 1999 study that surveyed all data available on marriage, divorce, and cohabiting in America. Conducting their own surveys as well, David Popenoe and Barbara Dafoe Whitehead of the National Marriage Project of Rutgers University reported on "The State of Our Unions: The Social Health of Marriage in America."[1] They conclude:

> Key social indicators suggest a substantial weakening of the institution of marriage. Americans have become less likely to marry. When they do marry, their marriages are less happy. And married couples face a high likelihood of divorce. Over the past four decades, marriage has declined as the first living-together experience for couples and as a status of parenthood. Unmarried cohabitation and unwed births have grown enormously, and so has the percentage of children who grow up in fragile families.

WHY IS THIS? The Whitehead/Popenoe studies selected groups of single, heterosexual men around the country to interview on the subject of marriage. In an essay titled, "Why Men Won't Commit," they validate the popular notion that men really are afraid to commit to marriage. The average age for marriage (27) is the oldest in the history of the United States. Why? There is less reason now to marry than ever before, the study reports. Society, including many churches, the family, employers, and the women they date put little pressure on men to marry. Sex is readily available in dating, and "trial marriage"—cohabitation without marriage—is the norm. Casual sex is just part of dating today. With the pressure off, young men (and women) first want a career to establish their own financial base by owning a home. This sets up the terrible fear for men, as comedian Rodney Dangerfield jokes, that they now are stuck with a nag or a loser, must give up real sex, lose their independence, and risk the possible loss of their fortunes through divorce.

Meanwhile, these very same men, young, single, and eligible, are waiting, longing and hoping; seeking, yes, a "soul mate" *even when they are living with a girlfriend.* That perfect partner. After their interviews across America, the study's authors define the Guy Ideal: "Notably they emphasize a soul mate's willingness to take them as they are and not try to change them." They want a woman who is "someone you are not putting on a show for," "a woman with whom 'you are completely compatible right now'"; in other words, someone you have that chemistry

1. ©2002.

thing with and who loves you just as you are. Hmm. Sound familiar?

What may also ring a bell for all of us is how these twenty-somethings are using a very common process: constructing a dream scenario and then doing everything they can to prevent its reality: dating based on appearance and quick sex (which they disrespect, they confide), working on their own careers, independently building their own asset bases, while fearing the loss of their independence to do and have the things they prize.

~~~~~~~~~~~~~~~~

BIBLIOGRAPHY.

Amen, Daniel. *Change Your Brain Change Your Life.* New York: Three Rivers Press, 1998.

Aron, Elaine. *The Highly Sensitive Person: How to Thrive When the World Overwhelms You.* Banton, Doubleday, Dell Publishing, 1997.

Byron, Katie. *Loving What Is.* New York: Harmony Books, 2002.

Dunn, Rita, Kenneth Dunn and Donald Treffinger. *Bringing Out the Giftedness in Your Child.* New York: John Wiley & Sons, Inc., 1992.

Farson, Richard. *Management of the Absurd.* New York: Simon & Schuster, 1996.

Gottman, John. *Why Marriages Succeed or Fail.* New York: Simon & Schuster, 1994.

Hamer, Dean, and Peter Copeland. *Living with Our Genes.* New York: Doubleday, 1998.

Levoy, Gregg. *Callings.* New York: Harmony Books, 1997.

Markova, Dawna. *How Your Child Is Smart.* Berkeley: Conari Press, 1992.

Pickover, Clifford. *Strange Brains and Genius.* New York: Plenum Publishing, 1998.

Prather, Hugh. *How to Live in the World and Still Be Happy.* New York: Doubleday & Company, Inc., 1986.

____. *Spiritual Notes to Myself.* Berkeley: Conari Press, 1998.

____. *I Will Never Leave You.* New York: Bantam Books, 1995.

____. *Spiritual Parenting.* New York: Three Rivers Press, 1996.

Rechtschaffen, Stephan. *Time Shifting.* New York: Doubleday, 1996.

Restak, Richard. *Mysteries of the Mind.* Willard: R.R. Donnelly & Sons, 2000.

Tolle, Eckhart. *The Power of Now.* Novato, CA: New World Library, 1999.

Walsch, Neale. *Conversations with God.* Charlottesville: Hampton Roads Publishing Company Inc., 1995.

Williamson, Marianne. *A Return to Love.* New York: HarperCollins Publishers, 1996.

Supplements to *A Course in Miracles. Foundation for Inner Peace.* New York: Viking Press, 1996.

ABOUT THE AUTHOR

MARLANE MILLER is an author and business consultant. She is also president of the consulting firm *BrainStyles*®, Inc./Miller Consulting Services, which licenses instructors and coaches around the world to teach her work. She has been a professional in the human development field since 1965 and is a graduate of UCLA, with graduate work in organizational behavior, group dynamics, and experiential adult learning. Marlane trained with Harvard and MIT professors in corporate cultural change and team dynamics as Manager of Executive and Organizational Development at Ciba-Geigy Corporation's American headquarters. Her clients have included P&G, PepsiCo, Monsanto, Allstate, Turner Broadcasting, educators in America and Mexico, nonprofit companies, and a wide variety of mid-sized and entrepreneurial firms. As a personal and corporate coach, she has helped hundreds of individuals define and leverage their strengths in the workplace and with their families.

Marlane is the author of two previous books on personal and professional success. The most recent, *BrainStyles*™: *Change Your Life Without Changing Who You Are*SM (Simon & Schuster, 1997) has been translated into five languages: Chinese, Japanese, Korean, Polish, and Portuguese.

Her firm is dedicated to helping people identify and master their brain-based strengths rather than trying to change themselves. The work is the result of extensive research on the brain and its impact on personality as well as qualitative research with entrepreneurs and corporate clients. After a career as a private coach to executives, seminar leader, and national public speaker, and a 21-city book tour, she is now devoted full time to training others to teach and coach this powerful work based on more than a decade of scientific research and two decades of disciplined spiritual study. To this end, the *BrainStyles* Instructor/Coaching network has been established globally to include China, Germany, Indonesia, and professors of ITESM, the largest private university in Mexico, to teach *The BrainStyles System* throughout Mexico and Latin America.

She has been married to David Cherry, the creator of the original *BrainStyles*® concepts, since 1980 and has two stepchildren and four grandchildren.